EMT-BASIC
EXAM FOR
FIREFIGHTERS

OTHER TITLES OF INTEREST FROM
LEARNINGEXPRESS

EMT-Basic Exam

EMT-BASIC
EXAM FOR
FIREFIGHTERS

1st Edition

LEARNINGEXPRESS®

NEW YORK

Library of Congress Cataloging-in-Publication Data

EMT-basic exam for firefighters. — 1st ed.
    p. cm.
  ISBN 978-1-57685-718-2
  1. Emergency medicine —United States —Examinations, questions, etc. 2. Emergency medical technicians—
Licenses —United States. 3. Fire fighters —Vocational guidance —United States. I. LearningExpress
(Organization)
  RC86.9.E485 2010
  616.02'5076 —dc22
                              2009031520
Printed in the United States of America

9 8 7 6 5 4 3 2 1

First Edition

    ISBN-10: 1-57685-718-2
    ISBN-13: 978-1-57685-718-2

Regarding the Information in This Book
We attempt to verify the information presented in our books prior to publication. It is always a good idea, however, to double-check such important information as minimum requirements, application and testing procedures, and deadlines with your local law enforcement agency, as such information can change from time to time.

For more information or to place an order, contact LearningExpress at:
    2 Rector Street
    26th Floor
    New York, NY 10006

Or visit us at:
    www.learnatest.com

Contents ▶

List of Contributors ▶

Mike Clumpner has over 15 years of service as a firefighter/paramedic and is currently a fire captain/paramedic with the Charlotte Fire Department and a flight paramedic with Regional One Helicopter in Spartanburg, SC. He is a member of the clinical faculty at the University of Maryland—Baltimore County and holds dual associate degrees in fire science and EMS, a bachelor's degree in business administration, a master's degree in business administration, and is currently working on a PhD in homeland security. Mike has published several critical care textbooks and has lectured globally at more than 150 conferences.

Nicol P. Jurotovac is currently a lieutenant with the San Francisco Fire Department, where she began her firefighting career in 1997. She has served on a number of busy engine and truck companies, and is a graduate of the National Fire Academy's Executive Fire Officer Program. She is also the California State Fire Training and Education System's certified Chief Officer, Fire Officer, and Fire Instructor.

Introduction ▶

If you've purchased this book you're probably well aware of the following fact: In addition to the basic hiring prerequisites of a high school diploma or GED, a local residency, a clean driver's license, and a Candidate Physical Agility Test (CPAT) card, most major metropolitan fire departments now require that candidates possess, at a minimum, a National Registry of Emergency Medical Technicians (NREMT) Emergency Medical Technician-Basic (EMT-B) certificate.

If you're a firefighter candidate, EMT-B certification can only improve your chances of getting hired; if you're a seasoned veteran, it can help you advance in your career and, in some cases, even increase your salary. Regardless of your present situation, the end-goal is the same—earning an EMT-B certification. *EMT-Basic Exam for Firefighters* will help you get there.

How to Use This Book

In the following two chapters you'll find information essential to any firefighter candidate pursuing his or her EMT-B certification. In Chapter 1 you'll learn about the advantages of certification, salaries, departments that require certification as well as those that prefer it, hiring trends, benefits, and invaluable and comprehensive information on searching for and securing a position. Chapter 2 outlines the National Registry of Emergency Medical Technicians' (NREMT) EMT-B certification requirements, so you know exactly what is expected of you.

The remainder of this book consists of four complete written practice tests—three tests that each contain 150 questions, similar to those on the National Registry EMT-Basic cognitive examination, and one 160-question free-response test. All practice tests and free-response items represent content from the NREMT-Basic examination.

An essential step in using this book to prepare for the EMT-Basic cognitive examination is to read Chapter 3, which presents the nine-step LearningExpress Test Preparation System; it introduces essential test-taking strategies that you can practice as you take the exams in this book.

Next, take one complete practice test and score your answers using the answer key. Complete explanations for the answers are included. Even though the EMT-Basic cognitive exam is pass/fail, LearningExpress recommends scoring at least a 70% on the practice tests in order to achieve the best results on your final EMT-Basic exam. This means you should shoot for 105 correct answers on tests 1–3 (multiple choice) and 112 correct answers on test 4 (free response).

If you score over 70% on your first practice test, congratulations! However, even if you do very well on the practice test, don't become overconfident and simply assume that you'll pass the actual exam easily—the items on that exam will be different from those on the practice test. You'll still need to do some test preparation. No matter what your initial score, follow the suggestions in the next paragraphs.

If you score below 70% on your first practice test, don't panic, but do put in some concentrated study time. Begin your studying by determining your major areas of weakness. For example, perhaps you answered 50 items on the practice test incorrectly, giving you a score of 100, or approximately 67%. Upon rereading the questions you missed, try to determine the content area in which they belong: Cardiology—12 questions missed; Airway and Breathing—3 questions missed; Trauma—13 questions missed; Medical—4 questions missed; Obstetrics and Pediatrics—12 questions missed; Operations—6 questions missed.

This analysis tells you that you need to concentrate your study in the areas of Cardiology, Trauma, and Obstetrics and Pediatrics. Try putting in one or two concentrated evenings of study in each area.

Review all the material on these topics in the textbook and printed materials from your EMS course. Then take a second practice test and check your total score and content area breakdown again. Chances are that your total will have improved.

In the time leading up to the EMT-Basic cognitive exam, use the remaining practice tests to further pinpoint areas of weakness and to find areas to review. For example, suppose that after additional study sessions, you take the third practice test. You now do well on all the questions about circulation *except* the ones that ask you to recognize signs and symptoms of shock. This information tells you which specific pages of your textbook you should review.

Once you have worked on and improved your areas of weakness, use the final days before the test to do some general reviewing. Devote a short period of time each day to reviewing one or two chapters of your textbook. Then use the fourth practice test to rehearse free-response testing. Although this method is not included on the official exam, it provides an alternative form of evaluation, and the challenge will help you achieve greater understanding of the concepts. After reading and studying this book, you'll be well on your way to obtaining EMT-Basic certification. Good luck!

EMT-BASIC
EXAM FOR
FIREFIGHTERS

CHAPTER 1

BECOMING A FIREFIGHTER

CHAPTER SUMMARY

The face of modern firefighting is changing rapidly, and earning your EMT certification is an important step towards making your dream of becoming a firefighter a reality. In this chapter you'll learn about all the advantages of certification—from getting hired, paid, and then promoted. You'll also get the essential information every firefighter candidate needs to know about getting selected for the fire academy.

The Advantages of EMT Certification

The nature of firefighting has changed dramatically from the days when firefighters only responded to fires. Many calls to the firehouse require emergency procedures unrelated to fires, such as providing help to a heart attack victim or dealing with hazardous materials. Firefighters also respond to terrorist attacks; earthquakes, hurricanes, and other natural disasters; vehicle accidents, vehicle fires, and many miscellaneous 911 emergency calls. According to the United States Fire Administration, just 5% of a typical fire department's total responses are actually fires, while approximately 80% of those responses are emergency medical incidents. Today, many firefighters are certified as EMTs or paramedics to meet the increasing need for such services.

Therefore, firefighters need a broad range of skills, which must be continually updated through additional training. As new technologies and equipment are created and responses to emergencies and disasters change in scope, the demands on firefighters have become increasingly complex. The cost of training firefighters for these new skill sets has put a serious strain on the already tight budgets of many major fire departments. It's only logical that many departments are coming to the realization that they are able to save hundreds of thousands of dollars yearly by simply hiring candidates that arrive at probationary fire academies already certified as EMTs.

A Competitive Edge

There are over 361,000 individuals employed in fire service in the United States. About 293,000 are line firefighters, whereas the rest are supervisors or other support staff. The majority of these individuals, about nine out of ten according to the Bureau of Labor Statistics (BLS), are employed by municipal or county fire departments, serving communities of 25,000 people or more. Large cities are the largest employers, but many intermediate sized municipalities also employ career firefighters. Full-time firefighters are also hired by federal and state government agencies to protect government owned property and special facilities. For example, the U.S. Forest Service, Bureau of Land Management, and Park Service offer both year-round and seasonal fire service jobs to protect the country's national parks, forests, and other lands.

In the private sector, many large industrial companies have their own firefighting forces, especially companies in the oil, chemical, aircraft, and aerospace industries. Other employers include airports, shipyards, and military bases. A growing number of companies are in the business of providing fire protection services—including on-call or on-site firefighting teams—to other businesses and institutions.

Most fire departments—especially large urban departments—have many more applicants than they do job openings. Obtaining an EMT-B certificate affords an individual the opportunity to apply to departments that require one. Certification reveals that the candidate possesses a certain level of skills, knowledge, and abilities that sets him or her apart from uncertified candidates. With increased competition for positions, certification is certainly an asset. It enhances a candidate's resume and increases his or her chances of getting hired.

For example, the San Francisco Fire Department (SFFD) did not require an EMT certificate until 2009. Yet, an EMT certificate was "highly desirable" in 2001—the last time that the SFFD tested for entry-level firefighter positions. Moreover, out of the approximately 50 candidates who were offered entry into the SFFD fire academy class of 2001, all but two were EMTs.

Lastly, many fire departments that do not currently require an EMT certificate do require that one is obtained within a year of hire. Check with the fire departments you're considering applying for to find out about their specific requirements, as requirements often differ.

SOME MAJOR METROPOLITAN FIRE DEPARTMENTS THAT REQUIRE EMT CERTIFICATION
Houston Fire Department
Los Angeles County Fire Department
Long Beach Fire Department
Nashville Fire Department
San Francisco Fire Department
San Jose Fire Department
Seattle Fire Department
Las Vegas Fire Rescue
Phoenix Fire Department

SOME MAJOR METROPOLITAN FIRE DEPARTMENTS THAT GIVE HIRING PREFERENCE TO EMTs
Miami Dade Fire Reserve
Salt Lake City Fire Department

Better Salary

Some major metropolitan fire departments boast a starting salary for a first year Firefighter/EMT at $65,000 with incremental yearly raises up to the fifth year—where a fifth year Firefighter/EMT could be making a base salary of $90,000. Many of these fire departments require at least an EMT certificate by the time a job offer is extended, with some of them requiring an EMT certificate in order to take the entry exam. Many Firefighter/EMTs, once hired, receive cost of living increases each year thereafter. This base salary also could be augmented with incentive pay if one possesses certain qualifications such as Hazardous Materials Technician, foreign language expertise, etc.

TYPICAL SALARIES

Here are some examples of base annual salaries for EMT firefighters in cities around the country.

Anchorage, Alaska $54,803

Lexington, Massachusetts $43,830

Kennedale, Texas $40,532

Gladstone, Missouri $34,295–$36,031

Upland, California $52,896–$64,296

Margate, Florida $42,988

Phoenix, Arizona $40,475–$47,475

Forest Park, Georgia $35,040

Washington, DC $48,731

Lateral Moves

Some fire departments, such as the FDNY, still hire single-functioning EMTs and paramedics, despite the fact that these departments have a fire-based EMS system. Often, these single functioning EMTs and paramedics find it less difficult to initially get hired into the department, with the hope of eventually cross-training as a firefighter. Some departments even allow for these newly transferred firefighters who have transferred to roll over their years of service to their current department.

For example, if you are a qualified FDNY EMT or paramedic you are afforded the opportunity to take the FDNY's "Promotion to Firefighter" examination. Passing all portions of the exam places the candidate on the "Promotion List for Firefighter," which is used by the department before the open competitive list.

This career opportunity is not always available however, as some departments require these single functioning employees to participate in the same application process for its entry-level firefighter position, while other departments allow a more informal path to cross-training.

Still, even if this hiring advantage isn't available, many fire departments consider EMT experience an attractive feature of a candidate's resume when evaluating a candidate in the hiring process, as we mentioned earlier. And of course, many private ambulance companies require that one possesses an EMT certificate to even work as an ambulance driver.

The Next Level

Once hired, many fire departments offer a myriad of additional training opportunities, as training in the Fire and Emergency Services never stops. The dynamics of the emergency incident can change, and emergency responders must be at a heightened level of preparedness for any and all emergencies. Consequently, many fire departments offer surf rescue, cliff rescue, SCUBA, Hazardous Materials Technician and Specialist, Paramedic, and Rescue Systems training to its employees while they are on duty.

EMT-B certification is often the first stop on the path to obtaining those advanced specializations. A handful of fire departments require a paramedic license for a candidate to apply for an entry-level firefighter position, with many more departments heading in that direction.

In addition, it is not uncommon for fire departments to require that a candidate possess a paramedic license to promote to the next rank, which often is the rank of lieutenant or captain, depending on the department's rank structure.

Because many more fire departments are likely to require a paramedic license in the near future, and EMT-B certification is needed to even get into a paramedic program, your decision to obtain an EMT-Basic certificate is a smart career move. But of course, no one can earn that certification without first passing the EMT-B Cognitive and Practical exams, and helping you prepare for those exams is what this book is all about.

The Firefighter Selection Process

Of course, earning your EMT-B certification doesn't guarantee you a job. All applicants must go through a rigorous testing and selection process that may last a few months to a year or more, so as to select only those who are qualified and prepared for the commitment. Although physical strength is still required, firefighters today must also have the academic skills to apply mathematics and sciences. Municipalities seek candidates with all the necessary skills and certifications but they also seek potential firefighters who are trustworthy. When all is said and done, a firefighter occupies a position in which people must trust him or her with their lives and property.

In most cases, there are far more applicants for each position than can be appointed. The selection process may be made up of an initial application, background checks, a written examination, an oral interview or board, a physical ability test, a drug screening, and psychological tests. Being informed and prepared will help you to remain confident through every stage of the process.

Networking

One of the best places to network with other candidates is the community college environment. EMT classes offered at community colleges are one of many classes where candidates may meet others—to discover which fire departments are hiring, what they need to do to enhance their resume, and so forth. Networking offers an individual the ability to interact with other like-minded candidates and share information that may be imperative in discovering which departments are hiring, what their requirements are, meeting important deadlines, the list goes on and on.

The Eligibility List

Most fire departments, or the city personnel departments that handle the selection process for them, establish a list of eligible candidates; many such lists rank candidates from highest to lowest. How ranks are determined varies from place to place; sometimes the rank is based solely on the written exam score, sometimes on the physical ability test, and sometimes on a combination of factors. Many municipalities are now combining scores on all the steps to develop an overall rating based on all aspects of the selection process. The point is, even if you make it through the entire selection process, the likelihood that you will be hired as a firefighter often depends on the quality of your performance in one or more parts of the selection process.

Make a commitment now: You need to work hard, in advance, to do well on the written exam, the physical ability test, and the oral interview (if there is one), so that your name will stand out at the top of your agency's eligibility list.

First, though, you need information. You need to know about the selection process for firefighters. The rest of this chapter outlines the basic process in its many steps. Not every fire department includes all of the steps discussed. The particulars of the process in the city where you are applying are usually available from the city human resources department or the fire department itself.

Basic Qualifications

The basic qualifications you need to even think about becoming a firefighter vary from city to city. It's worthwhile to find out what those qualifications are in the agency you want to serve. Some qualifications are pretty standard:

- A minimum age—sometimes this can be as low as 18, but 21 is the age that seems to be most common today. In some departments, there is a maximum age, but for the most part, these have been replaced by the requirements of physical ability tests and health.
- A high school diploma, or its equivalent, but now many departments require some college, and a few are looking for an associate's degree or perhaps a professional certification.
- A clean criminal record
- Excellent physical and mental health
- A valid driver's license and a satisfactory driving record

Many jurisdictions, but not all, require that you live nearby or in the jurisdiction. Some fire departments give preference to otherwise qualified veterans over civilians. This may take the form of a policy, sometimes called a "Veteran's Preference" policy, whereby points are automatically added to the written exam. Is this unfair? No. Fire companies are a lot like military units. They follow a strict chain of command, and firefighters on the line work as a team, knowing that their lives are in each other's hands. Military personnel have learned the discipline and teamwork that are vital to firefighting and emergency services, making them very well qualified.

In addition to the emergency medical certifications discussed earlier, fire departments are also increasing giving preference to applicants with fire certifications, such as National Board on Fire Professional Qualifications or ProBoard Accreditation Firefighter I, or other fire service certifications, such as vehicle and technical rescue. Some fire departments have successfully used these to screen candidates or as entry requirements. As fire departments continue to shift to all-hazards response agencies, these certifications and higher levels of education will be important for service.

The Exam or Position Announcement

Applying to be a firefighter differs from applying for most other jobs. The differences begin with the exam or position announcement. You rarely see fire department openings advertised in the Help Wanted ads. Instead, the city usually starts looking for potential firefighters by means of a special announcement. This announcement will outline the basic qualifications for the position as well as the steps you will have to go through in the selection process. It often tells you some of the duties you will be expected to perform. It may give the date and place of the written exam, which for most positions is the first step in the selection process. Search the Web, looking for the area where you desire to be a firefighter, and determine if the fire department or department of public safety has a Web site. Very often these sites will post calendars stating when the hiring process will begin and if and when they are hiring.

Get a copy of this announcement. Often your public library will have a copy, or you can get one directly from the fire department, city human resources department, or from the Internet. If exams are held irregularly, the fire or personnel department may maintain a mailing list so that you can receive an exam announcement the next time an exam is scheduled. If exams are held frequently, you will sometimes be told to simply show up at the exam site on a given day of the

City and County of San Francisco Class Specification Firefighter

Definition

Under general supervision, engages in firefighting and related activities for the saving of life and property; administers first responder treatment, including first aid; responds to a variety of emergency situations involving public safety and medical care; may be assigned duties in connection with fire prevention activities, including the inspection of business, schools, and homes to ensure fire safety; maintains station quarters; and performs other duties as assigned.

Distinguishing Features

An H-2 Firefighter is distinguished from an H-1 Fire Rescue Paramedic in that the H-1 performs advanced life support tasks, but does not perform interior fire attack tasks. The H-2 Firefighter is distinguished from the H-3 Firefighter Paramedic in that the H-3 performs advanced life support tasks. An H-2 Firefighter is distinguished from an H-20 Lieutenant in that the H-20 has supervision responsibilities, and the firefighter does not.

Supervision Exercised

None

Examples of Important and Essential Duties

According to Civil Service Commission Rule 9, the duties specified below are representative of the duties assigned to this class and are not intended to be an inclusive list.

1. In preparing for the tour of duty: attends roll call in uniform and receives orders, instructions, and assignments of work to be done; speaks with firefighters on other shifts to receive updated information regarding the previous day's activities; reads teletype or computer messages and general orders to receive Department and company information; calls in to fire house prior to tour to inform Department if he/she will not report to work due to sickness; relays messages to officer concerning sick or disabled crew members; while on watch, monitors computer printout to learn of obstructions, road work, broken hydrants, or other events that will require different route to any response; carries out station duties such as cooking, cleaning, and building and equipment maintenance; etc.

2. In performing tasks from receipt of alarm to arrival at scene: while on watch, listens for alarm and radio communications to inform company when to respond to call, address, and other pertinent information; dons protective gear and straps self into position in vehicle in preparation for departure; locates alarm using knowledge of first-alarm area to determine most efficient route and possible hazards for driving to alarm; drives engine/truck to and from locations of fires/emergencies using the most efficient route by considering traffic, safety, and road conditions; positions vehicle to fight fire as instructed by officer; positions vehicle to that there is access to the fire and to water sources; positions vehicle for use of hand and aerial ladders, paying special attention to overhead obstructions, such as power lines; positions vehicle so as not to interfere with later arriving equipment; dons Scott air pack to assist breathing in hazardous conditions; etc..

3. In performing tasks related to search and rescue: searches for victims under direction of officer; determines safest evacuation route of occupants; pries open vehicles, equipment, or structures using specialized equipment such as jaws-of-life or winch in order to free trapped persons; renders medical aid to victims, as appropriate, when victims are found; takes precautions for own safety when searching (e.g., has a way out, takes a rope or follows hose line); locates victims in smoky areas by crawling around room near walls, below smoke level, if possible, searching for victims by touch when visibility is limited; drags or carries conscious, or injured, or unconscious victims down ladders or stairway to remove them from building or entrapments to safety; works in team of two to perform search and rescue tasks; etc.

4. In performing fire extinguishing activities: adjusts throttle and relief valve to ensure necessary volume and pressure from pump for water supply in hoses; monitors gauges of pump (e.g., pressure) to ensure adequate water volume and pressure for hoses; connects hose and couplings to water sources, pumps, nozzles, and other hoses in order to set up water supply; secures garage door in an open position when attacking fire through a garage; sprays fire with charged hose for as long as necessary, until fire is extinguished, or until Scott air pack is expended, or until relieved by another firefighter; observes and responds to changes in condition of fire while fighting it; advances charged hose lines to fight fire, assisted by other firefighters; lifts and maneuvers hand-held and hand-raised ladders to rescue victims and to provide access to fire; lifts and pushes up 50-foot ladder, with assistance, and places against building or dwelling; uses foot to stabilize bottom of 50-foot ladder in positioning ladder against building or dwelling; pushes or pulls pole to stabilize 50-foot ladder; climbs ladders while wearing turnout gear, truckman's belt, ax, and Scott air pack and hand-held tools to ascend for rescue or firefighting; uses turntable controls to elevate, rotate, and extend aerial ladder for access to high building locations; walks or crawls through smoke-filled area to position self to fight fire; extinguishes fire in areas where there is no visibility and extreme heat; etc.

5. In performing ventilation activities: determines two means of egress from roof in case immediate evacuation is required to ensure fire-fighter safety; determines whether roof is safe to support weight of self and other firefighters and their equipment; ventilates structure based on location of fire; opens holes in structures using axes, ceiling hooks, and other equipment for the purpose of ventilation; operates power tools to make openings for ventilation; places ladders at appropriate positions to provide a means of egress for other firefighters; etc.

6. In performing salvage-related activities: carries by hand, materials and debris from fire areas to an area of safety in order to prevent smoke, fire, and water damage; carries with a carry-all, assisted by other firefighters, material, furniture, appliances, and debris from fire area in order to prevent smoke, fire, and water damage; turns in to superior officer valuable items found during salvage or overhaul; etc.

7. In performing overhaul-related activities: uses axes or ceiling hooks to open walls and floors to remove sheet rock and ceiling material to check for signs of fire, hot spots, potential rekindle, and extensions of fire; cuts holes in ceilings, walls, and floors, using power tools (e.g., chain or multi-purpose saws), and makes stairway and ladder chutes to drain water from floors; preserves evidence of arson for use by fire investigation squad; restores to working order all equipment used during the emergency; replaces all equipment on engine and truck used during emergency; inventories equipment used during fire to identify missing or damaged equipment; etc.

8. In performing activities related to administering first aid: dons protective equipment (e.g., gloves, Hepa Mask) to protect against infectious diseases; carries resuscitator and/or related emergency equipment (e.g., first aid bag) to scene of emergency in order to initiate treatment prior to arrival of paramedics; makes sure scene is safe before taking action at scene; checks pulse and respiration of victim to determine whether circulation and respiration are functional; inspects and clears oral and nasal airways to facilitate victim's breathing; inserts airway adjuncts to facilitate victim's breathing; controls bleeding of victims/patients; uses defibrillator to revive and stabilize victim; follows appropriate notification procedures when exposed to an infectious disease; etc.

9. In performing activities related to inspections and pre-planning: familiarizes self with buildings or transit system (e.g., building layout, type of occupancy, and structural information) during inspection in order to respond appropriately in an emergency; visually inspects hydrants, sprinkler systems, and standpipes in district to determine their location, and whether they can be opened for use in a firefighting situation; checks pressure of hydrant using a gauge during inspections to determine if pressure is correct; applies Gleeson valve to high-pressure hydrant to reduce pressure during inspection and testing of hydrants and hoses; conducts drills at schools to educate and pre-plan for emergency situation; etc.

10. In performing activities related to maintenance: tests equipment by operating it in order to determine if it is functioning properly; visually inspects and operates Scott and resuscitator equipment to ensure that all parts of the equipment are present and functioning properly, and tanks are fully charged; visually inspects equipment on truck and engine using an inventory list and knowledge of equipment and storage locations to determine whether all equipment is secured and available for use; visually inspects oil and fuel levels and parts of equipment (motor, tires, etc.) on engine and truck to ensure that equipment is ready and safe to function; cleans and refuels engine-powered equipment such as chain saws, generators, pumps, and extrication tools; reports verbally to officer and other drivers concerning conditions on truck or engine that need repair or replacement in order to function properly; visually inspects all medical equipment and performs daily tests; visually inspects water and cliff rescue equipment (e.g., wet suits, ropes); etc.

11. In performing activities related to training/drills: studies maps to familiarize self with locations of streets, buildings, etc., in first alarm area; exercises to maintain cardiovascular fitness and strength; attends in-service training classes for the purpose of maintaining and gaining knowledge of activities involved in firefighting; performs firefighting activities in fire drills, practices (e.g., ladder practice, hose practice, high-rise drills), and mock disasters as training exercise; discusses past fires and other emergencies with other firefighters and officers, in order to learn from experience and to prepare for similar situations in the future; attends training to maintain EMT and defibrillator certification; etc.

12. In performing activities related to community relations: presents general fire safety information (e.g., methods of eliminating fire hazards) in response to calls and other requests; refers citizen complaint to appropriate superiors; conducts public and private school fire drills (i.e., turns on alarm and observes how school responds); participates in community events (e.g., races, blood drives, neighborhood parties, toy program) to provide service to the city or raise awareness for the SFFD; etc.

13. In performing non-fire response activities: rescues persons who are stuck in elevators; gains entrance to residences by laddering building, picking locks, or using forcible entry to assist public or law enforcement during lock-outs or lock-ins; blocks off street with rig or flares when live wires are down to maintain scene safety until PG&E arrives; when there are reports of a gas leak, shuts off gas valves by using gas wrench to prevent possible explosion; shuts off refrigeration systems using appropriate tools; ensures scene safety at the scene of motor vehicle accidents (e.g., shutting off ignition, disconnecting battery); shores up building by using straps and any other available material (e.g., wood) to stabilize building with weakened structure until engineer can determine how to deal with situation; etc.

14. In performing tasks related to probationary activities at the Division of Training and during initial assignment: attends training classes daily in order to acquire the information necessary to become a certified firefighter; observes demonstrations by instructors in order to comprehend how firefighting tasks should be carried out; demonstrates the correct method of carrying out manipulative tasks (tying knots, raising ladders, etc.) in order to be graded as having satisfactorily mastered the material presented during training; practices performing the tasks which make up the job of a firefighter in order to perform the tasks satisfactorily on manipulative examinations given in fire college or the field; takes the physical ability test; participates in physical conditioning activities; at firehouse, seeks information from other personnel concerning firefighting; etc.

15. In performing tasks related to working with others: serves as a team member while performing job duties, firefighter training, or emergency missions; responds to, carries out, and completes work assignments in accordance with policy, procedure, and protocol; utilizes problem solving techniques in carrying out assignments; communicates effectively with peers and superiors from various cultural and ethnic backgrounds; understands and/or carries out oral instructions or information from superiors and/or peers at emergency incidents; etc.

Knowledge, Skills, and Abilities:

All candidates for this position must have knowledge of:

■ The streets, and traffic laws and patterns in the city; first responder and EMT procedures and equipment to assist in aiding injured individuals; methods of building construction; hazardous materials and their implications for firefighting situations; violations to look for during inspections; the Department's rules, regulations, policies, procedures, and training bulletins; department manuals; the general principles of fire science; the uses, capabilities, and limitations of firefighting equipment and apparatus; fire fighting techniques and strategies; and fire and building codes related to fire suppression systems and fire safety.

All candidates for this position must have the ability to:

■ Work effectively with others; successfully and expeditiously perform tasks associated with extinguishing a fire, administering first aid, searching for and rescuing victims, ventilating the fire building, going from receipt of alarm to arrival at the scene of the emergency, receiving training and performing drills, maintaining the fire house and job-related equipment, overhauling the fire building, preparing for the tour of duty, salvaging materials from the fire building, community relations, fire prevention inspections and pre-fire planning, non-fire response activities, and probationary activities.

Experience and Training:

1. High school diploma or equivalent at application.
2. Emergency Medical Technician certification prior to appointment.
3. Successful completion of fire academy post appointment.

Other Requirements:

1. Minimum of 19 years of age at application.
2. Minimum of 20 years of age at appointment.
3. A valid California Driver License at appointment.
4. Successful completion of the Candidate Physical Ability Test prior to appointment.

Disaster Service Workers

All City and County of San Francisco employees are designated Disaster Service Workers through state and local law (California Government Code Section 3100-3109). Employment with the city requires the affirmation of a loyalty oath to this effect. Employees are required to complete all Disaster Service Worker-related training as assigned, and to return to work as ordered in the event of an emergency.

- Neatness and accuracy count. Filling in your apartment number in the blank labeled "city" reflects poorly on your ability to follow directions.
- Most agencies don't want your resume. Save your time and energy for filling out the application form the agency gives you.
- Verify all information you put on the form. Don't guess or estimate; if you are not sure of, for instance, the exact address of the company you used to work for, look it up.
- If you are mailing your application, take care to submit it to the proper address. It might go to the personnel department rather than to the fire department. Follow the directions on the exam announcement.

week or month. In those cases you usually get more information about the job and the selection process if you pass the written exam. Study the exam announcement, as well as any other material, such as brochures, that the department sends you. You need to be prepared for the whole selection process to be successful.

One very useful exercise is to create a table with two columns—one column should contain each individual requirement of the announcement in its own box; in the second column, you should fill in your qualifications at the time of application. This will give you a graphic view of how well you fulfill the job requirements contained in the announcement.

The Application

Often the first step in the process of becoming a firefighter is filling out an application. Sometimes this is a complete application, asking about your education, employment experience, personal data, and so on. Sometimes there is just an application to take the written or physical test, with a fuller application coming later. In any case, at some point, you will probably be asked some questions you wouldn't expect to see on a regular job application. You might be asked things such as whether you have ever received any speeding tickets or been in trouble with the law, whether you've used illegal drugs, or even whether any relatives work

for the city or for the fire department. Your answers to these questions, as well as the more conventional ones, will serve as the starting point if the department conducts an investigation of your background, so it is important to answer all questions accurately and honestly. If you don't remember what year you worked for XYZ Company or your exact address your sophomore year of high school, don't guess; look it up.

The Written Firefighter Exam

In most jurisdictions, taking a written exam is the next step in the application process, though in some cases the physical ability test comes first.

The written exam is your first opportunity to show that you have what it takes to be a firefighter. As such, it is extremely important. Candidates who don't pass the written exam don't go any farther in the selection process. Furthermore, the written exam score often figures into applicants' rank on the eligibility list; in some cases, this score by itself determines your rank, whereas in others it is combined with other scores, such as physical ability or oral board scores. In those places, a person who merely passes the written exam with a score of, say, 70, is unlikely to be hired when there are plenty of applicants with scores in the 90s. The exam bulletin may specify what your rank will be based on.

- Ask for and use any material the fire department or personnel department puts out about the written test. Some agencies have study guides; some even conduct study sessions. Why let others get a vital advantage while you don't?
- Practice, practice, practice. And then practice some more.
- Try to find some people who have taken the exam recently, and ask them what was on the exam. Their hindsight—"I wish I had studied . . ."—can be your foresight.

What the Written Exam Is Like

Most written firefighter exams simply test basic skills and aptitudes: how well you understand what you read, your ability to follow directions, your judgment and reasoning skills, your ability to read and understand maps and floor plans, and sometimes your memory or your math skills. In this preliminary written exam, you may not be tested on your knowledge of fire behavior, firefighting procedures, or any other specific body of knowledge. This test is often designed only to see how well you can read, reason, and do basic math.

In some places, taking the exam involves studying written materials in advance and then answering questions about them on the exam. These written materials generally have to do with fire and firefighting—but all you have to do is study the guide you are given. You are still being tested on just your reading skills and memory, and there are good reasons for this.

Firefighters have to be able to read, understand, and act on complex written materials—not only fire law and fire procedures, but also scientific materials about fire, combustible materials, and chemicals. They have to be able to think clearly and independently because lives depend on decisions they make in a split second. They have to be able to do enough math to read and understand pressure gauges, or estimate the height of a building and the amount of hose needed to reach the third floor. They have to be able to read maps and floor plans so they can get to the emergency site quickly or find their way to an exit even in a smoke-filled building.

Most exams are multiple-choice tests of the sort you have often encountered in school. You get an exam book and an answer sheet where you have to fill in little circles (bubbles) or squares with a number 2 pencil.

When you are preparing to take your Firefighter written exam, be sure to purchase a copy of Learning-Express's *Firefighter Exam Fourth Edition*. It contains four practice exams that include the skills most commonly tested. There are also chapters on each kind of question you are most likely to encounter. Each chapter includes not only sample questions but also tips and hints on how to prepare for that kind of question and how to do well on the exam itself.

The Candidate Physical Ability Test (CPAT)

The Candidate Physical Ability Test is the next step in the process for many fire departments; some put this step first. You should expect to have a medical clearance, or at the very least sign a medical waiver stating that you are in good enough shape to undertake this stressful test, before you will be allowed to participate. The fire department wants to make sure that no one has a heart attack in the middle of the test. So, you can expect the test to be tough.

Firefighting is, after all, physically demanding work. Once again, lives depend on whether your strength, stamina, and overall fitness allow you to carry out the necessary tasks during an emergency. If you make it to the academy and later into a fire company, you can expect to continue physical training and exercises throughout your career. In fact, in some cities all firefighters are required to retake the Candidate Physical Ability Test every year.

What the Candidate Physical Ability Test Is Like

The exact events that make up the Candidate Physical Ability Test vary from place to place, but the tasks you have to perform are almost always job-related—they are a lot like the physical tasks you will actually have to perform as a firefighter. Some tests are set up as obstacle courses; others consist of a group of stations. In some, you are timed from start to finish with no breaks; others allow a break period between stations. The tests are timed. Your performance on the test is scored depending on that time. Often you have to wear full (heavy) protective gear, including an air pack, throughout these events. Here is an example of the events in a test that you would typically have ten minutes, 20 seconds to complete:

- Stair climb with weighted vest
- Hose drag
- Equipment carry
- Ladder raise and extension
- Forcible entry
- Search
- Rescue dummy drag
- Ceiling breach and pull

In an obstacle-course setup like this one, you might be given the opportunity to walk the course before you actually have to take the test. During the test itself, you would be timed as you went through the events, and you would have to complete the events within a set time limit to pass. In departments where the Candidate Physical Ability Test figures into your rank on the eligibility list, merely meeting the maximum time to pass isn't good enough; people who have lower times will be hired before you are.

Different departments have different policies on retesting if you fail. Some allow you to retest on the same day after a rest period. Some allow you to come back another time and try again—usually up to a set maximum number of tries. And in some departments, your first try is the only chance you get; if you fail, you are out, at least until the next testing period. Few departments will allow you to retest, if you have already passed, simply to improve your time.

You can usually find out just what tasks are included in the Candidate Physical Ability Test from the exam announcement or related materials.

The Background Investigation

Most fire departments conduct background investigations of applicants who pass the written and physical tests. Some departments prescreen applicants and may reject an applicant who has a criminal record. Firefighters have to be honest, upright citizens who can get along with both their company and the people they serve. You may not even know such an investigation is going on—until someone at the oral interview asks you why you wrote on your application that you never used drugs when your high school friends all say you regularly smoked marijuana on weekends. (That's why it is important to answer honestly on your application.)

What the Background Investigation Is Like

The rigorousness with which your background will be checked depends on the policies of your department. Some conduct a fairly superficial check, calling your former employers and schools simply to verify that you were there when you say you were there and didn't have any problems during that time.

Other departments will investigate you in a great deal more depth, asking their contacts how long and how well they knew you and what kind of person they found you to be. Did you meet your obligations? How did you deal with problems? Did they find you to be an honest person? Do they know of anything that might affect your fitness to be a firefighter? The references you provided will lead the investigator to other people who knew you, and when the investigator is finished, he or she will have a pretty complete picture of what kind of person you are.

A few fire departments include a polygraph, or lie detector test, as part of the background investigation. As long as you have been honest in what you have said when your stress reactions weren't being monitored by a polygraph machine, a lie detector test is nothing to worry about.

Oral Interviews and Boards

The selection process in your fire department is likely to include one or more oral interviews. There may be an individual interview with the chief or deputy chief, or there may be an oral board, in which you would meet with several people—or you may face both. Whether it is an individual interview or an oral board, the interviewers are interested in your interpersonal skills—how well you communicate with them—as well as in your qualifications to be a firefighter.

What the Oral Interview Is Like

In some cities, applicants who get this far in the process meet with the chief or deputy chief, who may conduct something like a typical job interview. The chief or deputy chief might describe in detail what the job is like, ask you how well you think you can do a job like that, and ask you why you want to be a firefighter in the first place. In the process, the chief will also be assessing your interpersonal skills, whether you seem honest and relatively comfortable in talking to him or her. You may also be asked questions about your background and experience.

This interview can be a make-or-break part of the process, with the chief approving or rejecting your candidacy, or the chief may rank you against other applicants, in which case the chief's assessment of you is likely to figure into your place on the eligibility list.

The chief's interview may also include situational questions like those typically asked by an oral board, or you may be facing an oral board in addition to your interview with the chief.

What the Oral Board Is Like

The oral board typically assesses such qualities as interpersonal skills, communication skills, judgment and decision-making abilities, respect for diversity, and adaptability. The board itself consists of two to five people, who may be firefighters or civilian personnel or interview specialists. There is usually some variety in the makeup of the board: It usually consists of officers of various ranks and/or civilians from the personnel department or from the community.

The way the interview is conducted depends on the practices of the individual department. You may be asked a few questions similar to those you would be asked at a normal employment interview: Why do you want to be a firefighter? What qualities do you have that would make you good at this job? You may be asked questions about your background, especially if your application or background investigation raised any questions in the board members' minds. Have answers prepared for such questions in advance.

In addition to such questions, you may be presented with hypothetical situations that you will be asked to respond to. A board member may say something like this: "A coworker on your shift is posting derogatory, racially based jokes in his gear rack and his locker. Another coworker on your shift finds the jokes tasteless and offensive. What would you do?" You would then have to come up with an appropriate response to this situation.

Increasingly, cities have standardized the oral board questions. The same questions are asked of every candidate, and when the interview is over, the board rates each candidate on a standard scale. This procedure helps the interviewers reach a somewhat more objective conclusion about the candidates they have interviewed and may result in a score that is included in the factors used to rank candidates in the eligibility list.

The Psychological Evaluation

Some cities, though not all, include a psychological evaluation as part of the firefighter selection process. The fire department wants to make sure that you are emotionally and mentally stable before putting you in a high-stress job in which you have to interact with peers, superiors, and the public. Don't worry, though;

the psychological evaluation is not designed to uncover your deep dark secrets. Its only purpose is to make sure you have the mental and emotional health to do the job.

What the Psychological Evaluation Is Like

If your fire department has a psychological evaluation, most likely that means you will be taking one or two written tests. A few cities have candidates interviewed by a psychologist or psychiatrist.

If you have to take a written psychological test, it is likely to be a standardized multiple-choice or true–false test licensed from a psychological testing company. The Minnesota Multiphasic Personality Inventory (MMPI) is one commonly used test. Such tests typically ask you about your interests, attitudes, and background. They may take one hour or several to complete; the hiring agency will let you know approximately how much time to allot.

If your process includes an oral psychological assessment, you will meet with a psychologist or psychiatrist, who may be either on the hiring agency's staff or an independent contractor. The psychologist may ask you questions about your schooling and jobs, your relationships with family and friends, your habits, and your hobbies. The psychologist may be as interested in the *way* you answer—whether you come across as open, forthright, and honest—as in the answers themselves.

The Medical Examination

Before passage of the Americans With Disabilities Act (ADA), many fire departments conducted a medical examination early in the process, before the physical ability test. Now, the ADA says it is illegal to do any examinations or ask any questions that could reveal an applicant's disability until after a conditional offer of employment has been made. That means that in most jurisdictions you will get such a conditional offer before you are asked to submit to a medical exam.

You should know, however, that almost any disability can prevent you from becoming a firefighter, even under the protections provided by ADA. Firefighting requires a high level of physical and mental fitness, and a host of disabilities that would not prevent a candidate from doing some other job would prevent a firefighter from fulfilling essential job functions. For example, a skin condition that requires a man to wear facial hair would disqualify that man from being a firefighter because facial hair interferes with proper operation of the breathing apparatus.

Drug Testing

Note, however, that a test for use of illegal drugs *can* be administered before a conditional offer of employment. Because firefighters have to be in tiptop physical shape, and because they are in a position of public trust, the fire department expects them to be drug-free. You may have to undergo drug testing periodically throughout your career as a firefighter.

What the Medical Exam Is Like

The medical exam itself is nothing to be afraid of. It will be just like any other thorough physical exam. The doctor may be on the staff of the hiring agency or someone outside the department with his or her own practice, just like your own doctor. Your blood pressure, temperature, weight, and so on will be measured; your heart and lungs will be listened to and your limbs examined. The doctor will probably peer into your eyes, ears, nose, and mouth. You will also have to donate some blood and urine. Because of those tests, you won't know the results of the physical exam right away. You will probably be notified in writing in a few weeks, after the test results come in.

And When You Succeed . . .

Congratulations! The end of the whole process for you is notification to attend the fire service academy. You are on the road to your career as a firefighter.

The road is hardly over, though. First, you have to make it through the academy. You will also have a lot of learning to do in your first year or so on the job. Throughout your career, you will need to keep up with new techniques, new equipment, and new procedures. And if you decide to go for a promotion, there will be more steps, more tests, and more evaluations. But you can do it, if you are determined and committed. You have already made a smart choice by choosing to pursue EMT certification. For information on how to get started, turn the page.

2 ▶ THE EMT-BASIC EXAM

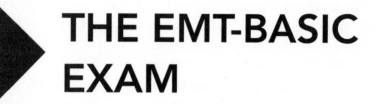

CHAPTER SUMMARY
This chapter tells you how to become certified as an Emergency Medical Technician-Basic (EMT-B). It outlines the certification requirements of the National Registry of Emergency Medical Technicians and tells you how to use this book to study for the written exam.

The National Registry of Emergency Medical Technicians (NREMT) was established in 1970 in response to a suggestion of the U.S. Committee on Highway Safety. Today, the NREMT is an independent, not-for-profit agency whose job is to certify that EMTs have the knowledge and skills to do their job—to save lives and preserve health. By setting uniform national standards for training, testing, and continuing education, the NREMT helps ensure patient safety throughout the United States.

In some states, the NREMT certification process is the only licensure process for EMTs. Other states have their own testing procedures. (A list of specific certification requirements for all 50 states, Washington, D.C., Puerto Rico, and the U.S. Virgin Islands appears in Chapter 9.) Nearly all states and U.S. territories base their curriculum and tests on the U.S. Department of Transportation's National Standard Curriculum for EMT-Basics. The NREMT exam uses the same curriculum to guide the construction of exam questions. Therefore, whether you will be taking a state test or the NREMT test, you will be learning and studying similar material. This book is based on the NREMT cognitive examination.

Minimum Requirements

To apply for national registration as an EMT-Basic with the NREMT, you must meet the following requirements:

- You must be at least 18 years old.
- You must have successfully completed a state-approved National Standard EMT-Basic training program within the last two years.
- If your state does not require national EMT-Basic registration, you must obtain official documentation of your current state EMT-Basic certification.
- You must have successfully completed all sections of a state-approved EMT-Basic practical exam within the past 12 months. This exam must equal or exceed all the criteria established by the National Registry.
- You must complete the felony statement on the application and submit the required documentation.
- You must submit current cardiopulmonary resuscitation (CPR) credentials from either the American Heart Association or the American Red Cross.
- You must submit an acceptable application attesting to the satisfaction of the previous requirements.
- You must send a $70 nonrefundable/nontransferable application fee (money order only). All fees must be made payable to the National Registry of Emergency Medical Technicians and submitted with the application to cover processing of the application.
- You must successfully complete the National Registry EMT-Basic cognitive examination.

How to Apply

When you have met all the requirements and are ready to take the exam, contact the NREMT to obtain an application and to find out where you can take the test in your state. Write or call the NREMT at:

National Registry of Emergency
Medical Technicians
P.O. Box 29233
Columbus, OH 43229
614-888-4484

When you contact the National Registry, you will find out whether the examination is administered through your state EMT office or whether you need to make individual arrangements to take the exam.

Finally, you must submit an application to the National Registry stating that you have met all the requirements, accompanied by the registration fee.

You can also fill out an NREMT application online by going to http://www.nremt.org/EMT Services/candidate_application.asp.

The EMT-Basic Cognitive Exam

The National Registry's EMT-Basic cognitive examination ranges from 70 to 120 items, and the maximum time allotted to take the exam is two hours from the time it begins. The exam is administered using a computer adaptive test (CAT). With the CAT method, each question is modified to fit your abilities. For example, if you answer a question correctly, the following question will be somewhat more challenging. If you answer a question incorrectly, the following question will be a bit easier. The more questions you answer correctly, the more likely you are to end the exam early. Once you complete each section of questions, the CAT will reevaluate your ability, and as the exam continues, the program will adapt to match your skill level.

The purpose of the CAT-administered cognitive exam is to find your highest ability level. The exam is pass/fail, and in order to pass, you must meet entry-level competency. Entry-level competency is the NREMT's criteria for an EMT-Basic candidate, which includes being able to practice carefully and capably.

The exam consists of six content areas:

CATEGORY	PERCENT OF OVERALL TEST
Airway and Breathing	18.0%
Cardiology	17.3%
Trauma	16.7%
Medical	15.3%
Obstetrics and Pediatrics	16.0%
Operations	16.7%
TOTAL	**100%**

For more information on the EMT-Basic cognitive exam, visit http://www.nremt.org/about/about_exams.asp.

The EMT-Basic Practical Exam

When you apply for National Registry EMT-Basic registration, you will fill out an application that consists of several sections. The application requires verification of your credentials. The verification may be in the form of your program director's electronic signature attesting to competency in the following skills:

1. Patient Assessment/Management—Trauma
2. Patient Assessment/Management—Medical
3. Cardiac Arrest Management/AED
4. Spinal Immobilization (Seated Patient)
5. Spinal Immobilization (Supine Patient)
6. Bag-Valve-Mask Apneic Patient with a Pulse
7. Long Bone Fracture Immobilization
8. Joint Dislocation Immobilization
9. Traction Splinting
10. Bleeding Control/Shock Management
11. Upper Airway Adjuncts and Suction
12. Mouth-to-Mask with Supplemental Oxygen
13. Supplemental Oxygen Administration

The National Registry EMT-Basic application also requires proof that you have successfully completed a state-approved practical examination within a 12-month period. At a minimum, the exam must evaluate your performance in the following skills. To pass the practical exam, you must meet or exceed the NREMT's criteria in the following six areas:

- **Station #1:** Patient Assessment/Management—Trauma
- **Station #2:** Patient Assessment/Management—Medical
- **Station #3:** Cardiac Arrest Management/AED
- **Station #4:** Spinal Immobilization (seated or supine patient)
- **Station #5:** Bag-Valve-Mask Apneic Patient with a Pulse
- **Station #6:** Random Skill Station. This will consist of one of the following skills:
  - Long bone immobilization
  - Joint dislocation immobilization
  - Traction splinting
  - Bleeding control/shock management
  - Upper airway adjuncts and suction
  - Mouth-to-mask with supplemental oxygen
  - Supplemental oxygen administration

Chapter 8 contains more detailed information about the NREMT practical exam.

EMT-Basic Application

The National Registry of Emergency Medical Technicians

I am submitting this application to test at

_____ in _____
Name of Facility | City

_____ on _____
State | Date (MM/DD/YY)

Application Date
[ ][ ] - [ ][ ] - [ ][ ][ ]

Social Security Number
[ ][ ][ ] - [ ][ ] - [ ][ ][ ][ ]

Have you ever applied for NREMT-B registration? ○ Yes ○ No

If you possess current state certification as an EMT, please list your current state EMT certification number in the space provided and attach a copy of your current EMT card

Current EMT Number
Please attach copy of card

Last Name

First Name

MI

Mailing Address

Program Code
[ ][ ][ ] - [ ][ ]

City

State

Zip Code + 4
[ ][ ][ ][ ][ ] - [ ][ ][ ][ ]

Gender
○ Male
○ Female

Date of Birth
[ ][ ] - [ ][ ] - [ ][ ]

APPROVED EMT-B COURSE: Applicant must have completed an approved EMT-Basic Training Program that equals or exceeds the objectives of the National Standard EMT-Basic Curriculum. Attach a copy of your course completion certificate or a copy of your current EMT-B card. If your initial EMT-Basic training program is more than two years old or you hold current state certification as an EMT-Basic, you must document completion of 24 hours of approved EMT-B refresher training within the past two years and attach official documentation to this application.

Name of initial training institution or agency	Street Address	City	State	Zip Code

Initial Course Instructor/Course Coordinator	Course Completion Date [ ][ ]-[ ][ ]-[ ][ ]	Classroom Hours [ ][ ][ ]
Refresher Course Instructor/Course Coordinator	Refersher Completion Date [ ][ ]-[ ][ ]-[ ][ ]	Classroom Hours [ ][ ][ ]

What is the highest level of education you have completed?
○ Didn't complete high school
○ High school graduate/GED
○ Associate's degree
○ Bachelor's degree
○ Graduate degree

Please indicate the type of EMT-B service you are or will be affiliated with. (mark all that apply)
○ Fire Department ○ U.S. Government
○ Private ○ Army
○ Hospital-Based ○ Navy
○ 3rd-Service ○ Air Force
○ Volunteer ○ Coast Guard
○ Other

Will you be paid for your services as an EMT-B?
○ Yes
○ No
○ Not yet affiliated

Ethnic Origin
○ Native American
○ Asian
○ Black
○ Hispanic
○ White
○ Other

Licensing Action and Felony Statement

○ Yes ○ No — Have you ever been subject to limitation, suspension, or termination of your right to practice in a health care occupation or voluntarily surrendered a health care licensure in any state or to an agency authorizing the legal right to work?

○ Yes ○ No — Have you ever been convicted of a felony

If you answered "yes" to either question, you must provide official documentation that fully describes the offense, current status, and disposition of the case

Candidate Statement and Signature: I hereby affirm and declare that the above information on this application is true and correct and that any fraudulent entry may be considered a sufficient cause for rejection or subsequent revocation. I further agree to abide by all policies and procedures of the National Registry of EMTs, and hereby authorize the NREMT to release my examination scores to the teaching institution/agency, any state office of Emergency Medical Services, or any agency authorizing the legal right to practice. I further permit the NREMT to release my current status (registered or not registered) with the NREMT to the public 30 days following mailing of my test scores.

Applicant Signature

EMT-Basic Practical Examination Verification

This is to verify that on [ ][ ]-[ ][ ][ ][ ], _____ completed a state-approved
Date (MM-YYYY) | Candidate's Name

practical examination at _____ _____ _____
Examination Site and State

equal to or exceeding the criteria established by the NREMT and performed satisfactorily so as to be deemed competent in the following skills:

Patient Assessment/Management - Trauma
Patient Assessment/Management - Medical
Cardiac Arrest Management/AED

Bag-Valve-Mask (Apneic Patient)
Spinal Immobilization (Seated or Supine Patient)
Random Skill Verification _____

Physician Name (Print or Type)

Agent or Assignee's Name (Print or Type)

Physician Signature

Agent or Assignee's Signature

License #

Agent or Assignee's Title

Section I: CPR Credential

As the candidate's CPR instructor/training officer, I hereby verify the candidate has been examined and performed satisfactorily so as to be deemed competent in each of the following skills:

Adult 1 & 2 Rescuer CPR
Adult Obstructed Airway Maneuvers
Child CPR
Child Obstructed Airway Maneuvers
Infant CPR
Infant Obstructed Airway Maneuvers

_____
Verifying Signature   Date

CPR Expiration Date

[ ] [ ] - [ ] [ ] - [ ] [ ] [ ] [ ]

Please submit a copy of your current CPR card and/or ensure the appropriate verification signatures are affixed to this section of the application

Section II: Statement of Competency in EMT-Basic Skills

As the EMT-Basic Training Program Director or service director of training/operations, I verify that _____ ____ __

has been examined and performed satisfactorily so as to be deemed competent in each of the following skills: (Candidate's Name)

Patient Assessment/Management - Trauma
Patient Assessment/Management - Medical
Cardiac Arrest Management/AED
Bleeding Control/Shock Management
Bag-Valve-Mask Apneic Patient
Supplemental Oxygen Administration
Upper Airway Adjuncts and Suction

Mouth-to-Mask with Supplemental Oxygen
Spinal Immobilization Supine Patient
Spinal Immobilization Seated Patient
Long Bone Immobilization
Joint Dislocation Immobilization
Traction Splinting

Signature: _____ _   Date: _____ _____

Name (Please Print) _____   _____

Title (Please Print) _____   Telephone # _____

Character Reference

Name	Street Address	City	State	Zip Code

National Registry EMT-Basic Application Information

Entry Requirements:

1. Successful completion of a state-approved EMT-Basic training program within the past 24 months, that equals or exceeds the behavioral objectives of the EMT-Basic National Standard Curriculum as developed and promulgated by the U.S. Department of Transportation.
2. If the candidate's initial EMT-Basic training completion date is beyond 24 months and the candidate has maintained state certification as an EMT-Basic, the candidate must document completion of 24 hours of state-approved EMT-Basic refresher training that meets all objectives of the current EMT-Basic National Standard Refresher Curriculum. Program completion date can be no older than 24 months from the date of testing.
3. Current CPR credential verifying competence in the skills listed in the "**CPR Credential**" section of this application.
4. The **EMT-Basic Practical Examination Verification** section of the application must be signed by the Physician Medical Director or the agent or assignee of the physician attesting to the candidates successful completion, within the past 12 months, of a practical examination that meets or exceeds the criteria established by the NREMT.
5. **Section II : Statement of Competency in EMT-Basic Skills** (above) must be signed by the EMT-Basic Training Program Director or the Director of Training/Operations. **Applications submitted for each re-examination must also be completed in their entirety and signed in an original fashion.**
6. Submission of a completed application and official course completion documentation attesting to the above requirements as well as all other published entry requirements of the National Registry of EMTs.
7. A non-refundable, non-transferable application fee of $20.00, payable to the National Registry of Emergency Medical Technicians, must be submitted with this application. Each attempt of the written examination requires submission of an application and a $20.00 non-refundable, non-transferable application fee.
8. Successful completion of the National Registry EMT-Basic written examinations.

Checklist for Submitting an Application for the National Registry EMT-Basic Examination Process:

1. Have you, your Physician Medical Director, and/or your training director or service director of training/operations signed the application? **Applications submitted for each re-examination must also be completed in their entirety and signed in an original fashion.**
2. Have you attached a copy of your CPR card which will be current and valid at the time of the examination or has your CPR instructor affixed his or her signature to the appropriate space in the "**CPR Credential**" section of this application?
3. Have you or your program director attached to this application official documentation of successful completion of state-approved EMT-Basic training which meets or exceeds the bahavioral objectives of the current EMT-Basic National Standard Curriculum?
4. Have you filled in all of the information requested on the application, including the felony statement?
5. Have you attached a check or money order in the appropriate amount to this application. Each attempt of the written examination requires submission of an application and a $20.00 non-refunable, non-transferable application fee.
6. Be sure to bring an official photo identification (driver's license) and two #2 pencils to the examination site.
7. For more information please visit our homepage at http://www.nremt.org or contact us via telephone at (614) 888-4484.

Payments or contributions to the NREMT are not deductible as charitable contributions for Federal Income Tax purposes. Payments may be deductible as a business expense. If in doubt, please contact your tax advisor.

477122

THE LEARNINGEXPRESS TEST PREPARATION SYSTEM

CHAPTER SUMMARY

Taking the EMT-Basic exam can be tough. It demands a lot of preparation if you want to achieve a top score. The LearningExpress Test Preparation System, developed exclusively for LearningExpress by leading test experts, gives you the discipline and attitude you need to be a winner.

First, the bad news: Taking the EMT-Basic exam is no picnic, and neither is getting ready for it. Your future career as a firefighter may depend on passing, but there are all sorts of pitfalls that can keep you from doing your best on this all-important exam. Here are some of the obstacles that can stand in the way of your success:

- being unfamiliar with the format of the exam
- being paralyzed by test anxiety
- leaving your preparation to the last minute
- not preparing at all!
- not knowing vital test-taking skills: how to pace yourself through the exam, how to use the process of elimination, and when to guess
- not being in tip-top mental and physical shape
- arriving late at the test site, working on an empty stomach, or shivering through the exam because the room is cold

What's the common denominator in all these test-taking pitfalls? One thing: *control*. Who's in control, you or the exam?

Now the good news: The LearningExpress Test Preparation System puts *you* in control. In just nine easy-to-follow steps, you will learn everything you need to know to ensure that you are in charge of your preparation and your performance on the exam. Other test takers may let the test get the better of them; other test takers may be unprepared or out of shape, but not you. You will have taken all the steps you need to get a high score on the EMT-Basic exam.

Here's how the LearningExpress Test Preparation System works: Nine easy steps lead you through everything you need to know and do to get ready to master your exam. Each of the following steps includes both reading about the step and one or more activities. It's important that you do the activities along with the reading, or you won't get the full benefits of the system. Each step tells you approximately how much time that step will take you to complete.

Step 1. Get Information	50 minutes
Step 2. Conquer Test Anxiety	20 minutes
Step 3. Make a Plan	30 minutes
Step 4. Learn to Manage Your Time	10 minutes
Step 5. Learn to Use the Process of Elimination	20 minutes
Step 6. Know When to Guess	20 minutes
Step 7. Reach Your Peak Performance Zone	10 minutes
Step 8. Get Your Act Together	10 minutes
Step 9. Do It!	10 minutes
TOTAL	**3 HOURS**

We estimate that working through the entire system will take you approximately three hours, though it's perfectly okay if you work more quickly or slowly than the time estimates assume. If you have a whole afternoon or evening free, you can work through the whole LearningExpress Test Preparation System in one sitting. Otherwise, you can break it up and do just one or two steps a day for the next several days. It's up to you—remember, *you're* in control.

Step 1: Get Information

Time to complete: 50 minutes
Activities: Read Chapter 2, "The EMT-Basic Exam" and Chapter 9, "State Certification Requirements"

Knowledge is power. The first step in the LearningExpress Test Preparation System is finding out everything you can about the EMT-Basic exam. Once you have your information, the next steps in the LearningExpress Test Preparation System will show you what to do about it.

Part A: Straight Talk about the EMT-Basic Exam

Why do you have to take this exam anyway? Simply put, because lives depend on your performance in the field. The EMT-Basic cognitive exam is just one part of a whole series of evaluations you have to go through to show that you can be trusted with the health and safety of the people you serve. The cognitive exam attempts to measure your knowledge of your trade. The practical skills exam attempts to measure your ability to apply what you know.

It's important for you to remember that your score on the EMT-Basic cognitive exam does not determine how smart you are or even whether you will make a good EMT. There are all kinds of things an exam like this can't test: whether you are likely to frequently show up late or call in sick, whether you can keep your cool under the stress of trying to revive a victim of cardiac arrest, whether you can be trusted with confidential information about people's health, etc. Those kinds of things are hard to evaluate, while whether you can click on the right answer on a computer is easy to evaluate.

This is not to say that clicking on the right answer is not important. The knowledge tested on the cognitive exam is knowledge you will need to do the EMS aspect of your firefighting job. Furthermore, your ability to enter the firefighter profession may depend on your first passing this exam. And that's why you're here—using the LearningExpress Test Preparation System to achieve control over the exam.

Part B: What's on the Test

If you haven't already done so, stop here and read the previous chapter of this book, which gives you an overview of EMT-Basic cognitive exams in general and the National Registry of Emergency Medical Technicians (NREMT) exam in particular.

Many states use the NREMT exam, but others do not. Turn to Chapter 9 for a state-by-state overview of certification requirements. If you haven't already gotten the full rundown on certification procedures as part of your training program, you can contact your state's EMT agency listed in Chapter 9 for details.

Step 2: Conquer Test Anxiety

Time to complete: 20 minutes
Activity: Take the Test Stress Exam

Having complete information about the exam is the first step in getting control of it. Next, you have to overcome one of the biggest obstacles to test success: anxiety. Test anxiety can not only impair your performance on the exam itself, it can even keep you from preparing! In Step 2, you'll learn stress-management techniques that will help you succeed on your exam. Learn these strategies now, and practice them as you work through the exams in this book, so they'll be second nature to you by exam day.

Combating Test Anxiety

The first thing you need to know is that a little test anxiety is a good thing. Everyone gets nervous before a big exam—and if that nervousness motivates you to prepare thoroughly, so much the better. It's said that Sir Laurence Olivier, one of the foremost British actors of the twentieth century, felt sick before every performance. His stage fright didn't impair his performance; in fact, it probably gave him a little extra edge—just the kind of edge you need to do well, whether on a stage or in an examination room.

The Test Stress Exam is on page 25. Stop here and answer the questions on that page to find out whether your level of test anxiety is cause for worry.

Stress Management before the Test

If you feel your level of anxiety is getting the best of you in the weeks before the test, here is what you need to do to bring the level down again:

- **Get prepared.** There's nothing like knowing what to expect and being prepared for it to put you in control of test anxiety. That's why you're reading this book. Use it faithfully, and remind yourself that you're better prepared than most of the people taking the test.

- **Practice self-confidence.** A positive attitude is a great way to combat test anxiety. This is no time to be humble or shy. Stand in front of the mirror and say to your reflection, "I'm prepared. I'm full of self-confidence. I'm going to ace this test. I know I can do it." Record it and play it back once a day. If you hear it often enough, you'll believe it.
- **Fight negative messages.** Every time someone starts telling you how hard the exam is or how it's almost impossible to get a high score, start telling them your self-confidence messages. If that someone with the negative messages is *you* telling yourself *you don't do well on exams, you just can't do this,* don't listen. Turn on your recording and listen to your self-confidence messages.
- **Visualize.** Imagine yourself reporting for duty on your first day as an EMT. Think of yourself responding to calls, interacting with patients, preserving health, and saving lives. Visualizing success can help make it happen—and it reminds you of why you're doing all this work preparing for the exam.
- **Exercise.** Physical activity helps calm your body and focus your mind. Besides, being in good physical shape can actually help you do well on the exam. Go for a run, lift weights, go swimming—and do it regularly.

Stress Management on Test Day

There are several ways you can lower your anxiety on test day. They'll work best if you practice them in the weeks before the test, so you know which ones work best for you.

- **Deep breathing.** Take a deep breath while you count to five. Hold it for a count of one, then let it out for a count of five. Repeat several times.
- **Move your body.** Try rolling your head in a circle. Rotate your shoulders. Shake your hands from the wrist. Many people find these movements very relaxing.

- **Visualize again.** Think of the place where you are most relaxed: lying on the beach in the sun, walking through the park, or whatever. Now close your eyes and imagine you're actually there. If you practice in advance, you'll find that you need only a few seconds of this exercise to experience a significant increase in your sense of well-being.

When anxiety threatens to overwhelm you right there during the exam, there are still things you can do to manage the stress level.

- **Repeat your self-confidence messages.** You should have them memorized by now. Say them quietly to yourself, and believe them!
- **Visualize one more time.** This time, visualize yourself moving smoothly and quickly through the test, answering every question correctly and finishing just before time is up. Like most visualization techniques, this one works best if you've practiced it ahead of time.
- **Find an easy question.** Skim over the test until you find an easy question, and answer it. Entering even one answer choice helps get you into the test-taking groove.
- **Take a mental break.** Everyone loses concentration once in a while during a long test. It's normal, so you shouldn't worry about it. Instead, accept what has happened. Say to yourself, "Hey, I lost it there for a minute. My brain is taking a break." Close your eyes and do some deep breathing for a few seconds. Then, you'll be ready to go back to work.

Try these techniques ahead of time, and watch them work for you!

You need to worry about test anxiety only if it is extreme enough to impair your performance. The following questionnaire will diagnose your level of test anxiety. In the blank before each statement, write the number that most accurately describes your experience.

0 = Never   1 = Once or twice   2 = Sometimes   3 = Often

_____   I have gotten so nervous before an exam that I simply put down the books and didn't study for it.

_____   I have experienced disabling physical symptoms such as vomiting and severe headaches because I was nervous about an exam.

_____   I have simply not shown up for an exam because I was scared to take it.

_____   I have experienced dizziness and disorientation while taking an exam.

_____   I have had trouble filling in the little circles because my hands were shaking too hard.

_____   I have failed an exam because I was too nervous to complete it.

_____   **Total: Add up the numbers in the blanks above.**

Your Test Stress Score

Here are the steps you should take, depending on your score. If you scored:

- **Below 3:** Your level of test anxiety is nothing to worry about; it's probably just enough to give you that little extra edge.

- **Between 3 and 6:** Your test anxiety may be enough to impair your performance, and you should practice the stress-management techniques listed in this section to try to bring your test anxiety down to manageable levels.

- **Above 6:** Your level of test anxiety is a serious concern. In addition to practicing the stress-management techniques listed in this section, you may want to seek additional personal help. Call your local high school or community college and ask for the academic counselor. Tell the counselor that you have a level of test anxiety that sometimes keeps you from being able to take the exam. The counselor may be willing to help you or may suggest someone else with whom you should talk.

Step 3: Make a Plan

Time to complete: 30 minutes
Activity: Construct a study plan
Maybe the most important thing you can do to get control of yourself and your exam is to make a study plan. Too many people fail to prepare simply because they fail to plan. Spending hours the day before the exam poring over sample test questions not only raises your level of test anxiety, it also is simply no substitute for careful preparation and practice over time.

Don't fall into the cram trap. Take control of your preparation time by mapping out a study schedule. On the following pages are two sample schedules based on the amount of time you have before you take the EMT-Basic cognitive exam. If you're the kind of person who needs deadlines and assignments to motivate you for a project, here they are. If you're the kind of person who doesn't like to follow other people's plans, you can use the following suggested schedules to construct your own.

Even more important than making a plan is making a commitment. You can't review everything you learned in your EMT course in one night. You have to set aside some time every day for study and practice. Try for at least 20 minutes a day. Twenty minutes daily will do you much more good than two hours on Saturday.

Don't put off your studying until the day before the exam. Start now. A few minutes a day, with half an hour or more on weekends, can make a big difference in your score.

Schedule A: The 30-Day Plan

If you have at least a month before you take the EMT-Basic exam, you have plenty of time to prepare—as long as you don't waste it! If you have less than a month, turn to Schedule B.

TIME	PREPARATION
Days 1–4	Skim over the written materials from your training program, particularly noting 1) areas you expect to be emphasized on the exam and 2) areas you don't remember well. On Day 4, concentrate on those areas.
Day 5	Take the first practice exam in Chapter 3.
Day 6	Score the first practice exam. Use the outline of skills in Chapter 2 to reveal your strongest and weakest areas. Identify two areas that you will concentrate on before you take the second practice exam.
Days 7–10	Study the two areas you identified as your weak points. Don't worry about the other areas.
Day 11	Take the second practice exam in Chapter 5.
Day 12	Score the second practice exam. Identify one area to concentrate on before you take the third practice exam.
Days 13–18	Study the one area you identified for review. In addition, review both practice exams you've already taken, with special attention to the answer explanations.
Day 19	Take the third practice exam in Chapter 6.
Day 20	Once again, identify one area to review, based on your score on the third practice exam.
Days 20–21	Study the one area you identified for review.
Days 22–25	Take an overview of all your training materials, consolidating your strengths and improving on your weaknesses.
Days 26–27	Review all the areas that have given you the most trouble in the three practice exams you've already taken.
Day 28	Take the fourth practice exam in Chapter 7 and score it. Note how much you've improved!
Day 29	Review one or two weak areas.
Day before the exam	Relax. Do something unrelated to the exam, and go to bed at a reasonable hour.

Schedule B: The 10-Day Plan

If you have two weeks or less before you take the exam, you have your work cut out for you. Use this 10-day schedule to help you make the most of your time.

TIME	PREPARATION
Day 1	Take the first practice exam in Chapter 4 and score it using the answer key at the end. Turn to the list of subject areas on the exam in Chapter 2 and find out which areas need the most work based on your exam score.
Day 2	Review one area that gave you trouble on the first practice exam.
Day 3	Review another area that gave you trouble on the first practice exam.
Day 4	Take the second practice exam in Chapter 5 and score it.
Day 5	If your score on the second practice exam doesn't show improvement on the two areas you studied, review them. If you did improve in those areas, choose a new weak area to study.
Day 6	Take the third practice exam in Chapter 6 and score it.
Day 7	Choose your weakest area from the third practice exam to review.
Day 8	Review any areas that you have not yet reviewed in this schedule.
Day 9	Take the fourth practice exam in Chapter 7 and score it. Brush up on any remaining trouble areas.
Day before the exam	Relax. Do something unrelated to the exam, and go to bed at a reasonable hour.

Step 4: Learn to Manage Your Time

Time to complete: 10 minutes to read, many hours of practice!

Activities: Practice these strategies as you take the sample tests in this book

Steps 4, 5, and 6 of the LearningExpress Test Preparation System put you in charge of your exam by showing you test-taking strategies that work. Practice these strategies as you take the sample tests in this book, and then you'll be ready to use them on test day.

First, you'll take control of your time on the exam. Most EMT-Basic exams have a time limit of three hours, which may give you more than enough time to complete all the questions—or may not. It's a terrible feeling to hear the examiner say, "Five minutes left," when you're only three-quarters through the test. Here are some tips to avoid that happening to *you*.

- **Follow directions.** If the directions are given orally, listen to them. If they're written on-screen, read them carefully. Ask questions *before* the exam begins if there's anything you don't understand. If you're allowed to take notes, write down the beginning and ending time of the exam.
- **Pace yourself.** Glance at your watch every few minutes, and compare the time to how far you've gotten in the test. When one-quarter of the time has elapsed, you should be one-quarter through

the test, and so on. If you're falling behind, pick up the pace a bit.

- **Keep moving.** Don't dither around on one question. If you don't know the answer, skip the question and move on. Jot down the number of the question on a piece of scrap paper in case you have time to come back to it later.
- **Don't rush.** Though you should keep moving, rushing won't help. Try to keep calm and work methodically and quickly.

Step 5: Learn to Use the Process of Elimination

Time to complete: 20 minutes
Activity: Complete worksheet on Using the Process of Elimination

After time management, the next most important tool for taking control of your exam is using the process of elimination wisely. It's standard test-taking wisdom that you should always read all the answer choices before choosing your answer. This helps you find the right answer by eliminating wrong answer choices. And, sure enough, that standard wisdom applies to your exam, too.

Let's say you're facing a question that goes like this:

13. Which of the following lists of signs and symptoms indicates cardiac compromise?
a. headache, dizziness, nausea, confusion
b. dull chest pain, sudden sweating, difficulty breathing
c. wheezing, labored breathing, chest pain
d. difficulty breathing, high fever, rapid pulse

You should always use the process of elimination on a question like this, even if the right answer jumps out at you. Sometimes the answer that jumps out isn't right after all. Let's assume, for the purpose of this exercise, that you're a little rusty on your signs and symptoms of cardiac compromise, so you need to use

a little intuition to make up for what you don't remember. Proceed through the answer choices in order.

Start with answer **a**. This one is pretty easy to eliminate; none of these signs and symptoms is consistent with cardiac compromise. On a piece of scrap paper, mark an X next to choice **a** so you never have to look at it again.

On to the next. "Dull chest pain" looks good, though if you're not up on your cardiac signs and symptoms you might wonder if it should be "acute chest pain" instead. "Sudden sweating" and "difficulty breathing"? Check. And that's what you write next to answer **b** on your scrap paper—a check mark, meaning, "Good answer, I might use this one."

Choice **c** is a possibility. Maybe you don't really expect wheezing in cardiac compromise, but you know "chest pain" is right, and let's say you're not sure whether "labored breathing" is a sign of cardiac difficulty. Put a question mark next to **c**, meaning, "Well, maybe."

Choice **d** strikes you about the same; "difficulty breathing" is a good sign of cardiac compromise. But wait a minute. "High fever"? Not really. "Rapid pulse"? Well, maybe. This doesn't really sound like cardiac compromise, and you've already got a better answer picked out in choice **b**. If you're feeling sure of yourself, put an X next to this one. If you want to be careful, put a question mark.

Now your notes on the question look like this:

13. Which of the following lists of signs and symptoms indicates cardiac compromise?
X a. headache, dizziness, nausea, confusion
✔ b. dull chest pain, sudden sweating, difficulty breathing
? c. wheezing, labored breathing, chest pain
? d. difficulty breathing, high fever, rapid pulse

You've got just one check mark for a good answer. It's good to have a system for marking good, bad, and maybe answers. We're recommending this one:

   X = bad

   ✔ = good

   ? = maybe

If you don't like these marks, devise your own system. Just make sure you do it long before test day (while you're working through the practice exams in this book) so you won't have to worry about it during the test.

Even when you think you're absolutely clueless about a question, you can often use the process of elimination to get rid of one answer choice. If so, you're better prepared to make an educated guess, as you'll see in Step 6. More often, the process of elimination helps you get down to only *two* possibly right answers. Then you're in a strong position to guess. And sometimes, even though you don't know the right answer, you find it simply by getting rid of the wrong ones, as you did in the previous example.

Try using your powers of elimination on the questions in the worksheet Using the Process of Elimination beginning on the next page. The questions aren't about EMT work; they're just designed to show you how the process of elimination works. The answer explanations for this worksheet show one way you might use the process to arrive at the right answer.

The process of elimination is your tool for the next step, which is knowing when to guess.

Using the Process of Elimination

Use the process of elimination to answer the following questions.

1. Ilsa is as old as Meghan will be in five years. The difference between Ed's age and Meghan's age is twice the difference between Ilsa's age and Meghan's age. Ed is 29. How old is Ilsa?
   a. 4
   b. 10
   c. 19
   d. 24

2. "All drivers of commercial vehicles must carry a valid commercial driver's license whenever operating a commercial vehicle." According to this sentence, which of the following people need NOT carry a commercial driver's license?
   a. a truck driver idling his engine while waiting to be directed to a loading dock
   b. a bus operator backing her bus out of the way of another bus in the bus lot
   c. a taxi driver driving his personal car to the grocery store
   d. a limousine driver taking the limousine to her home after dropping off her last passenger of the evening

3. Smoking tobacco has been linked to
   a. increased risk of stroke and heart attack.
   b. all forms of respiratory disease.
   c. increasing mortality rates over the past ten years.
   d. juvenile delinquency.

4. Which of the following words is spelled correctly?
   a. incorrigible
   b. outragous
   c. domestickated
   d. understandible

Answers

Here are the answers, as well as some suggestions on how you might have used the process of elimination to find them.

1. d. You should have eliminated answer **a** off the bat. Ilsa can't be four years old if Meghan is going to be Ilsa's age in five years. The best way to eliminate other answer choices is to try plugging them into the information given in the problem. For instance, for answer **b**, if Ilsa is 10, then Meghan must be 5. The difference in their ages is 5. The difference between Ed's age, 29, and Meghan's age, 5, is 24. Is 24 two times 5? No. Then answer **b** is wrong. You could eliminate answer **c** in the same way and be left with answer **d**.

2. c. Note the word *not* in the question, and go through the answers one by one. Is the truck driver in choice **a** "operating a commercial vehicle"? Yes, idling counts as "operating," so he needs to have a commercial driver's license. Likewise, the bus operator in answer **b** is operating a commercial vehicle; the question doesn't say the operator must be on the street. The limo driver in **d** is operating a commercial vehicle, even if it doesn't have a passenger in it. However, the cabbie in answer **c** is *not* operating a commercial vehicle, but his own private car.

3. a. You could eliminate answer **b** simply because of the presence of *all*. Such absolutes hardly ever appear in correct answer choices. Choice **c** looks attractive until you think a little about what you know—aren't *fewer* people smoking these days, rather than more? So how could smoking be responsible for a higher mortality rate? (If you didn't know that *mortality rate* means the rate at which people die, you might keep this choice as a possibility, but you'd still be able to eliminate two answers and have only two to choose from.) And choice **d** is plain silly, so you could eliminate that one, too. And you're left with the correct choice, **a**.

4. a. How you used the process of elimination here depends on which words you recognized as being spelled incorrectly. If you knew that the correct spellings were *outrageous, domesticated,* and *understandable,* then you were home free. Surely you knew that at least one of those words was wrong!

Step 6: Know When to Guess

Time to complete: 20 minutes
Activity: Complete worksheet on Your Guessing Ability

Armed with the process of elimination, you're ready to take control of one of the big questions in test taking: Should I guess? The first and main answer is "Yes." Some exams have what's called a "guessing penalty," in which a fraction of your wrong answers is subtracted from your right answers—but EMT-Basic exams don't often work that way. The number of questions you answer correctly yields your raw score, so you have nothing to lose and everything to gain by guessing.

The more complicated answer to the question "Should I guess?" depends on you—your personality and your "guessing intuition." There are two things you need to know about yourself before you go into the exam:

- Are you a risk taker?
- Are you a good guesser?

You'll have to decide about your risk-taking quotient on your own. To find out if you're a good guesser, complete the worksheet Your Guessing Ability that begins on page 33. Frankly, even if you're a play-it-safe person with lousy intuition, you're probably still safe guessing every time. The best thing would be if you could overcome your anxieties and go ahead and mark an answer. But you may want to have a sense of how good your intuition is before you go into the exam.

Step 7: Reach Your Peak Performance Zone

Time to complete: 10 minutes to read; weeks to complete!
Activity: Complete the Physical Preparation Checklist

To get ready for a challenge like a big exam, you have to take control of your physical as well as your mental state. Exercise, proper diet, and rest will ensure that your body works with your mind, rather than against it, on test day, as well as during your preparation.

Exercise

If you don't already have a regular exercise program going, the time during which you're preparing for an exam is actually an excellent time to start one. If you're already keeping fit—or trying to get that way—don't let the pressure of preparing for an exam fool you into quitting now. Exercise helps reduce stress by pumping wonderful good-feeling hormones called endorphins into your system. It also increases the oxygen supply throughout your body, including your brain, so you'll be at peak performance on test day.

A half hour of vigorous activity—enough to raise a sweat—every day should be your aim. If you're really pressed for time, every other day is okay. Choose an activity you like and get out there and do it. Jogging with a friend or exercising to music always makes the time go faster.

But don't overdo it. You don't want to exhaust yourself. Moderation is the key.

The following are ten really hard questions. You're not supposed to know the answers. Rather, this is an assessment of your ability to guess when you don't have a clue. Read each question carefully, just as if you did expect to answer it. If you have any knowledge at all of the subject of the question, use that knowledge to help you eliminate wrong answer choices. Use this answer grid to fill in your answers to the questions.

ANSWER GRID

1. (a) (b) (c) (d)   5. (a) (b) (c) (d)   9. (a) (b) (c) (d)
2. (a) (b) (c) (d)   6. (a) (b) (c) (d)   10. (a) (b) (c) (d)
3. (a) (b) (c) (d)   7. (a) (b) (c) (d)
4. (a) (b) (c) (d)   8. (a) (b) (c) (d)

1. September 7 is Independence Day in
   a. India.
   b. Costa Rica.
   c. Brazil.
   d. Australia.

2. Which of the following is the formula for determining the momentum of an object?
   a. $p = mv$
   b. $F = ma$
   c. $P = IV$
   d. $E = mc^2$

3. Because of the expansion of the universe, the stars and other celestial bodies are all moving away from each other. This phenomenon is known as
   a. Newton's first law.
   b. the big bang.
   c. gravitational collapse.
   d. Hubble flow.

4. American author Gertrude Stein was born in
   a. 1713.
   b. 1830.
   c. 1874.
   d. 1901.

5. Which of the following is NOT one of the Five Classics attributed to Confucius?
   a. the *I Ching*
   b. the *Book of Holiness*
   c. the *Spring and Autumn Annals*
   d. the *Book of History*

6. The religious and philosophical doctrine that holds that the universe is constantly in a struggle between good and evil is known as
   a. Pelagianism.
   b. Manichaeanism.
   c. neo-Hegelianism.
   d. Epicureanism.

7. The third chief justice of the U.S. Supreme Court was
   a. John Blair.
   b. William Cushing.
   c. James Wilson.
   d. John Jay.

8. Which of the following is the poisonous portion of a daffodil?
   a. the bulb
   b. the leaves
   c. the stem
   d. the flowers

9. The winner of the Masters golf tournament in 1953 was
   a. Sam Snead.
   b. Cary Middlecoff.
   c. Arnold Palmer.
   d. Ben Hogan.

10. The state with the highest per capita personal income in 1980 was
   a. Alaska.
   b. Connecticut.
   c. New York.
   d. Texas.

Answers

Check your answers against the correct answers below.

1. c	**5.** b	**9.** d
2. a	**6.** b	**10.** a
3. d	**7.** b	
4. c	**8.** a	

How Did You Do?

You may have simply gotten lucky and actually known the answer to one or two questions. In addition, your guessing was more successful if you were able to use the process of elimination on any of the questions. Maybe you didn't know who the third chief justice was (question 7), but you knew that John Jay was the first. In that case, you would have eliminated answer **d** and therefore improved your odds of guessing right from one in four to one in three.

According to probability, you should get 2.5 answers correct, so getting either two or three right would be average. If you got four or more right, you may be a really terrific guesser. If you got one or none right, you may be a really bad guesser.

Keep in mind, though, that this is only a small sample. You should continue to keep track of your guessing ability as you work through the sample questions in this book. Circle the numbers of questions you guess on as you make your guess; or, if you don't have time while you take the practice tests, go back afterward and try to remember on which questions you guessed. Remember, on a test with four answer choices, your chances of getting a correct answer are one in four. So keep a separate "guessing" score for each exam. How many questions did you guess on? How many did you get right? If the number you got right is at least one-fourth the number of questions you guessed on, you are at least an average guesser, maybe better—and you should always go ahead and guess on the real exam. If the number you got right is significantly lower than one-fourth of the number you guessed on, you would, frankly, be safe in guessing anyway, but maybe you'd feel more comfortable if you guessed only selectively, when you can eliminate a wrong answer or at least have a good feeling about one of the answer choices.

Diet

First of all, cut out the junk. Go easy on caffeine and nicotine, and eliminate alcohol and any other drugs from your system at least two weeks before the exam. Promise yourself a binge the night after the exam, if need be.

What your body needs for peak performance is simply a balanced diet. Eat plenty of fruits and vegetables, along with protein and carbohydrates. Foods high in lecithin (an amino acid), such as fish and beans, are especially good brain foods.

The night before the exam, you might carboload the way athletes do before a contest. Eat a big plate of spaghetti, rice and beans, or your favorite carbohydrate.

Rest

You probably know how much sleep you need every night to be at your best, even if you don't always get it. Make sure you do get that much sleep, though, for at least a week before the exam. Moderation is important here, too. Extra sleep will just make you groggy.

If you're not a morning person and your exam will be given in the morning, you should reset your internal clock so that your body doesn't think you're taking an exam at 3 A.M. You have to start this process well before the exam. The way it works is to get up half an hour earlier each morning, and then go to bed half an hour earlier that night. Don't try it the other way around; you'll just toss and turn if you go to bed early without having gotten up early. The next morning, get up another half an hour earlier, and so on. How long you will have to do this depends on how late you're used to getting up. Use the Physical Preparation Checklist on page 36 to make sure you're in tip-top form.

Step 8: Get Your Act Together

Time to complete: 10 minutes to read; time to complete will vary

Activity: Complete Final Preparations worksheet

You're in control of your mind and body; you're in charge of test anxiety, your preparation, and your test-taking strategies. Now it's time to take charge of external factors, such as the testing site and the materials you need to take the exam.

Find Out Where the Test Center Is and Make a Trial Run

The testing agency or your EMS instructor will notify you when and where your exam is being held. Do you know how to get to the testing site? Do you know how long it will take to get there? If not, make a trial run, preferably on the same day of the week at the same time of day. On the Final Preparations worksheet on page 37, note the amount of time it will take you to get to the exam site. Plan on arriving 10 to 15 minutes early so you can get the lay of the land, use the bathroom, and calm down. Then figure out how early you will have to get up that morning, and make sure you get up that early every day for a week before the exam.

Gather Your Materials

The night before the exam, lay out the clothes you will wear and the materials you have to bring with you to the exam. Plan on dressing in layers; you won't have any control over the temperature of the examination room. Have a sweater or jacket you can take off if it's warm. Use the checklist on the Final Preparations worksheet on page 37 to help you pull together what you'll need.

Don't Skip Breakfast

Even if you don't usually eat breakfast, do so on exam morning. A cup of coffee doesn't count. Don't eat doughnuts or other sweet foods either. A sugar high will leave you with a sugar low in the middle of the exam. A mix of protein and carbohydrates is best: Cereal with milk and just a little sugar, or eggs with toast, will do your body a world of good.

Physical Preparation Checklist

For the week before the test, write down 1) what physical exercise you engaged in and for how long and 2) what you ate for each meal. Remember, you're trying for at least half an hour of exercise every other day (preferably every day) and a balanced diet that's light on junk food.

Exam minus 7 days

Exercise: _____ for _____ minutes

Breakfast: _____

Lunch: _____

Dinner: _____

Snacks: _____

Exam minus 6 days

Exercise: _____ for _____ minutes

Breakfast: _____

Lunch: _____

Dinner: _____

Snacks: _____

Exam minus 5 days

Exercise: _____ for _____ minutes

Breakfast: _____

Lunch: _____

Dinner: _____

Snacks: _____

Exam minus 4 days

Exercise: _____ for _____ minutes

Breakfast: _____

Lunch: _____

Dinner: _____

Snacks: _____

Exam minus 3 days

Exercise: _____ for _____ minutes

Breakfast: _____

Lunch: _____

Dinner: _____

Snacks: _____

Exam minus 2 days

Exercise: _____ for _____ minutes

Breakfast: _____

Lunch: _____

Dinner: _____

Snacks: _____

Exam minus 1 day

Exercise: _____ for _____ minutes

Breakfast: _____

Lunch: _____

Dinner: _____

Snacks: _____

Step 9: Do It!

Time to complete: 10 minutes, plus test-taking time
Activity: Ace the EMT-Basic exam!

Fast-forward to exam day. You're ready. You made a study plan and followed through. You practiced your test-taking strategies while working through this book. You're in control of your physical, mental, and emotional state. You know when and where to show up and what to bring with you. In other words, you're better prepared than most other people taking the EMT-Basic exam with you. You're psyched.

Just one more thing. When you're done with the exam, you will have earned a reward. Plan a celebration. Call up your friends and plan a party, have a nice dinner for two, or go see a good movie—whatever your heart desires. Give yourself something to look forward to.

And then do it. Go into the exam, full of confidence, armed with test-taking strategies you've practiced until they became second nature. You're in control of yourself, your environment, and your performance on the exam. You're ready to succeed. So do it. Go in there and ace the exam—and look forward to your career!

Final Preparations

Getting to the Exam Site

Location of exam site: _____

Date: _____

Departure time: _____

Do I know how to get to the exam site?   Yes ___   No ___

If no, make a trial run.

Time it will take to get to the exam site: _____

Things to Lay Out the Night Before

Clothes I will wear   ___

Sweater/jacket   ___

Watch   ___

Photo ID   ___

4 No. 2 pencils   ___

Other   ___

CHAPTER

4 ▶ EMT-BASIC PRACTICE EXAM 1

CHAPTER SUMMARY
This is the first of four practice exams in this book based on the National Registry EMT-Basic cognitive exam.

L ike the other tests in this book, this test is based on the National Registry's cognitive exam for EMT-Basics. See Chapter 2 for a complete description of this exam.

Take this first exam in as relaxed a manner as you can, and don't worry about timing. You can time yourself on the other three exams. You should, however, allow sufficient time to take the entire exam at one sitting, at least two hours. Find a quiet place where you can work without being interrupted.

The answer sheet you should use is on page 41, followed by the exam itself. The correct answers, each fully explained, come after the exam. Once you have read and understood the answer explanations, turn to Chapter 2 for an explanation of how to assess your score.

Practice Exam 1

1.	ⓐ	ⓑ	ⓒ	ⓓ	51.	ⓐ	ⓑ	ⓒ	ⓓ	101.	ⓐ	ⓑ	ⓒ	ⓓ
2.	ⓐ	ⓑ	ⓒ	ⓓ	52.	ⓐ	ⓑ	ⓒ	ⓓ	102.	ⓐ	ⓑ	ⓒ	ⓓ
3.	ⓐ	ⓑ	ⓒ	ⓓ	53.	ⓐ	ⓑ	ⓒ	ⓓ	103.	ⓐ	ⓑ	ⓒ	ⓓ
4.	ⓐ	ⓑ	ⓒ	ⓓ	54.	ⓐ	ⓑ	ⓒ	ⓓ	104.	ⓐ	ⓑ	ⓒ	ⓓ
5.	ⓐ	ⓑ	ⓒ	ⓓ	55.	ⓐ	ⓑ	ⓒ	ⓓ	105.	ⓐ	ⓑ	ⓒ	ⓓ
6.	ⓐ	ⓑ	ⓒ	ⓓ	56.	ⓐ	ⓑ	ⓒ	ⓓ	106.	ⓐ	ⓑ	ⓒ	ⓓ
7.	ⓐ	ⓑ	ⓒ	ⓓ	57.	ⓐ	ⓑ	ⓒ	ⓓ	107.	ⓐ	ⓑ	ⓒ	ⓓ
8.	ⓐ	ⓑ	ⓒ	ⓓ	58.	ⓐ	ⓑ	ⓒ	ⓓ	108.	ⓐ	ⓑ	ⓒ	ⓓ
9.	ⓐ	ⓑ	ⓒ	ⓓ	59.	ⓐ	ⓑ	ⓒ	ⓓ	109.	ⓐ	ⓑ	ⓒ	ⓓ
10.	ⓐ	ⓑ	ⓒ	ⓓ	60.	ⓐ	ⓑ	ⓒ	ⓓ	110.	ⓐ	ⓑ	ⓒ	ⓓ
11.	ⓐ	ⓑ	ⓒ	ⓓ	61.	ⓐ	ⓑ	ⓒ	ⓓ	111.	ⓐ	ⓑ	ⓒ	ⓓ
12.	ⓐ	ⓑ	ⓒ	ⓓ	62.	ⓐ	ⓑ	ⓒ	ⓓ	112.	ⓐ	ⓑ	ⓒ	ⓓ
13.	ⓐ	ⓑ	ⓒ	ⓓ	63.	ⓐ	ⓑ	ⓒ	ⓓ	113.	ⓐ	ⓑ	ⓒ	ⓓ
14.	ⓐ	ⓑ	ⓒ	ⓓ	64.	ⓐ	ⓑ	ⓒ	ⓓ	114.	ⓐ	ⓑ	ⓒ	ⓓ
15.	ⓐ	ⓑ	ⓒ	ⓓ	65.	ⓐ	ⓑ	ⓒ	ⓓ	115.	ⓐ	ⓑ	ⓒ	ⓓ
16.	ⓐ	ⓑ	ⓒ	ⓓ	66.	ⓐ	ⓑ	ⓒ	ⓓ	116.	ⓐ	ⓑ	ⓒ	ⓓ
17.	ⓐ	ⓑ	ⓒ	ⓓ	67.	ⓐ	ⓑ	ⓒ	ⓓ	117.	ⓐ	ⓑ	ⓒ	ⓓ
18.	ⓐ	ⓑ	ⓒ	ⓓ	68.	ⓐ	ⓑ	ⓒ	ⓓ	118.	ⓐ	ⓑ	ⓒ	ⓓ
19.	ⓐ	ⓑ	ⓒ	ⓓ	69.	ⓐ	ⓑ	ⓒ	ⓓ	119.	ⓐ	ⓑ	ⓒ	ⓓ
20.	ⓐ	ⓑ	ⓒ	ⓓ	70.	ⓐ	ⓑ	ⓒ	ⓓ	120.	ⓐ	ⓑ	ⓒ	ⓓ
21.	ⓐ	ⓑ	ⓒ	ⓓ	71.	ⓐ	ⓑ	ⓒ	ⓓ	121.	ⓐ	ⓑ	ⓒ	ⓓ
22.	ⓐ	ⓑ	ⓒ	ⓓ	72.	ⓐ	ⓑ	ⓒ	ⓓ	122.	ⓐ	ⓑ	ⓒ	ⓓ
23.	ⓐ	ⓑ	ⓒ	ⓓ	73.	ⓐ	ⓑ	ⓒ	ⓓ	123.	ⓐ	ⓑ	ⓒ	ⓓ
24.	ⓐ	ⓑ	ⓒ	ⓓ	74.	ⓐ	ⓑ	ⓒ	ⓓ	124.	ⓐ	ⓑ	ⓒ	ⓓ
25.	ⓐ	ⓑ	ⓒ	ⓓ	75.	ⓐ	ⓑ	ⓒ	ⓓ	125.	ⓐ	ⓑ	ⓒ	ⓓ
26.	ⓐ	ⓑ	ⓒ	ⓓ	76.	ⓐ	ⓑ	ⓒ	ⓓ	126.	ⓐ	ⓑ	ⓒ	ⓓ
27.	ⓐ	ⓑ	ⓒ	ⓓ	77.	ⓐ	ⓑ	ⓒ	ⓓ	127.	ⓐ	ⓑ	ⓒ	ⓓ
28.	ⓐ	ⓑ	ⓒ	ⓓ	78.	ⓐ	ⓑ	ⓒ	ⓓ	128.	ⓐ	ⓑ	ⓒ	ⓓ
29.	ⓐ	ⓑ	ⓒ	ⓓ	79.	ⓐ	ⓑ	ⓒ	ⓓ	129.	ⓐ	ⓑ	ⓒ	ⓓ
30.	ⓐ	ⓑ	ⓒ	ⓓ	80.	ⓐ	ⓑ	ⓒ	ⓓ	130.	ⓐ	ⓑ	ⓒ	ⓓ
31.	ⓐ	ⓑ	ⓒ	ⓓ	81.	ⓐ	ⓑ	ⓒ	ⓓ	131.	ⓐ	ⓑ	ⓒ	ⓓ
32.	ⓐ	ⓑ	ⓒ	ⓓ	82.	ⓐ	ⓑ	ⓒ	ⓓ	132.	ⓐ	ⓑ	ⓒ	ⓓ
33.	ⓐ	ⓑ	ⓒ	ⓓ	83.	ⓐ	ⓑ	ⓒ	ⓓ	133.	ⓐ	ⓑ	ⓒ	ⓓ
34.	ⓐ	ⓑ	ⓒ	ⓓ	84.	ⓐ	ⓑ	ⓒ	ⓓ	134.	ⓐ	ⓑ	ⓒ	ⓓ
35.	ⓐ	ⓑ	ⓒ	ⓓ	85.	ⓐ	ⓑ	ⓒ	ⓓ	135.	ⓐ	ⓑ	ⓒ	ⓓ
36.	ⓐ	ⓑ	ⓒ	ⓓ	86.	ⓐ	ⓑ	ⓒ	ⓓ	136.	ⓐ	ⓑ	ⓒ	ⓓ
37.	ⓐ	ⓑ	ⓒ	ⓓ	87.	ⓐ	ⓑ	ⓒ	ⓓ	137.	ⓐ	ⓑ	ⓒ	ⓓ
38.	ⓐ	ⓑ	ⓒ	ⓓ	88.	ⓐ	ⓑ	ⓒ	ⓓ	138.	ⓐ	ⓑ	ⓒ	ⓓ
39.	ⓐ	ⓑ	ⓒ	ⓓ	89.	ⓐ	ⓑ	ⓒ	ⓓ	139.	ⓐ	ⓑ	ⓒ	ⓓ
40.	ⓐ	ⓑ	ⓒ	ⓓ	90.	ⓐ	ⓑ	ⓒ	ⓓ	140.	ⓐ	ⓑ	ⓒ	ⓓ
41.	ⓐ	ⓑ	ⓒ	ⓓ	91.	ⓐ	ⓑ	ⓒ	ⓓ	141.	ⓐ	ⓑ	ⓒ	ⓓ
42.	ⓐ	ⓑ	ⓒ	ⓓ	92.	ⓐ	ⓑ	ⓒ	ⓓ	142.	ⓐ	ⓑ	ⓒ	ⓓ
43.	ⓐ	ⓑ	ⓒ	ⓓ	93.	ⓐ	ⓑ	ⓒ	ⓓ	143.	ⓐ	ⓑ	ⓒ	ⓓ
44.	ⓐ	ⓑ	ⓒ	ⓓ	94.	ⓐ	ⓑ	ⓒ	ⓓ	144.	ⓐ	ⓑ	ⓒ	ⓓ
45.	ⓐ	ⓑ	ⓒ	ⓓ	95.	ⓐ	ⓑ	ⓒ	ⓓ	145.	ⓐ	ⓑ	ⓒ	ⓓ
46.	ⓐ	ⓑ	ⓒ	ⓓ	96.	ⓐ	ⓑ	ⓒ	ⓓ	146.	ⓐ	ⓑ	ⓒ	ⓓ
47.	ⓐ	ⓑ	ⓒ	ⓓ	97.	ⓐ	ⓑ	ⓒ	ⓓ	147.	ⓐ	ⓑ	ⓒ	ⓓ
48.	ⓐ	ⓑ	ⓒ	ⓓ	98.	ⓐ	ⓑ	ⓒ	ⓓ	148.	ⓐ	ⓑ	ⓒ	ⓓ
49.	ⓐ	ⓑ	ⓒ	ⓓ	99.	ⓐ	ⓑ	ⓒ	ⓓ	149.	ⓐ	ⓑ	ⓒ	ⓓ
50.	ⓐ	ⓑ	ⓒ	ⓓ	100.	ⓐ	ⓑ	ⓒ	ⓓ	150.	ⓐ	ⓑ	ⓒ	ⓓ

EMT-Basic Practice Exam 1

1. EMTs should wear high-efficiency particulate air (HEPA) respirators when they are in contact with patients who have which of the following?
   a. HIV (human immunodeficiency virus) or AIDS (acquired immune deficiency syndrome)
   b. tuberculosis (TB)
   c. open wounds
   d. hepatitis B

2. In which of these situations should you wear a gown over your uniform?
   a. A 55-year-old male is suspected of having a myocardial infarction.
   b. The victim of a fall has no obvious wounds but is still unresponsive.
   c. A full-term pregnant woman is experiencing crowning with contractions.
   d. A 72-year-old female is experiencing dizziness and difficulty breathing.

3. The blue portion of the 704 hazardous materials placard stands for which of the following hazards?
   a. health
   b. fire
   c. reactivity
   d. special hazard

4. The most common electrical rhythm disturbance that results in sudden cardiac arrest is called
   a. pulseless electrical activity.
   b. ventricular fibrillation.
   c. ventricular tachycardia.
   d. asystole.

5. Which of the following is the highest priority patient?
   a. 57-year-old male with chest pain and systolic blood pressure of 80
   b. 40-year-old female with moderate pain from a leg injury
   c. 75-year-old male who appears confused but responds to commands
   d. 25-year-old female in labor with contractions six minutes apart

6. Of the following, which body fluid has the most potential to transmit blood-borne diseases?
   a. nasal discharge
   b. vomitus
   c. amniotic fluid
   d. feces

7. Your patient is an 11-month-old female. How can you determine if she has a decreased mental status and is responsive to verbal stimuli?
   a. She will be upset when you take her from her mother's arms.
   b. She will be unable to tell you how old she is if you ask her.
   c. She will attempt to locate her parents' voices when they speak.
   d. She will try to pull away from a painful stimulus on her toe.

8. What is the best method to assess circulation in an infant?
   a. Palpate the carotid pulse.
   b. Palpate the brachial pulse.
   c. Palpate the radial pulse.
   d. Observe capillary refill time.

9. A 45-year-old male is experiencing chest discomfort. After placing him in his position of comfort, your next action should be to
   a. ventilate the patient with a nonrebreather mask at 15 L/min.
   b. ventilate the patient with the bag-valve mask at 15 L/min.
   c. administer oxygen by nonrebreather mask at 15 L/min.
   d. administer oxygen by the nasal cannula at 6 L/min.

10. Which patient is at highest risk for hidden injury?
   a. 9-year-old child who fell seven feet off a swing set onto mulch-covered ground
   b. 30-year-old female who got out of her car after a low-speed collision
   c. 45-year-old male who was ejected from his car after a high-speed collision
   d. 25-year-old male who fell 12 feet from a low-angle roof onto the grass

11. You respond to the scene of a possible carbon monoxide exposure. When you question the patient he gives the following statements. Which of the following would be the most accurate statement regarding the nature of carbon monoxide?
   a. "I've been smelling carbon monoxide for the last several days."
   b. "I've tasted carbon monoxide and my vision is blurry."
   c. "I've been using my electric stove all day and I think it is leaking because I feel bad."
   d. "I haven't smelled anything but I have a headache and don't feel good."

12. Which of the following is a sign of increased pressure in the circulatory system?
   a. flat neck veins
   b. palpable carotid pulse
   c. distended jugular veins
   d. decreased radial pulse

13. An automated external defibrillator (AED) will shock which of the following rhythms?
   a. sinus rhythm
   b. asystole
   c. ventricular fibrillation
   d. pulseless electrical activity

14. When performing the rapid trauma assessment, what is the next step after assessing the neck?
   a. Assess the clavicles, scapula, and chest.
   b. Clear the airway and administer oxygen.
   c. Assess the head, eyes, ears, and nose.
   d. Apply a cervical immobilization device.

15. To assess the motor function in the lower extremities of a responsive patient, you would
   a. ask the patient to bend his knees.
   b. ask the patient to wiggle his toes.
   c. carefully move the patient's leg.
   d. touch the skin of the patient's foot.

16. Which patient can safely receive only a focused physical examination rather than a rapid trauma assessment?
   a. 10-year-old male with a deformed right lower leg who is responsive after falling off his bicycle
   b. 20-year-old female who complains of severe pain in her ankle after stepping off a curb
   c. 70-year-old male who complains of neck pain after a medium-speed car collision
   d. 30-year-old male who is unresponsive but has only minor cuts on the extremities

17. You are using the OPQRST acronym to assess a responsive medical patient. What question would you ask to assess the P component?
 a. What were you doing when the pain started?
 b. Can you describe the character of the pain for me?
 c. What makes the pain feel worse or better?
 d. On a scale of 1 to 10, how would you rank the pain?

18. What is the first step in the physical assessment of an unresponsive medical patient?
 a. Perform the initial assessment.
 b. Assess a complete set of vital signs.
 c. Position the patient to protect the airway.
 d. Obtain SAMPLE history from a family member.

19. Which patient needs a detailed physical examination?
 a. 48-year-old male with a history of heart disease who is complaining of chest pain
 b. 35-year-old female who has been in a single-car collision and who briefly lost consciousness
 c. 28-year-old full-term pregnant female whose water has broken and who is having contractions every two minutes
 d. 53-year-old female with a history of smoking who is distressed and short of breath

20. Where is a detailed physical exam typically performed?
 a. at the scene of the accident or injury
 b. in the hospital emergency department
 c. in the ambulance during transport
 d. in the triage area of the trauma center

21. The electrical rhythm disturbance that should be treated with the use of an AED is called
 a. ventricular fibrillation.
 b. atrial fibrillation.
 c. asystole.
 d. pulseless electrical activity (PEA).

22. The purpose of the ongoing assessment is to re-evaluate the patient's condition and to
 a. find any injuries missed during the initial assessment.
 b. reassure the patient that you are still caring for him or her.
 c. check the adequacy of each intervention performed.
 d. protect the EMT against liability from malpractice.

23. Immediately after delivering a shock with an AED to a patient in cardiac arrest, you should
 a. check for a pulse.
 b. check breathing and provide rescue breaths as necessary.
 c. analyze with the AED and shock again if indicated.
 d. do CPR.

24. Your patient is found lying on his stomach on the ground. This position would best be described as
 a. prone.
 b. semi-fowlers.
 c. supine.
 d. trendelenburg.

25. Your patient tells you that he just can't seem to catch his breath. You would describe the nature of the illness as
 a. chest pain.
 b. respiratory distress.
 c. apnea.
 d. emphysema.

26. You should apply an AED to
    a. adult patients experiencing chest discomfort.
    b. adult patients with significant traumatic injuries.
    c. adult patients without respirations or a pulse.
    d. adult patients with low blood pressure.

27. Which of the following would lead you to suspect that the scene is not safe when arriving at a call?
    a. people yelling and screaming
    b. several people outside directing the ambulance to the patient
    c. multiple calls to 911
    d. the call is at a large apartment complex

28. The trachea divides into two
    a. carina.
    b. bronchi.
    c. alveoli.
    d. lungs.

29. What is the structure that prevents food and liquid from entering the trachea during swallowing?
    a. larynx
    b. cricoid cartilage
    c. epiglottis
    d. diaphragm

30. The air sacs in the lungs where oxygen–carbon dioxide exchange occurs are the
    a. bronchioles.
    b. bronchi.
    c. epiglottis.
    d. alveoli.

31. A condition of the eye in which the internal pressure increases and the patient's sight worsens is called
    a. cataracts.
    b. glaucoma.
    c. Marfan syndrome.
    d. pinkeye.

32. Pink or bloody sputum is often seen in patients with
    a. pulmonary edema.
    b. anaphylaxis.
    c. allergic reaction.
    d. flu.

33. Which occurs during capillary–cellular exchange?
    a. Oxygen enters the capillaries as carbon dioxide enters the alveoli.
    b. Oxygen-poor blood from the capillaries passes into the alveoli.
    c. Body cells give up carbon dioxide and capillaries give up oxygen.
    d. Body cells obtain nourishment from the capillaries.

34. Cardiac arrest in children is most often caused by
    a. chest trauma.
    b. respiratory compromise.
    c. hypovolemia.
    d. irregular rhythm.

35. Which of the following terms means "away from the body"?
    a. adduction
    b. abduction
    c. posterior
    d. ipsilateral

36. Your patient has a large abrasion just below his elbow, above his hand. This injury would best be described as
    a. superior to the elbow, but distal to the hand.
    b. inferior to the hand, but superior to the elbow.
    c. inferior to the elbow, but superior to the hand.
    d. superior to the hand and superior to the elbow.

37. A gurgling sound heard with artificial ventilation is a sign that
    a. the patient must be suctioned immediately.
    b. supplemental oxygen should be added to the gas-valve mask.
    c. the airway is most likely open, patent, and clear.
    d. the patient is trying to communicate with you.

38. The first step in artificial ventilation with a bag-valve-mask unit in patients with no suspected trauma is to
    a. position the mask correctly on the face using both hands.
    b. place the patient's head in a hyperextended, sniffing position.
    c. insert an airway adjunct and select the correct mask size.
    d. have an assistant squeeze the bag until the patient's chest rises.

39. You take a report from a first responder who describes a patient as *postictal*; based on this report, you would expect to find the patient
    a. alert and oriented.
    b. confused.
    c. unresponsive.
    d. hallucinating.

40. When suctioning a patient, how far should you insert a soft suction catheter?
    a. as far as you can see
    b. as far as the base of the tongue
    c. until resistance is encountered
    d. past the vocal cords

41. What is the correct procedure for a patient who has secretions or emesis that suctioning cannot easily remove?
    a. Insert an oropharyngeal or nasopharyngeal airway immediately.
    b. Suction for 15 seconds, ventilate for two minutes, and then repeat.
    c. Logroll the patient and clear the oropharynx and nasopharynx.
    d. Hyperventilate the patient with a bag-valve-mask unit.

42. During active inhalation, the diaphragm
    a. contracts and flattens, increasing the size of the chest cavity.
    b. relaxes, decreasing the size of the thoracic cavity.
    c. moves upward, forcing the lungs to contract.
    d. moves upward, forcing the ribs to move downward and inward.

43. What is the purpose of the head-tilt/chin-lift technique?
    a. to position the patient for insertion of an airway adjunct
    b. to remove foreign bodies from the upper airway
    c. to help the rescuer better visualize the larynx and vocal cords
    d. to lift the tongue and epiglottis out of their obstructing position

44. After opening the airway, the next step in patient management is to
   a. insert an endotracheal tube.
   b. assess adequacy of respirations.
   c. begin mouth-to-mouth ventilation.
   d. apply bag-valve-mask ventilation.

45. If a patient has a radial pulse, you can expect a systolic blood pressure of at least
   a. 100 mm Hg.
   b. 80 mm Hg.
   c. 60 mm Hg.
   d. 70 mm Hg.

46. You respond to a doctor's office for an unknown emergency. When you arrive, the doctor greets you at the door and tells you that the patient has had an epistaxis. Which of the following describes the patient's condition?
   a. The patient had an allergic reaction.
   b. The patient had a miscarriage.
   c. The patient had a bloody nose.
   d. The patient had a fracture to a bone (similar to a Greenstick fracture).

47. The first step in the delivery of high-flow oxygen via a nonrebreather mask is to
   a. select the correct size mask.
   b. regulate the flow of oxygen.
   c. inflate the reservoir bag with oxygen.
   d. turn on the oxygen source.

48. Agonal respirations are best described as
   a. ineffective gasping breaths of a dying patient.
   b. fast breathing (respirations greater than 20 a minute).
   c. slow breathing (respirations less than 8 a minute).
   d. the sound heard from asthmatics (similar to wheezing).

49. Which of the following is true regarding bag-mask-ventilation in adult cardiac arrest patients?
   a. The patient should be ventilated a minimum of 20 breaths a minute.
   b. The patient should be ventilated 10–12 breaths a minute.
   c. The patient should be ventilated 5–8 times a minute to prevent air in the stomach.
   d. The patient should not be ventilated unless they are intubated.

50. When using the two-person bag-valve-mask procedure, one EMT ventilates the patient while the other
   a. suctions the patient and administers CPR.
   b. administers mouth-to-mask ventilation.
   c. inserts the oral or nasopharyngeal airway.
   d. maintains the mask seal and monitors chest rise.

51. Where is the cricoid cartilage located?
   a. inferior to the larynx
   b. superior to the epiglottis
   c. at the carina
   d. in the oropharynx

52. Your patient is awake, confused, and disoriented. How would you grade her using the AVPU scale?
   a. A
   b. V
   c. P
   d. U

53. Which of the following is not one of the differences between a child's and adult's airway?
  a. The child's trachea is softer and more pliable.
  b. The child's tongue takes up relatively more space in the mouth.
  c. The child's airway is less susceptible to airway obstructions than an adult's.
  d. The child tends to rely on the diaphragm more to assist with breathing.

54. The right ventricle pumps blood into the
  a. body via the aorta.
  b. lungs via the pulmonary vein.
  c. lungs via the pulmonary artery.
  d. left atrium.

55. A 56-year-old female patient complains of mild chest discomfort. You should
  a. decide what type of heart problem it might be.
  b. decide whether the patient has a heart problem.
  c. maintain a high index of suspicion for cardiac compromise.
  d. apply the AED.

56. Modern cars are often fitted with supplemental restraint systems. What system is this referring to?
  a. automatic seat belts
  b. child seat using factory-installed mounting points
  c. child booster seat
  d. air bags

57. Your patient is a 62-year-old male with a history of heart disease. He is experiencing chest pain. Your first action should be to
  a. place the pads for the AED on his chest.
  b. begin CPR while preparing the AED.
  c. ask him if he has taken his nitroglycerin, and if not, offer to assist him.
  d. place him in a comfortable position and administer high-flow oxygen.

58. Your patient is a 78-year-old female with a history of heart disease. While you are transporting her to the hospital, her level of consciousness decreases. You feel a carotid pulse but no radial pulse. What should you do?
  a. Request permission to administer nitroglycerin.
  b. Begin CPR and request advanced cardiac life support (ACLS) services.
  c. Defibrillate the patient with an AED.
  d. Assess her ABCs and maintain her airway.

59. The EMT-Basic should request prehospital ACLS for the care of the cardiac arrest patient
  a. because ACLS intervention provides higher survival rates.
  b. because EMT-Basics must have prehospital ACLS present to perform defibrillation.
  c. because only paramedics can transport cardiac arrest patients.
  d. because the EMT-Basic is not adequately trained to manage cardiac arrest.

60. Your patient is a 29-year-old male who has fallen off a ladder. He is bleeding profusely from a wound on his right forearm and has severe pain in his left thigh. Which of the following is an appropriate initial treatment for this patient?
  a. Perform a quick initial assessment to assess his ABCs.
  b. Stop the bleeding by applying a tourniquet near the elbow.
  c. Maintain an open airway and ventilate the patient with a gas-valve mask.
  d. Elevate the patient's legs 20–30 cm to treat him for shock.

61. Touching the patient when the semiautomatic external defibrillator (SAED) is analyzing the rhythm
    a. is acceptable with today's modern defibrillators.
    b. is indicated to maintain cardiac compressions.
    c. is indicated to maintain artificial ventilation.
    d. can cause the SAED to misinterpret a rhythm.

62. What should you do for the cardiac arrest patient found in the rain?
    a. Perform one rapid defibrillation, then move the patient inside.
    b. Defibrillate three times, then move the patient inside.
    c. Move the patient inside, away from the rain.
    d. Perform one rapid defibrillation, then start CPR if pulseless.

63. Your patient is bleeding profusely from a wound on her right forearm. Where is the pressure point for this injury?
    a. carotid artery
    b. ulnar artery
    c. brachial artery
    d. femoral artery

64. Kinetic energy is described as
    a. the energy an object has while in motion.
    b. the measure of matter.
    c. the capacity to do work.
    d. the tendency for an object to stay in motion.

65. A bystander is performing CPR when you arrive. You evaluate the scene, practice body substance isolation, and begin your initial assessment by having the bystander
    a. verify pulselessness.
    b. continue CPR.
    c. stop CPR.
    d. provide a history of cardiac arrest.

66. Your patient is bleeding from a wound to the forearm. The blood flows in a steady, dark-red stream. What type of bleeding should you suspect?
    a. venous
    b. arterial
    c. capillary
    d. internal

67. Your patient is restless, anxious, and complaining of thirst. She exhibits increased heart rate and pale, clammy skin. You should do all the following EXCEPT
    a. maintain an open airway and provide oxygen.
    b. elevate her legs if not contraindicated.
    c. cover the patient with a blanket to keep her warm.
    d. give the patient small amounts of liquid to drink.

68. Which of the following statements regarding the use of "ten codes" for radio traffic is accurate?
    a. Ten codes are recommended because they do not let the listening public know specifics about emergency calls.
    b. Ten codes are no longer recommended and plain text should be used.
    c. Ten codes should only be used by dispatchers when communicating to ambulances.
    d. Ten codes are no longer allowed because of the Freedom of Information Act.

69. Which of the following patients should be connected to the AED?
   a. 70-year-old male with a history of angina and a prescription for nitroglycerin; he is experiencing mild chest pain on exertion.
   b. 68-year-old female experiencing severe, crushing chest pain; she is breathing on her own and has an irregular pulse.
   c. 56-year-old male who suddenly collapsed; he is not breathing on his own, and there is no carotid pulse.
   d. 80-year-old female who suddenly collapsed; her breathing is shallow, and there is a weak carotid pulse.

70. You are teaching a class to other EMTs at your service regarding automatic external defibrillators. Which of the following statements are true?
   a. Automatic defibrillators can jumpstart a heart that isn't beating.
   b. Automatic defibrillators work by stopping abnormal electrical activity, allowing the heart's normal rhythm to restart.
   c. Automatic defibrillators should not be used in patients who have had a cardiac arrest because of respiratory problems.
   d. Automatic defibrillators cannot be used in children.

71. Which of the following statements regarding CPR in adult patients is not accurate?
   a. Chest compressions should be performed at a rate of 100 per minute.
   b. Interruptions should be minimized in order to increase survivability.
   c. The patient's sternum should be compressed 2–3 inches with every compression.
   d. The chest should be allowed to fully recoil after each compression.

72. What does Newton's second law of motion explain?
   a. An object will remain at rest or continue to move at a constant velocity unless a resultant force acts on it.
   b. Net force on an object is proportionate to its mass multiplied by its acceleration.
   c. For every force acting on an object, the object will exert an equal yet opposite force on its cause.
   d. What goes up must come down.

73. Which of the following is not an advantage of AEDs over standard manual defibrillators?
   a. AEDs are easier to operate
   b. AEDs allow for safer operations
   c. AEDs can be used on infants
   d. AEDs can be used by lay people

74. You are transporting a patient who has been resuscitated but is still unresponsive. You should check the patient's pulse
   a. every 30 seconds.
   b. every minute.
   c. every five minutes.
   d. every ten minutes.

75. The medical direction physician orders you to deliver additional shocks to a patient in cardiac arrest while en route to the hospital. What is the correct procedure to follow?
   a. Wait for the arrival of the ACLS team.
   b. Deliver the shocks without stopping CPR.
   c. Stop the vehicle before reanalyzing the rhythm.
   d. Refuse to defibrillate the patient while en route.

76. Which of the following blood sugars is within normal range for an adult?
  a. 50
  b. 100
  c. 150
  d. 200

77. Patients commonly describe heart attack pain as which of the following characteristics?
  a. like pins and needles
  b. crushing or squeezing
  c. intermittent (comes and goes)
  d. less severe than indigestion

78. In pedestrian versus automobile impacts, which of the following statements is true?
  a. Children often turn toward the impact and are often thrown down and under the vehicle.
  b. Adults tend to turn toward the vehicle before impact.
  c. Children often turn toward the impact and are often scooped and thrown over the vehicle.
  d. There tends to be no difference in the way adults and children respond in these situations.

79. Your patient is a 19-year-old male with a severe nosebleed and no other signs of trauma. In what position should you place him?
  a. flat on his back, with lower extremities elevated
  b. sitting up and leaning forward
  c. prone
  d. supine

80. Your patient has profuse bleeding from a wound on her lower leg but no signs of skeletal injury. The steps you should take to stop the bleeding, in the correct order, are
  a. direct pressure, elevation, pressure dressing, and pressure point.
  b. pressure point, tourniquet, and concentrated or diffuse direct pressure.
  c. pneumatic anti-shock garments (PASG), lower extremity elevation, and diffuse direct pressure.
  d. elevation, pressure point, pressure dressing, and PASG.

81. Where should you place your hands when using the head-tilt/chin-lift maneuver to open an unconscious patient's airway?
  a. on the nose, with the fingertips pinching it closed, and under the neck
  b. on the nose, with the fingertips pinching it closed, and on the forehead
  c. on the forehead, with the other hand under the neck
  d. on the forehead, with the fingertips of the other hand under the lower jaw

82. Your patient is found lying on the ground after falling off a roof. He is unconscious and apneic. Which method should you use to open the patient's airway?
  a. head-tilt/chin-lift
  b. modified jaw thrust
  c. head-tilt only
  d. head-tilt/neck-lift

83. With of the following is not a link in the chain of survival?
 a. early access to EMS
 b. early CPR
 c. early intra-cardiac medication
 d. early defibrillation

84. When splinting an injured limb, you should assess pulse, motor function, and sensation distal to the injury
 a. after applying the splint.
 b. before applying the splint.
 c. while applying the splint.
 d. before and after applying the splint.

85. When performing the modified jaw-thrust maneuver to open your patient's airway, which of the following steps is NOT correct?
 a. Stabilize the patient's cervical spine with your forearms.
 b. Rest your elbows on the same surface as the patient.
 c. Tilt the head by applying gentle pressure to the forehead.
 d. Use your index fingers to push the angles of the lower jaw forward.

86. The *golden hour* in emergency medicine refers to
 a. the first 60 minutes after the arrival of EMS.
 b. the first 60 minutes after the occurrence of multisystem trauma.
 c. the first 60 minutes after the arrival at the emergency room.
 d. the first 60 minutes after the start of surgery.

87. Which of the following devices can be used to secure the spine of a patient seated in a car?
 a. Kendrick Extrication Device
 b. Miller style backboard
 c. full body vacuum splint
 d. scoop stretcher

88. Your unconscious patient has blood in his airway. You should
 a. use a suction unit to immediately clear the airway.
 b. apply oxygen using a nonrebreather mask at 15 L/min.
 c. use a bag-valve mask to clear the airway.
 d. perform a finger sweep to remove the blockage.

89. Your patient is behaving abnormally but refuses treatment after falling down a flight of stairs. Before transporting the patient without consent, you should
 a. document the presence of any injury.
 b. ask bystanders to serve as witnesses.
 c. have bystanders help talk him into care.
 d. contact medical direction for advice.

90. You should not suction a patient's airway for more than 15 seconds because
 a. the patient's tongue may be injured.
 b. the suction unit's battery may drain too quickly.
 c. the patient will become hypoxic during this time.
 d. you may cause the patient to vomit.

91. Which of the following is true regarding using a pocket mask to ventilate a nonbreathing patient?
   a. There is direct contact between the rescuer and the patient's mouth.
   b. Oxygen cannot be connected to the mask.
   c. A one-way valve prevents exhaled air from contacting the rescuer.
   d. Oxygen levels of 100% may be achieved.

92. You are ventilating an apneic trauma patient using the jaw-thrust maneuver and a bag-valve mask. You should
   a. tilt the head as far as it can go.
   b. use your ring and little fingers to lift the jaw upward.
   c. kneel at the patient's side.
   d. do nothing. Use of airway adjuncts is not necessary.

93. To which patient should you administer oral glucose?
   a. 60-year-old female behaving as if she is intoxicated, and whose daughter informs you that she takes insulin by injection
   b. 45-year-old male with a history of diabetes behaving erratically after falling and hitting his head in the bathtub
   c. 70-year-old male with a long history of diabetes who is unconscious and cannot swallow
   d. 52-year-old female who tells you that she is feeling dizzy and has low blood sugar

94. You respond to a patient who is not acting appropriately and yelling obscenities at people on the street. Which of the following should you suspect first?
   a. diabetic crisis
   b. alcohol abuse
   c. psychological emergency
   d. heart attack

95. Using a reservoir with a bag-valve-mask system will allow oxygen levels to increase to nearly
   a. 70%.
   b. 90%.
   c. 80%.
   d. 100%.

96. All of the following may be signs of allergic reaction EXCEPT
   a. headache and dizziness.
   b. rapid, labored breathing.
   c. decreased blood pressure.
   d. decreased heart rate.

97. Which of the following patients would require the administration of epinephrine during an allergic reaction?
   a. a five-year-old patient who is itching after being exposed to poison ivy
   b. a 49-year-old patient who is having trouble breathing and has very low blood pressure after being stung by a bee
   c. a 13-year-old patient who is sneezing and has hives on her arm after eating shellfish
   d. a 56-year-old patient who has high blood pressure and has a rapid heart rate after eating peanuts

98. Ethics is best described as
   a. the principles of conduct; concerns for what is right or wrong, good or bad.
   b. a code of conduct put forward by a society or some other group such as a religion.
   c. the principle of doing good for the patient.
   d. the obligation to treat all patients fairly.

99. Your patient is a 48-year-old homeless man that was found lying in a parking lot in the winter. He is severely hypothermal. Which of the following is an appropriate treatment for this patient?
   a. rapid rewarming to achieve normal body temperature
   b. giving the patient hot coffee or hot tea to drink
   c. keeping the patient cold unless you can warm them to normal temperature
   d. gradual rewarming and gentle handling of the patient

100. Predisposing factors for hypothermia include all the following EXCEPT
   a. age.
   b. depression.
   c. exposure to cold.
   d. alcohol.

101. A sign of generalized cold emergency, or hypothermia, is cool skin on the
   a. feet or hands.
   b. ears.
   c. face.
   d. abdomen.

102. Two important principles in the emergency treatment of local cold injuries are to remove the patient from the cold environment and to
   a. rewarm the cold extremity quickly.
   b. warm the whole body as soon as possible.
   c. prevent further tissue damage.
   d. prevent or treat pain.

103. Which of the following indicates a true heat emergency?
   a. a patient with leg cramps and vomiting after running a marathon
   b. a patient who is sweating very heavily and feels dizzy after working outside all day
   c. a patient who has altered mental status after football practice for three hours outside
   d. a patient who has hot skin and is sweating heavily after working at a construction site all day

104. Which of the following treatments is recommended for all unwitnessed drowning?
   a. relieving gastric distention by compressing the stomach
   b. spinal immobilization
   c. placing the patient in the shock (Trendelenburg) position
   d. transportation to a hospital with a hyperbaric chamber

105. Your patient has been stung by a bee, and the stinger is present in the wound. You should attempt to remove it by
   a. grabbing it with sterile tweezers.
   b. cutting around it with a knife.
   c. scraping it away with a rigid object.
   d. grabbing it with your fingers.

106. The Health Insurance Portability and Accountability Act (HIPAA) requires EMTs to do all of the following EXCEPT
   a. respect patient confidentiality.
   b. submit all run reports to the State Office of EMS.
   c. safeguard patient information from unauthorized access.
   d. secure reports including paper reports and electronic documentation.

107. In legal terms, a *tort* is
  a. a civil wrong committed by one individual against another.
  b. a criminal wrongdoing.
  c. an action by an employee for a workers' compensation claim.
  d. a breach of contract.

108. Which of the following are the signs of early respiratory distress in children and infants?
  a. breathing rate of less than ten per minute, limp muscle tone, slow or absent heart rate, weak or absent distal pulses
  b. increased rate of breathing, nasal flaring, intercostal or supraclavicular retractions, mottled skin color, abdominal muscle use
  c. altered mental status, respiratory rate of over 60 or under 20 breaths per minute, severe retractions, severe use of accessory muscles
  d. inability to cough, crying with tears but no sounds, cyanosis, abdominal or chest-wall movements with absent breath sounds

109. Your patient is an 8-year-old female who had a single, brief seizure at school. Her mother arrives at the same time you do and reports that she has seizures often, and is under medical treatment. What should you do?
  a. Request advanced life support (ALS) and law enforcement backup so you can transport the child.
  b. Administer a dose of the child's prescribed seizure-control medication.
  c. Maintain ABCs, monitor vital signs, and transport the patient immediately.
  d. Ensure a patent airway and request medical direction regarding transport.

110. All of the following are signs of possible child abuse EXCEPT
  a. the presence of multiple bruises in various stages of healing.
  b. a single, severe traumatic event that occurred for no reason.
  c. injuries inconsistent with the mechanism described.
  d. conflicting histories of the injury from the guardians/parents.

111. The head of a newborn infant has just been delivered. You should
  a. suction the baby's mouth and nostrils with a bulb syringe.
  b. push down on the baby's upper shoulder to facilitate the rest of the delivery.
  c. push up on the baby's lower shoulder to facilitate the rest of the delivery.
  d. ventilate the baby with a pediatric bag-valve mask and high-flow oxygen.

112. Emergency care for a responsive 7-year-old child with a foreign-body airway obstruction includes
  a. holding the child on your knee and performing back blows.
  b. standing behind the child and performing sub-diaphragmatic thrusts.
  c. placing the child supine on the floor and attempting to see the obstruction.
  d. placing the child supine on the floor and performing abdominal thrusts.

113. A 2-year-old male is in respiratory failure when he has
- **a.** altered mental status and breathing rate of 68 per minute.
- **b.** limp muscle tone and weak or absent distal pulses.
- **c.** nasal flaring and mottled skin color.
- **d.** breathing rate of six per minute and heart rate of 50 per minute.

114. A sign or symptom of a predelivery emergency is
- **a.** the mother's skin is dry.
- **b.** profuse vaginal bleeding.
- **c.** the presence of a bloody show.
- **d.** a contraction every 20 minutes.

115. Select the correct-size oral airway for a small child by measuring from the corner of the patient's mouth to what structure?
- **a.** central incisor
- **b.** angle of the jaw
- **c.** tip of the nose
- **d.** pinnea of the ear

116. Vitreous humor is found
- **a.** behind the lens of the eye.
- **b.** in the bone marrow of the upper arm.
- **c.** in front of the lens of the eye.
- **d.** in the joint lubrication of the upper arm.

117. You are assisting with childbirth in the field. As the infant's head is delivered, you discover that the umbilical cord is wrapped tightly around the neck. You should immediately
- **a.** place the mother on her side and transport rapidly.
- **b.** deliver the infant with the cord wrapped around its neck.
- **c.** clamp the cord in two places and cut it between clamps.
- **d.** suction the infant's mouth and nose to clear secretions.

118. You are helping an EMT student study for his upcoming final exam. You are quizzing the student on newborn assessment, and he cannot remember what the "R" stands for in APGAR. You reply
- **a.** "rate."
- **b.** "respirations."
- **c.** "redness of the skin."
- **d.** "resting state of the newborn."

119. Asking all of the following questions will help you decide whether delivery is imminent EXCEPT
- **a.** when is the baby due?
- **b.** do you feel increasing pressure in your vaginal area?
- **c.** do you feel the urge to move your bowels?
- **d.** when did you last eat or drink?

120. Which of the following is not a disease causing microorganism?
- **a.** ricotta
- **b.** fungus
- **c.** bacteria
- **d.** parasites

121. The presence of a bloody show during the first stage of labor is a sign that
- **a.** the delivery of the infant is imminent.
- **b.** the newborn is in danger of respiratory distress.
- **c.** labor is progressing normally.
- **d.** the second stage of labor has begun.

122. Your patient has experienced a spontaneous abortion or miscarriage. You should
- **a.** remove any tissue from the vagina.
- **b.** discard any expelled tissue.
- **c.** place a sanitary napkin in the vagina.
- **d.** treat the patient for shock.

123. Your patient is a 28 year old that just gave birth. She is having severe vaginal bleeding. Which of the following is not an appropriate treatment?
   a. administer oxygen
   b. treat for shock
   c. pack her vagina with gauze
   d. massage her abdomen gently

124. Which of the following is the primary difference in adult and child cardiac arrest?
   a. Children suffer cardiac arrest primarily from congenital heart defects.
   b. Adults usually suffer from cardiac arrest because of trauma, whereas children suffer cardiac arrest because of illness.
   c. Children suffer cardiac arrest from breathing problems, whereas adults suffer cardiac arrest because of heart problems.
   d. There is no difference between child and adult cardiac arrest.

125. In addition to caring for injuries, emergency care for a rape victim should focus on which of the following?
   a. performing a pelvic or rectal exam on the patient
   b. collecting evidence of the rape and bagging it in plastic
   c. allowing the patient to shower and change clothes
   d. preserving evidence in a paper bag and reassuring the victim

126. The reason to position a pregnant woman on her left side is to
   a. reduce the pressure of the fetus on maternal circulation.
   b. make labor proceed more slowly by slowing down contractions.
   c. help turn a breech fetus in the birth canal to the vertex position.
   d. ensure that there is sufficient blood flow to the placenta.

127. You respond to a small local hospital to transport a pregnant patient to a large hospital in another city. The labor and delivery nurse tells you that the patient is "gravid 5, para 3." This means
   a. the patient has a communicable disease and universal precautions should be taken.
   b. the patient's water has broken five minutes before, and contractions are three minutes apart.
   c. the patient has been pregnant five times, and has given birth to three children.
   d. the patient has given birth to five children, and has been pregnant three times.

128. The average length of labor for a woman's first baby is
   a. 45 to 60 minutes.
   b. 2 to 3 hours.
   c. 12 to 18 hours.
   d. more than 24 hours.

129. The patient is said to be crowning when the
   a. placenta separates from the uterine wall.
   b. placenta is formed in an abnormal location.
   c. umbilical cord presents at the vaginal opening.
   d. baby's head is visible at the vaginal opening.

130. When arriving at the scene of a possible hazardous materials incident, you would identify hazards by
   a. thoroughly investigating the scene yourself.
   b. interviewing victims and bystanders.
   c. scanning with binoculars from a safe distance.
   d. assisting law enforcement officers in the search.

131. For which of these procedures should you wear gloves, gown, mask, and protective eyewear?
   a. performing endotracheal intubation
   b. performing oral/nasal suctioning
   c. cleaning contaminated instruments
   d. bleeding control with spurting blood

132. Which of the following situations represents your abandonment of a patient?

   a. You begin assessing a patient, but turn responsibility for that patient over to a first responder.

   b. You begin CPR on a cardiac arrest patient, but stop when the ALS team takes over care.

   c. With the approval of medical direction, you do not transport a patient who feels fine after having a seizure.

   d. You refuse to help a patient administer nitroglycerin that has been prescribed for someone else.

133. You are called to a store where a holdup has been committed. Police are already on the scene searching for the gunman. Through the store window, you see the store manager, who has been shot. You should

   a. enter the store immediately to care for the manager.

   b. leave immediately and seek cover a distance away.

   c. wait until the police tell you it is safe to enter the scene.

   d. request medical direction to determine if you can enter.

134. You respond to a pregnant patient in labor at a doctor's office. The doctor advised that she has had "rupture of membranes." What has occurred?

   a. she is having placenta previa

   b. she is having placenta abruption

   c. she has serious vaginal bleeding

   d. her bag of waters (amniotic fluid) has broken

135. What is the first thing you should do after receiving orders from the medical direction physician?

   a. carry out the orders immediately

   b. repeat the orders exactly as you heard them

   c. question anything you did not understand

   d. document the orders in your report

136. Which of the following represents proper communication with the patient?

   a. When talking to a 12-year-old female: "Do you want to hold your mommy's hand while I bandage you?"

   b. When talking to an intoxicated 27-year-old male: "Get up. You are intoxicated and are not injured."

   c. When talking to a 75-year-old female: "Ma'am, we think you should go to the hospital to make sure you're okay. Will you come with us?"

   d. When talking to a 4-year-old male: "I think you've fractured your femur. We'll stabilize you here and transport you to the hospital for surgery."

137. Your pregnant patient is experiencing contractions. She feels like she needs to move her bowels. This may indicate that

   a. birth is still some time away.

   b. birth is imminent.

   c. she is going into shock.

   d. the baby is still very high in the birth canal.

138. Which statement about a patient's right to refuse care is correct?
  a. A child who is old enough to understand danger is old enough to refuse care and transport.
  b. An adult patient who is of sound mind and understands the consequences can refuse treatment.
  c. No one can authorize treatment or transport for any other individual, regardless of his or her age.
  d. EMTs should leave immediately whenever a patient says that he or she will refuse care.

139. Which situation requires that an emergency patient be moved?
  a. Your patient has undergone cardiac arrest while seated in a chair.
  b. Your patient is found on the ground, unresponsive, and alone.
  c. Your patient is found in his bed, displaying early symptoms of shock.
  d. Your patient is showing signs of inadequate breathing and shock.

140. Which of the following is not a sign or symptom of an infectious disease?
  a. night sweats
  b. fevers
  c. increased thirst, increased hunger, increased urination
  d. flu-like symptoms

141. Which of the following is not a risk factor during pregnancy?
  a. history of twins
  b. history of diabetes
  c. history of hypertension
  d. history of a sexually transmitted disease

142. The purpose of incident management systems is to provide
  a. a clear chain of command in case of legal liability.
  b. a means of evaluating the EMS system's response to an event.
  c. an orderly method for communications and decision making.
  d. a training program for first responders.

143. A 23-year-old pregnant female is bleeding profusely from her vagina. All of the following actions are appropriate EXCEPT
  a. providing high-concentration oxygen.
  b. placing a sanitary napkin in the vagina.
  c. replacing pads as they become soaked.
  d. rapid transport to the hospital.

144. In a multiple-casualty situation, which patient should be assigned the highest priority?
  a. adequate breathing, responsive, venous bleeding
  b. adequate breathing, responsive, suspected spine injury
  c. inadequate breathing, responsive, suspected broken tibia
  d. inadequate breathing, unresponsive, suspected internal bleeding

145. In a multiple-casualty situation, the lowest priority would be assigned to a patient who
  a. has moderate burns.
  b. is in respiratory distress.
  c. has died.
  d. is in shock.

146. Your patient is an 84-year-old female having difficulty breathing. Her daughter, age 45, is with her. When communicating with this patient, you should assume that she is
   a. incompetent; speak directly with the daughter.
   b. hard of hearing; speak extremely slowly and loudly.
   c. competent and able to understand; speak respectfully.
   d. confused; explain your treatment clearly to the daughter.

147. Which statement about patient confidentiality is correct?
   a. Patients who are cared for in a public place lose their right to confidentiality.
   b. The right to confidentiality does not apply to minors or to wards of the state.
   c. The patient who signs a statement releasing confidential information relinquishes all rights to privacy.
   d. A patient must sign a written release before any confidential information can be disclosed.

148. A pregnant female who is about to deliver a baby should be positioned
   a. on her right side with legs apart.
   b. in a sitting position on the stretcher.
   c. in the knee-chest position.
   d. supine with knees drawn up and spread apart.

149. Your ambulance is dispatched to the home of a terminally ill patient. The patient is in full cardiac arrest. His wife states that the patient is a Do Not Resuscitate (DNR), but cannot find the document. You should
   a. begin CPR and contact medical control for further instructions.
   b. have your partner assist the wife in locating the document.
   c. respect the wife's wishes and stop resuscitation.
   d. tell the wife that she will need to have the patient's doctor call you.

150. Your patient is a 6-year-old female who fell off her bicycle. She has a suspected broken ankle, no respiratory compromise, and no suspected internal injuries. After providing necessary care at the scene, you are transporting the child and her father to the hospital. The father loudly insists that you use your siren and lights en route. You should
   a. request medical direction in dealing with the father.
   b. request permission from dispatch to use lights and siren.
   c. refuse, because it may cause an unnecessary hazard.
   d. comply, it will relax the father and comfort the patient.

Answers

1. b. HEPA respirators are worn when in contact with patients who have airborne infections such as TB. HIV/AIDS and hepatitis B are both blood-borne pathogens. Contaminants from open wounds would also be blood borne.

2. c. Gowns should be worn when you expect to be exposed to large amounts of blood or body fluids, such as when assisting with childbirth.

3. a. The blue portion of the 704 placard stands for health hazards, red is fire, yellow is reactivity, and white is special hazards.

4. b. Because ventricular fibrillation is the most common cause of sudden cardiac arrest, it is critical to apply an AED on an unconscious apneic and pulseless patient as quickly as possible. The other rhythms can also cause a patient to be in cardiac arrest, but they do not occur as frequently as "V-fib."

5. a. The patient with chest pain and systolic blood pressure less than 100 is the highest priority patient of the four. A leg injury may be life threatening if the femoral artery is injured, but most often, a single extremity injury is not a threat to life. The elderly gentleman may be exhibiting his normal mental status, or he may be having problems due to an ongoing health problem. You need more information before you can make that determination, but he is not in any imminent danger right now. Labor with contractions six minutes apart is not considered imminent delivery. If you have any questions, however, you should continue assessing this patient as well by asking pertinent questions and checking for crowning.

6. c. Fluids containing blood have the highest potential for disease transmission.

7. c. An infant who is alert to verbal stimuli will still try to locate the parents' voices; choice **a** describes an alert infant; choice **d** describes an infant who is responsive to painful stimuli; choice **b** is incorrect because infants of this age are not developed enough to tell you their age regardless of their mental status.

8. b. Assess circulation in an infant by palpating the brachial pulse in the upper arm. The carotid and radial pulses are difficult to locate in infants. Capillary refill time shows that the patient has impaired circulation, but it is not the first tool to use in assessing circulation because it is affected by external factors (like the environment) as well as internal factors like poor perfusion.

9. c. There is no information to indicate that the patient requires ventilatory support. Any patient experiencing chest discomfort should receive the highest possible concentration of oxygen.

10. c. A person who is ejected from a vehicle after a collision is at highest risk for hidden injury and death. In fact, ejected patients have 300 times a greater chance of dying than patients who remain inside the vehicle during a crash. Regarding falls, patients are considered to be at risk for hidden injury if they fall a distance greater than three times their height. The surface they land on is also considered with falls. Both patients **a** and **d** had falls two times their height and landed on relatively soft surfaces.

11. d. Carbon monoxide is odorless, colorless, and tasteless. The primary signs and symptoms of carbon monoxide exposure are headache, nausea and vomiting, and general lethargy.

12. c. A supine patient may or may not have jugular veins that are prominent enough to palpate. However, even if the neck veins are normally present when an individual is supine, they will not be engorged in blood and overly firm to the touch. This is what is meant by the phrase *distended neck veins*. Distended neck veins (in any position) are a sign of increased circulatory pressure. The carotid pulse should always be palpable. A decreased radial pulse may indicate hypovolemic shock or an injured extremity.

13. c. The other rhythms do not benefit from an electrical shock. The purpose of early defibrillation is to stop a highly chaotic, disorganized electrical rhythm such as ventricular fibrillation, with the hope that an organized rhythm will begin and generate a pulse.

14. d. The rapid trauma assessment starts with the top of the head and proceeds downward. You should immobilize the spine as soon as you have finished assessing the neck.

15. b. Assess motor function by asking the patient to wiggle his toes; moving the leg or having the patient bend the knee can compromise spinal stability; option **d** describes assessment of sensation, not motor function.

16. b. Patient **b** is the only one both responsive and who has no significant mechanism of injury.

17. c. The P component of the OPQRST acronym refers to provocation or palliation, or what makes the pain feel worse or better.

18. a. You should perform the initial assessment first, because the unresponsive patient cannot direct you to the specific complaint. Vital signs are completed during your second phase of patient assessment after you determine treatment priority and have a baseline ABC assessment. You cannot determine the appropriate course of treatment of any airway problem (including the need for positioning—choice **c**) until you have first assessed the airway. The SAMPLE history is important information to gather, but it should never come before any treatment that may be needed to correct an ABC abnormality.

19. b. Trauma and medical patients who are unresponsive, and all patients who have altered mental status, should receive a detailed physical assessment. It is easy to overlook something

when the patient is not conscious enough to tell you what hurts or if the MOI and nature of illness (NOI) are unclear.

20. c. The detailed physical assessment is usually performed in the back of the ambulance during transport; its purpose is to reveal hidden injuries that escaped the initial rapid assessment.

21. a. Defibrillation is not currently recommend as a treatment for atrial fibrillation, asystole, or PEA.

22. c. The purpose of ongoing assessment is to check the adequacy of your initial interventions. The detailed examination is designed to find missed injuries.

23. d. Do CPR. American Heart Association guidelines advise that even if there is an organized rhythm, a pulse will not be palpable immediately after a shock. CPR is crucial to maintain blood flow and ventilation during this time.

24. a. The prone position is described as lying on one's stomach.

25. b. The NOI is the chief complaint, or the reason the patient called the ambulance.

26. c. Only those patients who are unresponsive, pulseless, and apneic should have the AED applied.

27. a. People yelling and screaming as you arrive on scene are indicators that the scene may not be safe for responders.

28. b. The trachea divides into the right and left bronchi; the carina is the point at which the division takes place; the alveoli are the minute air sacs in the lungs; and the lungs are the organs of air exchange.

29. c. The epiglottis is the leaf-shaped structure that closes off the trachea during swallowing. The larynx is the voice box, the structure that produces speech vibrations; the cricoid cartilage forms the lower portion of the larynx; the diaphragm is a large muscle that contracts to initiate inhalation.

30. d. The alveoli are the numerous minute air sacs that make up the lungs; bronchioles are small branches of the bronchi, which are the two main tubes branching from the trachea; the epiglottis is the structure that closes off the trachea during swallowing.

31. b. In glaucoma, high pressure distorts the optic disk and damages the optic nerve if the aqueous humor is not removed rapidly enough.

32. a. Other symptoms of pulmonary edema may include difficulty breathing, excessive sweating, anxiety, and pale skin.

33. c. During capillary–cellular exchange, oxygen enters the body cells and carbon dioxide enters the capillaries; choices **a** and **b** describe alveolar-capillary exchange; choice **d** describes cellular digestion.

34. b. The most common complication causing pediatric cardiac arrest is inadequate breathing or other respiratory compromise.

35. b. Abduction is the medical term meaning "away from the body."

36. c. The injury is inferior to (below) the elbow, and superior to (above) the hand.

37. a. A gurgling sound means that the patient needs to be suctioned immediately; ventilation cannot be adequate when the airway is blocked from mucous, blood, or other secretions.

38. b. Correct order of steps would be **b, c, a, d**.

39. b. The seizure event is referred to as *ictal,* hence *postictal* refers to the period after the seizure wherein a patent is often confused for a period of time.

40. b. Choice **b** is the correct procedure. Choice **a** is correct for a rigid catheter, choice **c** is the correct method for inserting an oropharyngeal airway, and choice **d** is applicable only to endotracheal intubation.

41. c. Choice **c** is the correct procedure for clearing the airway when simple suctioning is not working. Choice **b** is appropriate for a patient with copious frothy secretions like the kind produced with pulmonary edema. Choices **a** and **d** are inappropriate without first clearing the airway.

42. a. Choice **a** describes what happens during active inhalation; choices **b, c,** and **d** describe what happens during exhalation.

43. d. The purpose of the head-tilt/chin-lift is to move the tongue and epiglottis out of the way of the airway; it is not useful for intubation (use the sniffing position), to remove foreign bodies, or to visualize the larynx.

44. b. After opening the airway, the EMT should assess the rate and depth of ventilations; choices **a, c,** and/or **d** would occur only after respiratory adequacy has been assessed and they are appropriate to use.

45. b. While only an estimate, it is assumed that a blood pressure of at least 80 mm Hg would be required in order to palpate a pulse at the wrist.

46. c. Epistaxis is the medical term for a bloody nose.

47. a. Masks come in adult and pediatric sizes. In order to deliver the highest possible concentration of oxygen to the patient, you must have a properly fitting mask. Steps **d, b,** and **c** must then be completed (in that order) before placing the mask on the patient's face.

48. a. Agonal respirations are ineffective gasping respirations of a dying patient.

49. b. The 2005 American Heart Association guidelines for bag-mask-ventilation of adult patients is one breath every 5–6 seconds or 10–12 breaths per minute.

50. d. During a two-person bag-valve-mask procedure, one EMT ventilates the patient while the other maintains the airway and monitors the patient's chest rise.

51. a. The cricoid cartilage forms a ring of firm cartilage and is located inferior to (below) the larynx.

52. a. A means alert. The other letters in the acronym stand for verbal, pain, and unresponsive.

53. c. The child's airway is more susceptible to airway obstruction than an adult's because of the narrowed diameter and increased risk of swelling with infection.

54. c. The right ventricle receives oxygen-poor blood from the right atrium. It then pumps the blood to the lungs via the pulmonary artery, where it receives oxygen and releases carbon dioxide.

55. c. The role of the EMT-Basic is not to diagnose the exact cause of the patient's chief complaint. Maintaining a high suspicion for a cardiac emergency will guide your next step in managing this patient appropriately.

56. d. This refers to air bags. The word *supplemental* implies that other restraint systems such as seat belts are also required.

57. d. Your first action would be to administer oxygen and place the patient in a comfortable position; next, if not contraindicated, you would request permission to administer nitroglycerin. You should first obtain a set of vital signs to ensure he is not in cardiogenic shock. Never put defibrillator pads onto a conscious patient with a pulse; this procedure is contraindicated. AED pads are not serving the same function as the electrodes used by ALS providers to monitor the heart rhythm.

58. d. Any change in a patient's mental status should result in immediate assessment of the ABCs. If not already done, place this patient on supplemental oxygen and ventilate as needed. Neither CPR nor defibrillation (AED use) is appropriate for a patient with a pulse. Nitroglycerin is not administered to patients with altered levels of consciousness or in the absence of chest pain. You should first know the patient's blood pressure before assisting her in self-administering nitroglycerine.

59. a. Prehospital ACLS provides additional medications and other therapies that may help either terminate the cardiac arrest state or help prevent the patient who has regained a pulse from going back into cardiac arrest.

60. a. Although you note several injuries, you still need to perform a rapid initial assessment to determine if any problems with the ABCs that you have not noted may be more life threatening than what you can obviously see. Stop the bleeding (but do not use a tourniquet) and treat the patient for shock, but do not elevate the patient's legs if there is an injury to the legs, pelvis, head, neck, chest, abdomen, or spine. There is no indication that this patient needs ventilation at this time.

61. d. When the SAED is attempting to analyze the patient's electrical rhythm, any movement of the patient or the unit could cause the machine to misinterpret the signal.

62. c. Safety is critical when performing defibrillation. Any defibrillation attempt in the rain may possibly harm anyone near the patient during the discharge of the unit.

63. c. The pressure point for wounds of the forearm is the brachial artery.

64. a. Kinetic energy is the energy an object has while in motion. Choice **b** describes mass, choice **c** describes energy, and choice **d** describes inertia.

65. c. Having the bystander stop CPR will allow you to reassess the patient's ventilatory and circulatory status. This will tell you whether you need to continue CPR or whether the patient has regained a pulse or is breathing.

66. a. Venous bleeding flows in a steady, dark-red stream. Arterial bleeding is bright red and spurts from the wound, while capillary bleeding oozes. Internal bleeding may or may not present externally recognizable signs or symptoms.

67. d. This patient has the classic signs and symptoms of shock. Do not offer anything to eat or drink to a patient you suspect of being in shock, since surgery may be necessary later.

68. b. In March of 2004, the Department of Homeland Security regulated that all emergency responders should stop using ten codes and use plain text in order to increase agency inter-operability (National Incident Management Systems or NIMS).

69. c. The AED should be used only on patients who are not breathing and have no carotid pulse.

70. b. Automatic external defibrillators work by stopping chaotic, disorganized electrical rhythms in the heart in hopes that the heart will intrinsically start over with a normal perfusing rhythm.

71. c. Effective adult CPR includes a rate of 100 a minute, minimizing interruptions of chest compressions, and allowing the chest to fully recoil after each compression.

72. b. Net force on an object is proportionate to its mass multiplied by its acceleration. Choice **a** describes Newton's first law, and choice **c** describes his third law.

73. c. AEDs are currently not recommended for infants under the age of one.

74. a. If the patient has been resuscitated but is still unresponsive, check the pulse every 30 seconds during transport and keep the AED leads attached to the patient.

75. c. If it becomes necessary to deliver shocks while en route with the patient, the proper procedure is to stop the vehicle before reanalyzing the rhythm because the AED has a motion detector sensor in place that will not allow the unit to operate in the presence of motion.

76. b. The normal range of blood sugar in adults is 80–120.

77. b. Myocardial pain is often difficult to determine because it can take on many different characters; however, patients most commonly (over 40% of the time) describe the pain of a myocardial infarction as a crushing, squeezing, pressure that radiates outward to the arms and upper back.

78. a. Children often turn toward the impact and are often thrown down and under the vehicle.

79. b. Have the patient sit up and lean forward so the blood does not enter the airway or stomach.

80. a. The combination of direct pressure, elevation, pressure dressing, and pressure point pressure is almost always successful in stopping bleeding in the extremities. Tourniquets are seldom needed. PASG use is performed cautiously under direct medical control, and it is never the first line of treatment.

81. d. Lifting the jaw is necessary to dislodge the tongue from the back of the throat and provide a patent airway.

82. b. The head-tilt/chin-lift may jeopardize the patient's cervical spine. The other two procedures will not adequately open the airway.

83. c. Early intra-cardiac medication is not a link in the chain of survival.

84. d. Assess pulse, motor function, and sensation distal to a splint both before and after applying the splint to ensure that the splint is not adversely affecting circulation to the limb.

85. c. Tilting the head may compromise the stabilization of the cervical spine when using the modified jaw thrust.

86. b. The first 60 minutes after the occurrence of multisystem trauma is the *golden hour.*

87. a. The Kendrick Extrication Device (KED) is used to secure the spine of a patient seated in a car.

88. a. Blood is too fluid to be cleared adequately by a finger sweep. The other answers are not appropriate unless the airway was cleared first by suction.

89. d. Before transporting a patient without consent, it is best to always seek medical direction.

90. c. While the other answers may be true, they may occur regardless of the time interval.

91. c. The one-way valve minimizes potential cross-exposure of the patient's secretions and exhaled breath to the rescuer.

92. b. Doing this will allow you to maintain the cervical spine while keeping the tongue from blocking the back of the pharynx.

93. a. Administer oral glucose on medical direction (through protocol or standing order) only to patients with altered mental status and history of diabetes. Patient **b** should be first treated as a trauma patient, and because research shows poor outcomes following brain injuries and glucose administration, it is best to withhold its use until blood sugar can be checked (which is an ALS-provider skill in many areas). Patient **c** is not appropriate because of an inability to swallow properly; ALS should be called to provide IV dextrose to this patient. Glucose should be withheld until you can better determine if patient **d** is actually diabetic or not. (A blood glucose reading would be helpful with this patient as well.)

94. a. Patient's with altered mental status should be suspected of having a diabetic crisis, before suspecting other causes.

95. d. The use of a reservoir ensures that the patient receives the highest concentration of oxygen available.

96. d. Signs of allergic reactions include increased heart rate, as the heart attempts to compensate for hypoperfusion. The two primary life-threatening events that occur during an allergic reaction are profound vasoconstriction (resulting in shock) and compromised airway due to swelling, constriction, or mucous production.

97. b. A patient in anaphylaxis, with difficulty breathing and hypotension, is an indication for the administration of epinephrine.

98. a. This is the principles of conduct; concerns for what is right or wrong, good or bad. Choice **b** describes morals, choice **c** is a better description of bioethics, and choice **d** describes justice for the patient.

99. d. Severely hypothermial patients should be handled gently to prevent ventricular fibrillation, and should be gradually rewarmed.

100. b. Cold environments, immersion in water, age, alcohol, and shock are the most important factors that predispose patients to hypothermia.

101. d. Cool skin on the abdomen is a reliable sign of hypothermia in a patient because the abdomen is in the central core of the body and is generally covered under layers of clothing.

102. c. The goal of care in cases of localized cold damage is to prevent further damage by removing the patient from the cold environment and protecting the damaged tissues from further injury. Rewarming is best accomplished in the hospital setting, where pain medication can be administered and the danger of reinjury due to recooling is diminished.

103. c. A patient with a heat emergency who has altered mental status is experiencing a life-threatening emergency.

104. b. Spinal immobilization is recommended for all unwitnessed drowning because of the potential for spinal cord injury.

105. c. Grabbing a stinger with tweezers or your fingers can squeeze more venom into the wound (also, there is personal risk of accidental exposure to the venom if you use your hands). Instead, scrape the stinger out of the skin with a piece of cardboard or rigid plastic (a credit card is ideal). Cutting around the stinger causes more tissue damage.

106. b. HIPAA does not require EMTs to submit run reports to the State Office of EMS.

107. a. A *tort* is a civil wrong committed by one individual against another. Improper or negligent patient care would be considered a tort.

108. b. Choice **b** describes early respiratory distress. Choice **a** describes the signs of impending respiratory arrest from insufficiency, choice **c** describes respiratory failure, and choice **d** describes airway obstruction.

109. d. For patients who have routine seizures and whose condition returns to normal quickly after a seizure, you should request medical direction about whether to transport.

110. b. Multiple injuries, conflicting stories of the cause, and repeated calls to the same address are characteristic of child abuse.

111. a. Suctioning the baby's mouth and nose will help to open the airway while the baby has not yet begun breathing. You should not force any part of the delivery process.

112. b. Care for a responsive child consists of standing behind the child and attempting to relieve the obstruction with a series of sub-diaphragmatic thrusts.

113. a. Signs of respiratory failure include altered mental status and a slow or fast breathing rate with fatigue. There is not enough information to determine if patients **b** and **c** are in respiratory insufficiency, respiratory failure, or impending respiratory arrest. Patient **d** is in impending respiratory arrest.

114. b. Profuse vaginal bleeding may indicate a true obstetrical emergency such as uterine rupture or torn placenta.

115. b. Select the correct-size oral airway for an infant or child by measuring from the corner of the patient's mouth to the angle of the jaw.

116. a. Vitreous humor is found behind the lens of the eye. It is the clear gel that fills the space between the lens and the retina. Aqueous humor is a thick, watery substance that fills the space between the lens and the cornea.

117. c. If the cord is wrapped around the infant's neck and you cannot easily loosen and remove it, you should clamp it in two places and cut the cord.

118. b. APGAR stands for Appearance, Pulse, Grimace, Activity and Respirations.

119. d. As delivery becomes imminent, the woman will feel increasing pressure in her vaginal area and will feel the urge to bear down and push. Asking about the due date, prenatal care, and number of previous children helps determine if delivery is imminent as well. Oral intake has no bearing on delivery.

120. a. Ricotta is a form of cheese and is not a disease causing microorganism. Virus, fungus, bacteria, and parasites are all disease causing microorganisms.

121. c. The presence of a bloody show (which is the expulsion of the mucous plug from the mouth of the cervix) occurs during the first stage of labor. It is normal and indicates that the cervix is beginning to open or dilate and may occur several hours prior to delivery. The second stage of labor begins after the baby is born.

122. d. There can be large blood loss suffered by the mother during a miscarriage. The EMT-Basic should treat the patient for possible shock as well as provide emotional care.

123. c. Packing the vagina with gauze is not an appropriate treatment.

124. c. Children primarily suffer cardiac arrest because of respiratory failure, whereas adults suffer cardiac arrest because of cardiac dysfunction.

125. d. In addition to providing routine emergency care, care for a rape victim should focus on preserving evidence and providing comfort and reassurance. Although you want to provide comfort to the patient, you should not allow him or her to shower or change clothes, as this will destroy evidence. Any clothing or personal effects that are removed from the patient should be placed in paper bags to prevent the growth of bacteria that might occur if stored in plastic bags. You should not need to examine the genital or rectal area unless you note significant bleeding.

126. a. This condition, called supine hypotension syndrome, is the result of compression that the enlarged uterus causes on the vena cava of the maternal circulatory system. This corrective position, called the left lateral recumbent position, is accomplished by placing the mother on her left side with her legs bent slightly or kept straight. Maternal positional changes have no effect on the speed of labor or the position of the infant in the birth canal. By assisting in venous blood return in the mother, you will get the secondary effect of increasing blood flow to the uterus, but this is a secondary effect seen in correcting supine hypotension syndrome.

127. c. The term *gravid* means the number of pregnancies, and *para* means the number of live births. Gravid 5, para 3 indicates a patient who has been pregnant five times and given birth to three live babies.

128. c. The average length of labor for a first baby is 12 to 18 hours, but duration of labor varies greatly from one woman to another.

129. d. When the top of the baby's head is seen at the vaginal opening, birth is imminent.

130. c. Never enter a scene where hazardous materials are present until you have verified that the scene is safe. Use binoculars to survey the scene from a distance in order to identify hazardous materials placards. Consider victims and bystanders contaminated and take appropriate precautions.

131. d. Bleeding control with spurting blood carries maximum danger of contamination, and maximum protection is therefore required. Airway suctioning or intubation does not generally require the use of a cover gown, and cleaning contaminated instruments does not generally require eye/facial protection unless there is danger of splashing.

132. a. Abandonment occurs when you relinquish care without a patient's consent or without insuring that care is continued by someone of the same or higher level, such as a paramedic, ALS unit, or physician.

133. c. EMTs should not enter a crime scene until it has been secured by police. As you travel to the scene, you should determine where it is most appropriate to park your vehicle. Generally, you want cover (protection from attack) and concealment (out of direct visual range) in your staging area.

134. d. The term "rupture of membranes" means that the amniotic sac has ruptured.

135. b. To avoid misunderstanding, always repeat medical orders exactly as you heard them. Once you have done that, you can question any order you do not understand or about which you are unclear. When you complete your written patient-care report, you should include the order in your report.

136. c. Speak respectfully to all patients regardless of intoxication or mental impairment; when talking to a child, consider his or her developmental level.

137. b. The sensation of needing to move one's bowels during labor is the result of the head pressing down on the anal sphincter as the baby passes through the birth canal. The head is very close to the opening of the birth canal, and delivery is imminent.

138. b. An adult of sound mind can refuse treatment, but the EMT should first make an effort to clearly explain the consequences; refusal of treatment should be documented in writing.

139. a. An emergency move is required in a situation where a patient is in immediate life-threatening danger. Emergency moves require only cervical spine stabilization (if it is a trauma situation) and should be performed quickly. Once the patient is in a safer location, you should begin with your initial assessment as you do in all patient situations.

140. c. Increased thirst, increased hunger, and increased urination are signs of diabetes, not infectious disease.

141. a. History of twins is not an indication for a high-risk pregnancy.

142. c. An incident management system is a coordinated system of procedures that allows for smooth operations at the scene of an emergency.

143. b. Placing napkins in the birth canal will not stop the source of bleeding. Placing bulky dressings or sanitary napkins at the vaginal opening will help prevent the blood from spreading.

144. d. Patients with breathing difficulties and serious bleeding receive the highest priority in a multiple-casualty situation.

145. c. Patients who have already died are assigned to the lowest priority when there are still living patients who require care.

146. c. Do not assume that an elderly patient is incompetent, deaf, or confused. Address all patients respectfully.

147. d. Patient information can be released only if the patient has signed a specific consent form.

148. d. This position best allows the EMT-Basic to receive the newborn baby.

149. a. If a patient is in cardiac arrest and family states that the patient is a DNR (Do Not Resuscitate) but cannot locate the document, CPR should be initiated and medical control contacted for further direction.

150. c. You are responsible for helping make your patient feel at ease, but you are also responsible for operating your ambulance in the safest possible way.

5 ▶ EMT-BASIC PRACTICE EXAM 2

CHAPTER SUMMARY
This is the second of four practice exams in this book based on the National Registry EMT-Basic cognitive exam. Having taken one test before, you should feel more confident of your ability to pick the correct answers. Use this test to continue your study and practice. Notice how knowing what to expect makes you feel better prepared!

Like the first exam in this book, this test is based on the National Registry exam. It should not, however, look exactly like the first test you took, because you know more now about how the test is put together. You have seen how different types of questions are presented and are perhaps beginning to notice patterns in the order of questions. You see that questions on each area are grouped together. This pattern will help you develop your own test-taking strategy.

If you're following the advice of this book, you've done some studying between this exam and the first. This second exam will give you a chance to see how much you've improved.

The answer sheet, the test, and the answer key appear next (in that order). Read the answer explanations carefully, especially the explanations for the questions you missed.

Practice Exam 2

1.	ⓐ	ⓑ	ⓒ	ⓓ	51.	ⓐ	ⓑ	ⓒ	ⓓ	101.	ⓐ	ⓑ	ⓒ	ⓓ
2.	ⓐ	ⓑ	ⓒ	ⓓ	52.	ⓐ	ⓑ	ⓒ	ⓓ	102.	ⓐ	ⓑ	ⓒ	ⓓ
3.	ⓐ	ⓑ	ⓒ	ⓓ	53.	ⓐ	ⓑ	ⓒ	ⓓ	103.	ⓐ	ⓑ	ⓒ	ⓓ
4.	ⓐ	ⓑ	ⓒ	ⓓ	54.	ⓐ	ⓑ	ⓒ	ⓓ	104.	ⓐ	ⓑ	ⓒ	ⓓ
5.	ⓐ	ⓑ	ⓒ	ⓓ	55.	ⓐ	ⓑ	ⓒ	ⓓ	105.	ⓐ	ⓑ	ⓒ	ⓓ
6.	ⓐ	ⓑ	ⓒ	ⓓ	56.	ⓐ	ⓑ	ⓒ	ⓓ	106.	ⓐ	ⓑ	ⓒ	ⓓ
7.	ⓐ	ⓑ	ⓒ	ⓓ	57.	ⓐ	ⓑ	ⓒ	ⓓ	107.	ⓐ	ⓑ	ⓒ	ⓓ
8.	ⓐ	ⓑ	ⓒ	ⓓ	58.	ⓐ	ⓑ	ⓒ	ⓓ	108.	ⓐ	ⓑ	ⓒ	ⓓ
9.	ⓐ	ⓑ	ⓒ	ⓓ	59.	ⓐ	ⓑ	ⓒ	ⓓ	109.	ⓐ	ⓑ	ⓒ	ⓓ
10.	ⓐ	ⓑ	ⓒ	ⓓ	60.	ⓐ	ⓑ	ⓒ	ⓓ	110.	ⓐ	ⓑ	ⓒ	ⓓ
11.	ⓐ	ⓑ	ⓒ	ⓓ	61.	ⓐ	ⓑ	ⓒ	ⓓ	111.	ⓐ	ⓑ	ⓒ	ⓓ
12.	ⓐ	ⓑ	ⓒ	ⓓ	62.	ⓐ	ⓑ	ⓒ	ⓓ	112.	ⓐ	ⓑ	ⓒ	ⓓ
13.	ⓐ	ⓑ	ⓒ	ⓓ	63.	ⓐ	ⓑ	ⓒ	ⓓ	113.	ⓐ	ⓑ	ⓒ	ⓓ
14.	ⓐ	ⓑ	ⓒ	ⓓ	64.	ⓐ	ⓑ	ⓒ	ⓓ	114.	ⓐ	ⓑ	ⓒ	ⓓ
15.	ⓐ	ⓑ	ⓒ	ⓓ	65.	ⓐ	ⓑ	ⓒ	ⓓ	115.	ⓐ	ⓑ	ⓒ	ⓓ
16.	ⓐ	ⓑ	ⓒ	ⓓ	66.	ⓐ	ⓑ	ⓒ	ⓓ	116.	ⓐ	ⓑ	ⓒ	ⓓ
17.	ⓐ	ⓑ	ⓒ	ⓓ	67.	ⓐ	ⓑ	ⓒ	ⓓ	117.	ⓐ	ⓑ	ⓒ	ⓓ
18.	ⓐ	ⓑ	ⓒ	ⓓ	68.	ⓐ	ⓑ	ⓒ	ⓓ	118.	ⓐ	ⓑ	ⓒ	ⓓ
19.	ⓐ	ⓑ	ⓒ	ⓓ	69.	ⓐ	ⓑ	ⓒ	ⓓ	119.	ⓐ	ⓑ	ⓒ	ⓓ
20.	ⓐ	ⓑ	ⓒ	ⓓ	70.	ⓐ	ⓑ	ⓒ	ⓓ	120.	ⓐ	ⓑ	ⓒ	ⓓ
21.	ⓐ	ⓑ	ⓒ	ⓓ	71.	ⓐ	ⓑ	ⓒ	ⓓ	121.	ⓐ	ⓑ	ⓒ	ⓓ
22.	ⓐ	ⓑ	ⓒ	ⓓ	72.	ⓐ	ⓑ	ⓒ	ⓓ	122.	ⓐ	ⓑ	ⓒ	ⓓ
23.	ⓐ	ⓑ	ⓒ	ⓓ	73.	ⓐ	ⓑ	ⓒ	ⓓ	123.	ⓐ	ⓑ	ⓒ	ⓓ
24.	ⓐ	ⓑ	ⓒ	ⓓ	74.	ⓐ	ⓑ	ⓒ	ⓓ	124.	ⓐ	ⓑ	ⓒ	ⓓ
25.	ⓐ	ⓑ	ⓒ	ⓓ	75.	ⓐ	ⓑ	ⓒ	ⓓ	125.	ⓐ	ⓑ	ⓒ	ⓓ
26.	ⓐ	ⓑ	ⓒ	ⓓ	76.	ⓐ	ⓑ	ⓒ	ⓓ	126.	ⓐ	ⓑ	ⓒ	ⓓ
27.	ⓐ	ⓑ	ⓒ	ⓓ	77.	ⓐ	ⓑ	ⓒ	ⓓ	127.	ⓐ	ⓑ	ⓒ	ⓓ
28.	ⓐ	ⓑ	ⓒ	ⓓ	78.	ⓐ	ⓑ	ⓒ	ⓓ	128.	ⓐ	ⓑ	ⓒ	ⓓ
29.	ⓐ	ⓑ	ⓒ	ⓓ	79.	ⓐ	ⓑ	ⓒ	ⓓ	129.	ⓐ	ⓑ	ⓒ	ⓓ
30.	ⓐ	ⓑ	ⓒ	ⓓ	80.	ⓐ	ⓑ	ⓒ	ⓓ	130.	ⓐ	ⓑ	ⓒ	ⓓ
31.	ⓐ	ⓑ	ⓒ	ⓓ	81.	ⓐ	ⓑ	ⓒ	ⓓ	131.	ⓐ	ⓑ	ⓒ	ⓓ
32.	ⓐ	ⓑ	ⓒ	ⓓ	82.	ⓐ	ⓑ	ⓒ	ⓓ	132.	ⓐ	ⓑ	ⓒ	ⓓ
33.	ⓐ	ⓑ	ⓒ	ⓓ	83.	ⓐ	ⓑ	ⓒ	ⓓ	133.	ⓐ	ⓑ	ⓒ	ⓓ
34.	ⓐ	ⓑ	ⓒ	ⓓ	84.	ⓐ	ⓑ	ⓒ	ⓓ	134.	ⓐ	ⓑ	ⓒ	ⓓ
35.	ⓐ	ⓑ	ⓒ	ⓓ	85.	ⓐ	ⓑ	ⓒ	ⓓ	135.	ⓐ	ⓑ	ⓒ	ⓓ
36.	ⓐ	ⓑ	ⓒ	ⓓ	86.	ⓐ	ⓑ	ⓒ	ⓓ	136.	ⓐ	ⓑ	ⓒ	ⓓ
37.	ⓐ	ⓑ	ⓒ	ⓓ	87.	ⓐ	ⓑ	ⓒ	ⓓ	137.	ⓐ	ⓑ	ⓒ	ⓓ
38.	ⓐ	ⓑ	ⓒ	ⓓ	88.	ⓐ	ⓑ	ⓒ	ⓓ	138.	ⓐ	ⓑ	ⓒ	ⓓ
39.	ⓐ	ⓑ	ⓒ	ⓓ	89.	ⓐ	ⓑ	ⓒ	ⓓ	139.	ⓐ	ⓑ	ⓒ	ⓓ
40.	ⓐ	ⓑ	ⓒ	ⓓ	90.	ⓐ	ⓑ	ⓒ	ⓓ	140.	ⓐ	ⓑ	ⓒ	ⓓ
41.	ⓐ	ⓑ	ⓒ	ⓓ	91.	ⓐ	ⓑ	ⓒ	ⓓ	141.	ⓐ	ⓑ	ⓒ	ⓓ
42.	ⓐ	ⓑ	ⓒ	ⓓ	92.	ⓐ	ⓑ	ⓒ	ⓓ	142.	ⓐ	ⓑ	ⓒ	ⓓ
43.	ⓐ	ⓑ	ⓒ	ⓓ	93.	ⓐ	ⓑ	ⓒ	ⓓ	143.	ⓐ	ⓑ	ⓒ	ⓓ
44.	ⓐ	ⓑ	ⓒ	ⓓ	94.	ⓐ	ⓑ	ⓒ	ⓓ	144.	ⓐ	ⓑ	ⓒ	ⓓ
45.	ⓐ	ⓑ	ⓒ	ⓓ	95.	ⓐ	ⓑ	ⓒ	ⓓ	145.	ⓐ	ⓑ	ⓒ	ⓓ
46.	ⓐ	ⓑ	ⓒ	ⓓ	96.	ⓐ	ⓑ	ⓒ	ⓓ	146.	ⓐ	ⓑ	ⓒ	ⓓ
47.	ⓐ	ⓑ	ⓒ	ⓓ	97.	ⓐ	ⓑ	ⓒ	ⓓ	147.	ⓐ	ⓑ	ⓒ	ⓓ
48.	ⓐ	ⓑ	ⓒ	ⓓ	98.	ⓐ	ⓑ	ⓒ	ⓓ	148.	ⓐ	ⓑ	ⓒ	ⓓ
49.	ⓐ	ⓑ	ⓒ	ⓓ	99.	ⓐ	ⓑ	ⓒ	ⓓ	149.	ⓐ	ⓑ	ⓒ	ⓓ
50.	ⓐ	ⓑ	ⓒ	ⓓ	100.	ⓐ	ⓑ	ⓒ	ⓓ	150.	ⓐ	ⓑ	ⓒ	ⓓ

EMT-Basic Practice Exam 2

1. Which patient's vital signs are NOT within normal limits?
   a. newborn: pulse, 100; respirations, 30; BP, 70/30
   b. 3-year-old child: pulse, 90; respirations, 28; BP, 86/50
   c. 10-year-old child: pulse, 88; respirations, 18; BP, 100/60
   d. adult: pulse, 76; respirations, 17; BP, 116/86

2. Which of the following federal agencies establishes guidelines regarding the personal protective equipment that EMTs must wear?
   a. The Centers for Disease Control (CDC)
   b. The Occupational Safety and Health Administration (OSHA)
   c. The Department of Transportation (DOT)
   d. The National Registry of EMTs (NREMT)

3. Which of the following indicates that you are achieving adequate ventilation with a bag-valve mask?
   a. stomach rise and fall
   b. heart rate increases
   c. chest rise and fall
   d. the bag completely inflates between breaths

4. You should assess skin color by examining an adult patient's
   a. extremities.
   b. face.
   c. nailbeds.
   d. palms.

5. Which of the following patients would be described as alert and oriented?
   a. a 40-year-old female who appears to be asleep but answers you appropriately when questioned
   b. a 4-year-old male who refuses to tell you his name and cries to be returned to his mother's arms
   c. a 65-year-old male who grimaces when you pinch his shoulder but does not answer you
   d. a 59-year-old female who tells you her name but can't remember why you are there

6. A bag-valve mask that is not connected to supplemental oxygen will provide what oxygen concentration?
   a. 10%
   b. 21%
   c. 50%
   d. 100%

7. What is the most effective mode of transmission for hepatitis C?
   a. oral and nasal secretions
   b. airborne droplets or respiratory secretions
   c. contact with blood
   d. contact with contaminated objects

8. You would locate a patient's carotid pulse by first finding the Adam's apple and then
   a. pressing hard on only one side of the patient's neck.
   b. placing one hand gently on each side of the neck.
   c. pressing with your thumb on one side of the neck.
   d. sliding two fingers toward one side of the neck.

9. Your patient's pupils react unequally to light. You should suspect the presence of
   a. head injury.
   b. shock.
   c. airway obstruction.
   d. cardiac arrest.

10. A 70-year-old female is complaining of shortness of breath. She has a history of emphysema. You should
    a. withhold oxygen, since these patients do not respond to oxygen.
    b. withhold oxygen, because you could eliminate the hypoxic drive.
    c. administer oxygen, because in most cases, the hypoxic drive will not be a problem.
    d. withhold oxygen, because these patients become apneic if they receive high-flow oxygen.

11. A *contusion* refers to a
    a. cut.
    b. deformity.
    c. scrape.
    d. bruise.

12. *Ecchymosis* refers to
    a. an unreactive left pupil.
    b. bruising or discoloration.
    c. motion sickness.
    d. a bad taste in the mouth.

13. Which of the following is an example of a symptom?
    a. Your patient's blood pressure is 90/65 and falling.
    b. Your patient's skin color is slightly jaundiced.
    c. Your patient is complaining of pain and nausea.
    d. Your patient has a 102-degree fever.

14. In which situation should you determine the patient's blood pressure through palpation?
    a. Your patient is under 1 year old.
    b. The setting is unusually quiet, such as a private home.
    c. Your patient's pulse is very weak and difficult to hear.
    d. Your patient cannot tolerate pressure to the cartoid artery.

15. The correct way to select the proper size oropharyngeal airway (OPA) is to measure the distance from the
    a. corner of the mouth to the tip of the earlobe.
    b. nose to the tip of the earlobe.
    c. corner of the mouth to the nose.
    d. nose to the tip of the chin.

16. Which patient should receive only a focused physical exam and SAMPLE history?
    a. 46-year-old male, unresponsive after falling from a 10-meter scaffold
    b. 80-year-old male, responsive to painful stimuli after being hit by a car
    c. 5-year-old female, responsive and in pain after falling from a standing position
    d. 16-year-old female, responsive to verbal stimuli after a gunshot wound

17. Which of the following should you assess in the affected limb before and after splinting?
    a. blood pressure
    b. temperature
    c. color, sensation, and movement
    d. heart rate

18. Continuous monitoring of a patient's mental status is best accomplished by
    a. repeatedly asking the patient's name and address.
    b. continuously monitoring the patient's vital signs.
    c. continuously interacting with the patient.
    d. repeatedly assessing the peripheral circulation.

19. The reason for asking a patient her normal blood pressure reading is to determine
    a. if she is alert and oriented.
    b. if her general state of health is poor.
    c. whether you should perform a detailed exam.
    d. if a current reading is cause for concern.

20. You should assess the brachial pulse in patients who
    a. have a weak peripheral pulse.
    b. are younger than 1 year old.
    c. have a history of cardiac problems.
    d. have a pulse rate less than 60/min.

21. Which patient is showing early signs of shock (decreased tissue perfusion)?
    a. 23-year-old female: pulse, 104; respiration, 25/min; BP, 118/78; cool, clammy skin
    b. 45-year-old female: pulse, 68; respiration, 20/min; BP, 110/72; warm, moist skin
    c. 5-year-old male: pulse, 110; respiration, 22/min; BP, 88/52; cool, dry skin
    d. 60-year-old male: pulse, 76; respiration, 10/min; BP, 96/60; hot, dry skin

22. Which of the following is the most important sign of a diabetic emergency?
    a. altered mental status
    b. warm, dry skin
    c. decreased heart rate
    d. nausea and vomiting

23. An EMT should be especially vigilant for severe difficulty breathing in which of the following patients?
    a. stroke
    b. food poisoning
    c. anaphylaxis
    d. hypertension

24. Universal precautions include all of the following EXCEPT
    a. wearing a mask and gown.
    b. hand washing after each patient.
    c. treating all patients as if they have a communicable disease.
    d. vaccination for HIV.

25. Your patient is a 45-year-old homeless male who is suspected of hypothermia. The most important question to ask him is
    a. do you know who you are and where you are?
    b. are you having any trouble breathing?
    c. are you currently taking any prescription medications?
    d. what makes the pain feel better or worse?

26. Which of the following distinguishes heat exhaustion from heat stroke?
    a. hot, flushed skin
    b. severe sweating
    c. altered mental status
    d. cramps in the extremities

27. The zygomatic bones are found
    a. in the face.
    b. in the wrist.
    c. in the nasal passages.
    d. in none of the above. They do not exist in the human body.

28. What is the most common cause of airway obstruction in an unconscious patient?
   a. vomitus
   b. mucous
   c. the tongue
   d. blood

29. All of the following are reasons that infants and children are prone to respiratory difficulties EXCEPT that they
   a. breathe faster than adults.
   b. have smaller air passages.
   c. use their diaphragm rather than their intercostal muscles.
   d. are prone to respiratory infections.

30. Your patient is a newborn. You should consider the possibility of breathing difficulty if the respiratory rate is
   a. 40/min.
   b. 50/min.
   c. 60/min.
   d. 70/min.

31. When assessing your patient's airway, you hear snoring sounds. You should suspect that
   a. there is fluid in the airway.
   b. the tongue is blocking the airway.
   c. the bronchioles are constricted.
   d. the patient is forcefully exhaling.

32. What sign indicates that your patient's tidal volume might be inadequate?
   a. noisy, labored breathing
   b. rapid breathing
   c. inadequate chest movement
   d. slow breathing

33. How many vertebrae are there in the human spinal column?
   a. 33
   b. 66
   c. 44
   d. 77

34. You hear gurgling in your patient's airway. You should immediately
   a. administer high-flow oxygen.
   b. open and suction the airway.
   c. insert a nasopharyngeal airway.
   d. insert an oropharyngeal airway.

35. Your patient, a 49-year-old female with a history of heart disease, has collapsed in her home. What should you do first?
   a. Administer supplemental high-flow oxygen.
   b. Find out if the patient has taken nitroglycerin.
   c. Insert an oropharyngeal airway adjunct.
   d. Open the airway and assess breathing.

36. The rate of compressions to breaths in adult CPR is
   a. 15:2.
   b. 5:1.
   c. 30:1.
   d. 30:2.

37. The correct way to select the size of a nasopharyngeal airway is to measure
   a. from the corner of the mouth to the angle of the jaw.
   b. from the earlobe to the corner of the jaw.
   c. the diameter of the patient's little finger.
   d. from the chin to the Adam's apple.

38. In what position should you place a child's head for ventilation?
   a. in the neutral position
   b. slightly hyperextended
   c. slightly flexed foward
   d. in the recovery position

39. Your patient has a foreign-body airway obstruction. Three attempts to clear the airway have been unsuccessful. You should
   a. transport and attempt to clear the airway en route.
   b. call for an ALS unit as backup.
   c. request medical direction for further instructions.
   d. carry out three additional cycles before requesting help.

40. Wind can make the body lose heat at a much greater rate. Heat lost in this way describes the process of
   a. conduction.
   b. convection.
   c. radiation.
   d. diffusion.

41. After obtaining medical direction, you are helping your patient use a prescribed inhaler. You should tell the patient to
   a. take three quick, shallow breaths.
   b. inhale deeply and hold her breath.
   c. exhale as slowly as she can.
   d. lie down to prevent dizziness.

42. Your patient, a 78-year-old male, has no pulse and agonal respirations. You should
   a. begin CPR immediately.
   b. administer high-flow oxygen via bag-valve mask.
   c. transport immediately to the closest medical facility.
   d. request the patient's permission to administer nitroglycerin.

43. Most inhalers work by
   a. providing moisture to the lungs.
   b. dilating the bronchioles.
   c. increasing alveolar blood flow.
   d. increasing the respiratory rate.

44. You have assisted a patient in administering a prescribed inhaler. After one dose of the medication, the patient's pulse rate increases, and he reports feeling nauseated. You should
   a. administer another dose of the medication.
   b. assess respiratory rate, rhythm, and quality.
   c. document and report the signs and symptoms.
   d. begin cardiopulmonary resuscitation.

45. Which of the following is not true regarding oropharyngeal airways?
   a. They can be used in conscious patients with severe difficulty breathing.
   b. They come in a variety of sizes.
   c. They should be measured before they are inserted.
   d. They should be inserted either upside down or sideways and then rotated.

46. During the management of a cardiac arrest, the AED gives a "no shock indicated" message. Which of the following statements will most likely prompt this condition?
   a. The patient's rhythm is asystole.
   b. The patient has a pulse.
   c. The patient is in ventricular tachycardia.
   d. The patient is in ventricular fibrillation.

47. Which patient is breathing adequately?
   a. 3-month-old male: respiratory rate, 62/min, using diaphragm and muscles in chest and neck
   b. 7-year-old female: respiratory rate, 12/min, irregular rhythm, using diaphragm primarily
   c. 18-year-old male: respiratory rate, 28/min, shallow chest motions
   d. 43-year-old female: respiratory rate, 15/min, regular chest motions

48. The purpose of quickly opening and closing the valve on an oxygen tank before attaching the regulator is to
   a. ensure the valve is facing away from you and the patient.
   b. blow dirt or contamination out of the opening.
   c. ensure the tank is filled.
   d. check the pressure inside the tank.

49. Which of the following is the most ominous sign of impending respiratory failure in pediatric patients?
   a. wheezing
   b. see-saw breathing
   c. tachycardia
   d. nasal flaring

50. If a cardiac arrest is not witnessed, how long must the EMT provide CPR before defibrillating that patient?
   a. The patient should immediately be defibrillated if they are in a shockable rhythm.
   b. The patient should never be defibrillated during CPR.
   c. The patient should be defibrillated after one minute of CPR.
   d. The patient should be defibrillated after two minutes of CPR.

51. Adult defibrillators and adult defibrillation pads can be used on children as long as they are over what age?
   a. two
   b. four
   c. six
   d. eight

52. A danger of using a rigid suction catheter with infants and young children is that stimulating the back of the throat can
   a. cause changes in the heart rhythm.
   b. be ineffective in suctioning.
   c. lead to immediate vomiting.
   d. cause the tongue to fall into the airway.

53. Which of the following methods would you use to open the airway of a patient with a suspected spinal cord injury?
   a. head-tilt chin-lift method
   b. head-tilt neck-lift method
   c. modified jaw thrust
   d. two jaw/neck extension

54. The nasopharyngeal airway is preferred over the oropharyngeal airway for responsive patients because it
   a. is shorter and easier to insert.
   b. can move the tongue out of the airway.
   c. is unlikely to stimulate the gag reflex.
   d. comes in a wide variety of sizes.

55. The function of the white blood cells is to
   a. form clots.
   b. fight infection.
   c. carry oxygen.
   d. carry nutrients.

56. Angina differs from a heart attack because in an attack of angina, the
   a. patient feels severe chest pain.
   b. pain radiates outward from the heart.
   c. administration of nitroglycerin provides no relief.
   d. heart muscle is not permanently damaged.

57. The following patients all have signs and symptoms of cardiac chest pain and have their own prescriptions for nitroglycerin. Which patient should you NOT assist with taking nitroglycerin?
   a. 67-year-old male: pulse, 90; respirations, 26/min; BP, 98/72
   b. 72-year-old female: pulse, 88; respirations, 23/min; BP, 140/96
   c. 78-year-old male: pulse, 98; respirations, 26/min; BP, 160/112
   d. 51-year-old female: pulse, 72; respirations, 14/min; BP, 130/80

58. When deciding whether to assist a patient in administering nitroglycerin, you should check the medicine for the patient's name, the route of administration, the dose, and the
   a. doctor who prescribed it.
   b. quantity still available.
   c. pharmacy.
   d. expiration date.

59. The 2005 American Heart Association guidelines recommend CPR after each shock. How long should CPR be performed before the next shock is given (if indicated)?
   a. one minute
   b. two minutes
   c. three minutes
   d. four minutes

60. Your patient is showing signs and symptoms of shock and has a tender abdomen. She reports vomiting material that "looked like coffee grounds." You should suspect
   a. ruptured appendix.
   b. internal bleeding.
   c. fractured pelvis.
   d. inhaled poisoning.

61. Which of the following patients is showing signs of cardiac compromise?
   a. a 72-year-old female patient with emphysema who is wheezing, has labored breathing and a rapid heart rate
   b. an 18-year-old male patient who was in a motorcycle accident, with a femur fracture, is in a lot of pain, and has an elevated heart rate
   c. a 48-year-old male patient complaining of chest heaviness, has difficulty breathing and has vomited twice
   d. a 56-year-old female patient complaining of sudden dizziness, has a bad headache and numbness in her left arm

62. Which blood vessel carries oxygen-poor blood to the heart?
   a. vena cava
   b. aorta
   c. pulmonary artery
   d. pulmonary vein

63. Which chamber of the heart pumps oxygen-rich blood out to the body tissues?
   a. right atrium
   b. right ventricle
   c. left atrium
   d. left ventricle

64. Central pulses may be palpated at the
   a. carotid and radial arteries.
   b. radial and brachial arteries.
   c. carotid and femoral arteries.
   d. brachial and femoral arteries.

65. The diastolic blood pressure represents the pressure in the brachial artery when the
   a. ventricles contract.
   b. ventricles are at rest.
   c. cardiac artery is stressed.
   d. aorta is distended.

66. Stridor is a sign of
   a. mucus in the lower airway.
   b. accessory muscle use.
   c. upper-airway obstruction.
   d. altered mental status.

67. Your patient is complaining of chest pain. Which question would you ask to assess the O part of the OPQRST algorithm?
   a. What were you doing when the pain started?
   b. What does the pain feel like?
   c. How long ago did the pain begin?
   d. How bad is the pain now?

68. All of the following are contraindictions for the administration of nitroglycerin EXCEPT when the patient
   a. has a systolic blood pressure of less than 100 mm Hg.
   b. has taken a previous dose of nitroglycerin two minutes ago.
   c. has a heart rate less than 60 beats per minute.
   d. is an infant or child.

69. Which of the following is a side effect of nitroglycerin?
   a. hypertension
   b. drowsiness
   c. nausea
   d. headache

70. A patient is in greater danger of severe internal bleeding from fracturing which bone?
   a. pelvis
   b. rib
   c. femur
   d. tibia

71. Why is an infant more likely to suffer an airway obstruction than an adult?
   a. An infant's ribs are less flexible than an adult's.
   b. The shape of the infant's head will cause the neck to flex when the child is supine.
   c. The adult has a relatively larger tongue compared to an infant.
   d. The adult has a relatively smaller airway compared to the infant.

72. Your patient, the victim of a stabbing, is bleeding profusely from a wound on his upper arm. Your first action should be to
   a. apply concentrated direct pressure.
   b. apply diffuse direct pressure.
   c. manage the airway and breathing.
   d. elevate the limb and apply pressure points.

73. Which patient would be most likely to have a barrel chest?
- **a.** 10-month-old male: premature birth and history of respiratory problems
- **b.** 6-year-old female: history of asthma and frequent respiratory infections
- **c.** 58-year-old male: history of emphysema and years of smoking
- **d.** 70-year-old female: recent history of pneumonia and bronchitis

74. Which of the following is the only absolute contraindication to the administration of PASG (MAST) pants?
- **a.** fractured pelvis
- **b.** swelling to the lower legs
- **c.** suspected spinal cord injury
- **d.** pulmonary edema

75. The primary reason you auscultate both sides of the chest is to determine whether breath sounds are
- **a.** strong and regular.
- **b.** fast or slow.
- **c.** noisy or quiet.
- **d.** present and equal.

76. Your patient is bleeding heavily from a puncture wound on her right leg. Your attempt to stop the bleeding with a gloved fingertip placed over the wound is unsuccessful. Your next step should be to
- **a.** remove the gauze to ensure you have it over the right location.
- **b.** elevate the limb and apply more diffuse pressure on the leg.
- **c.** use pressure point pressure on the femoral artery.
- **d.** apply and inflate the right leg of the PASG garment.

77. What is the proper order for controlling bleeding?
- **a.** tourniquet, pressure point, elevation, direct pressure
- **b.** direct pressure, pressure point, elevation, tourniquet
- **c.** pressure point, elevation, direct pressure
- **d.** direct pressure, elevation, pressure point, tourniquet

78. Your patient is a 24-year-old female with a history of asthma. She is wheezing and gasping for air and has a pulse rate of 88/min. You may assist her in using an inhaler if
- **a.** she has not yet taken more than three doses of medication.
- **b.** she has her own inhaler and you obtain medical direction.
- **c.** her respiratory rate is greater than 24/min.
- **d.** her blood pressure is greater than 100/70.

79. After assisting a patient to administer nitroglycerin, you should
- **a.** transport the patient immediately.
- **b.** place the patient in Trendelenburg position.
- **c.** give a second dose two minutes later.
- **d.** reassess vital signs and chest pain.

80. The AED is used to detect
- **a.** the patient's pulse rate and rhythm.
- **b.** electrical activity of the heart.
- **c.** the contraction force of the heart.
- **d.** the degree of cardiac compromise.

81. Your patient, the victim of a car accident, has an obvious injury to her right leg. You should splint the injury before moving her unless
- **a.** transport time is less than 15 minutes.
- **b.** the patient is in severe pain.
- **c.** bones are protruding through the skin.
- **d.** life-threatening injuries are present.

82. Your 18-month-old patient is experiencing respiratory distress. Which of the following conditions is NOT a likely cause of the difficulty in breathing?
a. a partial foreign-body obstruction
b. the flu
c. epiglottitis
d. chronic obstruction pulmonary disease (COPD)

83. A seesaw (chest and abdomen move in opposite directions) pattern of breathing is a sign of
a. breathing difficulty in infants.
b. normal respirations in elderly patients.
c. adequate artificial respiration.
d. a disease such as COPD.

84. Your patient has been having breathing problems when she lays down. The medical term for this is
a. dyspnea.
b. eupnea.
c. tachypnea.
d. orthopnea.

85. A sign of early respiratory distress in the pediatric patient is
a. an increased blood pressure.
b. an increased heart rate.
c. flush, warm skin.
d. a decreased breathing rate.

86. Your patient is a 33-year-old female with a suspected spinal cord injury. After you have immobilized her to a long board, she vomits. What should you do?
a. reassess her vital signs
b. ask her what she last ate
c. remove the board and suction the airway
d. tilt the board to clear the airway

87. Your patient is a 28-year-old male who appears intoxicated. Bystanders report that the man seemed fine but suddenly began "acting strange." You should first suspect
a. alcohol abuse.
b. poisoning.
c. diabetic emergency.
d. allergic reaction.

88. Which of the following is not a description typically used when describing a patient's pulse?
a. rapid
b. regular
c. slow
d. rhythmic

89. Your patient is a 23-year-old female who calmly tells you that her thoughts are controlling the weather. Her body language and speech are nonthreatening and gentle. You should
a. request immediate police backup for protection.
b. talk quietly to this patient and keep her calm.
c. request permission to restrain the patient.
d. take a detailed medical history.

90. A 17-year-old male patient is experiencing difficulty breathing and abdominal pain after being struck with a bat in his left lower quadrant. He is alert, cool, and diaphoretic, with a tachycardic heart rate. You should provide oxygen using a
a. nonrebreather mask at 15 L/min.
b. nasal cannula at 6 L/min.
c. nasal cannula at 2 L/min.
d. nonrebreather mask at 8 L/min.

91. Which of the following is not a sign of hypoxia?
   a. anxiety
   b. hot, red skin
   c. elevated pulse
   d. poor skin color

92. The last vital sign to change in a patient going into shock is
   a. an increased pulse rate.
   b. a decreased blood pressure.
   c. an increased respiration rate.
   d. cool, clammy, pale skin.

93. The central nervous system consists of the brain and the
   a. spinal cord.
   b. spinal nerves.
   c. cranial nerves.
   d. spinal vertebrae.

94. Your male patient has climbed out of his car unassisted after a car crash, but he is now complaining of back pain. You should
   a. transport him in whatever position is the most comfortable.
   b. immobilize him to a long spine board with a standing take-down.
   c. immobilize him to a short spine board in the sitting position.
   d. immobilize him with a Kendrick Extrication Device.

95. Which of the following sign or symptom is NOT associated with hypoperfusion?
   a. nausea
   b. increased pulse rate
   c. decreased blood pressure
   d. diarrhea

96. Which of the following sets of vital signs would be indicative of hypovolemic shock in an adult patient?
   a. Pulse: 78, Respirations: 18, BP: 108/78
   b. Pulse: 120, Respirations: 20, BP 128/80
   c. Pulse: 140, Respirations: 28, BP 92/58
   d. Pulse: 130, Respirations: 20, BP 140/100

97. Which of the following signs or symptoms might you expect to see in a patient suffering from hypothermia?
   a. confused behavior
   b. excessive mucous production
   c. blood tinged sputum
   d. burning or itching in the underarms

98. With medical direction, you may administer epinephrine from a patient's own autoinjector if the patient displays signs and symptoms of respiratory distress or
   a. cardiac arrest.
   b. diabetic emergency.
   c. hypoperfusion.
   d. poisoning.

99. Emergency care for the early local cold injury includes
   a. gently massaging the affected area.
   b. preventing the affected area from any further cold exposure.
   c. covering the affected area with cold, moist dressings.
   d. forcing the patient to drink hot fluids.

100. Which patient is most likely suffering from hypothermia?
   a. 79-year-old female: living in an unheated house, outside temperature 40° Fahrenheit
   b. 65-year-old male: dressed appropriately, walking briskly, outside temperature 26° Fahrenheit
   c. 43-year-old female: swimming actively, outside temperature 85° Fahrenheit
   d. 10-year-old male: swimming actively, outside temperature 78° Fahrenheit

101. Which of the following would be expected in late stages of hypothermia?
   a. rapid breathing, slow pulse, pale skin, severe shivering
   b. slow breathing, fast pulse, pale skin, severe shivering
   c. slow breathing, slow pulse, pale skin, no shivering
   d. rapid breathing, fast pulse, pale skin, no shivering

102. A 2-year-old female is in severe respiratory distress. Her skin is mottled, and she does not respond to verbal or physical stimulus. You should
   a. administer oxygen by the blow-by method.
   b. assist her ventilations with a bag-valve mask and supplemental oxygen.
   c. administer blind finger sweeps to attempt removal of an obstruction.
   d. provide oxygen by pediatric nonrebreather mask.

103. What is the goal of emergency care for a hypothermic patient with a reduced level of consciousness?
   a. to actively warm the patient
   b. to keep the patient active
   c. to provide fluids and oxygen
   d. to prevent further heat loss

104. Which of the explanations of "trending" is correct?
   a. Trending is vital signs that are typically found in a particular race or gender.
   b. Trending is the process of comparing vital signs to determine a trend.
   c. Trending is vital signs that are typical for a certain disease.
   d. Trending is the process of changing vital sign normal values with current medical trends.

105. What does the presence of abdominal breathing signify in infants and small children?
   a. labored breathing
   b. noisy breathing
   c. shallow breathing
   d. normal breathing

106. A child's tongue is more likely to cause an airway obstruction than an adult's because it
   a. is relatively large compared to the size of the mouth.
   b. is more flexible than an adult's tongue.
   c. is softer than an adult's tongue.
   d. has weaker muscles than an adult's tongue.

107. While providing artificial ventilation to a 14-year-old near-drowning patient, you feel resistance in the airway. The possible cause of the resistance is that
   a. the trachea is too short.
   b. there is water in the stomach.
   c. the patient has chronic obstructive pulmonary disease.
   d. the epiglottis is swollen, causing an obstruction.

108. The correct rate for providing artificial ventilations to infants and children is
   a. 8 breaths per minute.
   b. 12 breaths per minute.
   c. 20 breaths per minute.
   d. 24 breaths per minute.

109. All of the following conditions are common causes of behavioral emergencies EXCEPT
    a. low blood sugar.
    b. lack of oxygen.
    c. head trauma.
    d. an allergic reaction.

110. Care for an unresponsive infant with a complete airway obstruction includes
    a. giving sub-diaphragmatic thrusts and ventilation.
    b. performing back blows and ventilation attempts.
    c. performing continuous chest thrusts until clear.
    d. giving back blows, chest thrusts, and ventilation.

111. It is important to recognize signs of early respiratory distress in a child. A sign of early respiratory distress includes
    a. audible wheezing.
    b. decreased heart rate.
    c. a breathing rate of 22.
    d. altered mental status.

112. A common side effect of high fever in infants and small children is
    a. shock.
    b. seizures.
    c. hives.
    d. cardiac arrest.

113. Your patient is an 8-month-old infant with a recent history of vomiting and diarrhea. Which signs should alert you to the possibility of shock?
    a. dry diaper and the absence of tears while crying
    b. capillary refill time of two seconds or less
    c. strong peripheral pulses; heart rate of 100
    d. skin that is flushed and hot to the touch

114. Which of the following indicates a life-threatening airway obstruction in a child?
    a. The child is coughing uncontrollably.
    b. The child is crying and tells you that he has food stuck in his mouth.
    c. The child is breathing at a rate of 30 breaths a minute.
    d. The child is making a high pitched noise when he breathes.

115. Your patient is a 26-year-old male who has been in a motor vehicle accident. The patient's radial pulse is weak, while the carotid pulse is strong. You should
    a. treat for signs and symptoms of shock.
    b. recheck by taking the brachial pulse.
    c. wait 15 minutes, then recheck vital signs.
    d. check for low blood pressure on the other arm.

116. The *sniffing position* refers to the
    a. way children position themselves when feeling respiratory distress.
    b. recovery position used for children in respiratory distress.
    c. position used to insert the oropharyngeal or nasopharyngeal airway.
    d. placement of a child's head for the head-lift/chin-tilt maneuver.

117. Diastolic pressure is a measure of the
    a. force exerted against the walls of the blood vessels when the heart contracts.
    b. force exerted against the walls of the blood vessels when the heart relaxes.
    c. rhythm and strength of the heart's contractions during arterial circulation.
    d. time it takes the capillary beds in the extremities to refill after being blanched.

118. A 5-year-old male is experiencing severe respiratory distress. He is altered with poor skin signs. You should
  a. assist ventilation with a pediatric bag-valve mask and supplemental oxygen.
  b. perform blind finger sweeps to attempt to remove an obstruction.
  c. provide oxygen by pediatric nonrebreather mask.
  d. provide oxygen by the blow-by method.

119. You are assisting in a delivery in the field. When the baby's head appears during crowning, the first thing you should do is
  a. exert gentle pressure on the mother's perineum and the baby's head to prevent too-rapid delivery and tearing of the perineum.
  b. pull gently downward to deliver the baby's upper shoulder, then tilt the child downward to deliver the other shoulder.
  c. break the amniotic sac, push it away from the baby's face, and check for the location of the umbilical cord.
  d. suction the baby's mouth and then the nose, and monitor the ventilatory efforts providing supplemental oxygen via blow-by.

120. Fontanels are the
  a. strong contractions that signal the end of labor.
  b. soft spots located on the infant's head.
  c. blood vessels in the umbilical cord.
  d. special forceps doctors use to assist the delivery.

121. Where does blood travel when it leaves the right ventricle of the heart?
  a. to the pulmonary veins, then to the lungs
  b. to the aorta, then out to the body
  c. to the vena cava, then to the left atrium
  d. to the pulmonary arteries, then to the lungs

122. The third stage of labor consists of the
  a. delivery of the placenta.
  b. full dilation of the cervix.
  c. birth of the baby.
  d. onset uterine contractions.

123. You have just assisted in the delivery of a newborn who has good color, a strong pulse, and is not yet breathing. You should
  a. suction the infant again.
  b. slap the baby's back vigorously.
  c. massage the baby's back gently.
  d. provide artificial ventilation.

124. Amniotic fluid with a yellow or brownish color means a high likelihood of
  a. miscarriage.
  b. infectious disease.
  c. excessive bleeding.
  d. fetal distress.

125. Your patient is a 68-year-old male who is complaining of chest pain. Your focused assessment findings include a pulse rate of 92, a BP of 140/90, and some difficulty breathing. After administering oxygen, you should focus your questioning to determine if the patient has a history of
  a. asthma.
  b. diabetes mellitus.
  c. cardiac problems.
  d. strokes.

126. When is the APGAR score done on a newborn?
  a. one hour post-birth and then two hours post-birth
  b. one minute post-birth and then five minutes post-birth
  c. APGAR is a trauma score, and is not done on newborns
  d. one minute post-birth and then ten minutes post-birth

127. One of the most common problems with the post-delivery mother is excessive bleeding. How much bleeding is considered excessive?
   a. any bleeding
   b. 100–200 cc's
   c. 250–400 cc's
   d. 500 cc's or more

128. Which of the following statements is incorrect regarding pregnant patients?
   a. Childbirth outside of the hospital is a true emergency.
   b. If a pregnant patient has not received any prenatal care, she should be considered "high risk."
   c. By the end of the third trimester, the mother's blood volume can increase 30-40%.
   d. By the end of the third trimester, the mother's blood pressure decreases about 10 mm Hg.

129. Which of the following signs and symptoms may indicate shock in children?
   a. an alert mental state
   b. increased urine output
   c. excessive tear production
   d. cool, clammy skin

130. As an EMT-Basic, you are acting as a patient advocate when you
   a. document the care you provide.
   b. treat patients with dignity and respect.
   c. continue your education and training.
   d. consult with medical direction in the field.

131. What are the earliest signs of shock?
   a. fatigue and depression
   b. weak pulse and low blood pressure
   c. anxiety and tachycardia
   d. cyanosis and shallow respirations

132. The following are all effective techniques for stress reduction EXCEPT
   a. getting more exercise.
   b. seeking professional help.
   c. working extra hours.
   d. eating a healthy diet.

133. Your ambulance responds to an eight-year-old girl who fell while roller skating. Both of her forearms have obvious open fractures. This injury would best be described as
   a. mirror injuries.
   b. duplication injuries.
   c. unilateral.
   d. bilateral.

134. It is necessary to wear a mask and eye protection when
   a. transporting a patient.
   b. suctioning a patient.
   c. splinting a closed injury.
   d. administering oxygen.

135. Which statement about disposable gloves is correct?
   a. You should remove gloves by grasping the ends of the fingers and pulling them off right side out.
   b. It is not necessary to wear gloves when suctioning or ventilating a patient with a bag-valve-mask device.
   c. Gloves protect both you and the patient from the transmission of infectious diseases.
   d. One pair of gloves is sufficient for any call, no matter how many patients there are.

136. Which of the following situations illustrates implied consent?
  a. You splint the broken arm and leg of a 6-year-old female with her mother's permission.
  b. You care for a cardiac patient who asks you to help him take a dose of nitroglycerin.
  c. You arrive at the scene of a car crash, and the injured driver says, "Please help my child first."
  d. You provide life support to a man who was found unconscious by bystanders who called EMS.

137. Your partner instructs you to put your patient in the "recovery position." Which of the following is the most accurate description of your actions?
  a. The patient is placed with her head down and her feet up.
  b. The patient is placed sitting up.
  c. The patient is placed on her side.
  d. The patient is placed on her stomach.

138. The Incident Command System (ICS) was originally developed to handle what type of disaster?
  a. wildfires in California
  b. hurricanes in the Southeast
  c. earthquakes in Alaska
  d. tornados in the Midwest

139. Which of the following patient-related information should not be given when calling in a report to a hospital?
  a. sex
  b. age
  c. complaint
  d. name

140. Which of the following is NOT part of the standard medical report you give to the receiving facility?
  a. mental status
  b. history of present illness
  c. medical diagnosis
  d. vital signs

141. You are splinting the injured leg of a 5-year-old male. What should you say?
  a. "It is necessary to immobilize the extremity to prevent further injury."
  b. "After I strap your leg to this board, it won't hurt so much."
  c. "Stop crying! I can't work when you're making loud noises."
  d. "Mom, if your child stops crying, I'll explain what I'm doing."

142. Which of the following is NOT an indication for the use of PASG (MAST) pants?
  a. pregnancy
  b. pelvic fracture
  c. signs of shock
  d. ruptured abdominal aortic aneurysm

143. Which of the following is an example of a subjective statement that could be included in a prehospital care report?
  a. bystander stated, "He was drunk as a skunk"
  b. patient vomited two times during transport
  c. bystanders assisted EMTs in moving patient
  d. patient is unsure of the reason for the call

144. Your patient has a wound on her anterior left lower leg that is spurting large amounts of blood. Direct pressure alone is ineffective. Where should you apply indirect pressure?
  a. on the left side of the groin
  b. medially to the left knee
  c. in the medial mid-thigh area
  d. both above and below the wound

145. Your patient is an 84-year-old female who is complaining of severe abdominal pain. The abdomen is rigid and tender. What should you suspect?
   a. cardiac disease
   b. internal bleeding
   c. pregnancy
   d. thoracic aneurysm

146. Which of the following is an example of care that would be provided by the EMT performing triage at a mass-casualty incident?
   a. covering the patient to prevent shock
   b. opening the airway
   c. starting CPR
   d. applying PASGs

147. Which patient would be given the lowest priority during triage?
   a. 80-year-old male: multiple fractures on extremities without severe bleeding
   b. 56-year-old female: compromised airway
   c. 34-year-old male: signs of internal bleeding from pelvic injury
   d. 28-year-old female: second-degree burns, intact airway

148. Which of the following describes an emergency patient move?
   a. The patient cannot be cared for adequately in the present location.
   b. Because of danger, there is no time to immobilize the spine.
   c. The patient is being moved to a more comfortable location.
   d. The patient is being moved against his or her will.

149. Your patient has a large laceration to his back. The location of this injury is best described as
   a. posterior.
   b. superior.
   c. anterior.
   d. inferior.

150. Which of the following is the largest organ in the human body?
   a. heart
   b. lungs
   c. pelvic girdle
   d. skin

Answers

1. a. Normal values for a newborn are: pulse, 120–160; respirations, 40–60; BP, 80/40.

2. b. The Occupational Safety and Health Administration (OSHA) has established strict guidelines about precautions against exposure to bloodborne pathogens. Failure to follow these guidelines is a violation of federal law.

3. c. Chest rise and fall indicates that bag-mask ventilations are adequate.

4. c. Assess skin color in an adult patient by examining the nailbeds, oral mucosa, and conjunctiva.

5. b. An alert child of any age will prefer his or her parent to a stranger and may refuse to answer your questions.

6. b. A bag-valve mask that does not have supplemental oxygen will only deliver 21% oxygen (the concentration of oxygen in room air).

7. c. Of the choices given, contact with blood is the most effective mode of transmission. Other forms of hepatitis have different transmission methods.

8. d. When assessing the carotid pulse, first locate the Adam's apple and then slide two fingers toward one side of the neck; never exert strong pressure or assess the carotid pulse on both sides of the neck at the same time.

9. a. Head injury, eye injury, or drug use may cause the pupils to be nonreactive or unequally reactive. Shock, airway obstruction, and cardiac arrest will cause both pupils to dilate equally.

10. c. While it may be true that providing high levels of oxygen over prolonged time periods may cause the hypoxic drive to fail, it is a rare occurrence in the prehospital field. With the complaint of shortness of breath, it is better to ensure that the patient is fully oxygenated rather than taking a chance that she is hypoxic.

The EMT-Basic is prepared to ventilate the patient if she goes into respiratory arrest due to the high levels of oxygen.

11. d. A contusion is a bruise, or damage to the underlying tissues without a break in the skin. A scrape is called an abrasion. A cut is a laceration, and a deformity is an oddly shaped body structure.

12. b. Blood under the skin, appearing on the surface as a bruise, is also known as ecchymosis.

13. c. A symptom is subjective information, something your patient described to you, such as pain or nausea; the other options are objective signs, or conditions you note, such as vital signs.

14. c. Use palpation only when it is difficult to hear the pulse, either because the setting is extremely noisy or because the patient's pulse is very weak.

15. a. The other methods will provide an either too large or too small measurement of an OPA.

16. c. You can omit the detailed physical exam if your patient shows no alterations in consciousness and if the mechanism of injury does not suggest high risk of trauma.

17. c. Color, sensation, and movement (CSM) or pulse, movement, and sensation (PMS) should always be assessed in all patients before and after splinting.

18. c. The best way to monitor the patient's mental status is to interact with the patient so that you are immediately aware of any changes.

19. d. Always ask the patient her normal pulse or blood pressure reading, since it will help you determine if the current reading is abnormal or normal for the particular patient.

20. b. Assess the brachial pulse instead of the radial or carotid in patients less than 1 year old.

21. a. Patient **a**, with elevated pulse and respiratory rate and cool, clammy skin is showing early signs of shock. Patients **b** and **c** have normal vital signs. Patient **d** has a normal pulse, low blood pressure, and slow respiratory rate but hot and dry skin, so shock is not clearly evident in this patient.

22. a. The most important sign of a diabetic emergency is altered mental status; patients may appear intoxicated or act anxious or combative. Patients who present an altered level of consciousness should have an evaluation for diabetic emergency.

23. c. Anaphylaxis is most often accompanied with severe difficulty breathing

24. d. Universal precautions do not include general vaccination for HIV

25. a. Assessing the patient's level of consciousness will help you find out the stage of hypothermia and what treatment the patient needs.

26. c. Altered mental status is the distinguishing symptom between heat exhaustion and heat stroke. The absence of sweating is no longer considered as the distinguishing symptom because some heat stroke patients can still sweat.

27. a. The zygomatic bones are found in the face. They are also known as cheekbones.

28. c. Although all the choices can cause airway obstruction, the tongue is the most common cause, especially in unconscious patients.

29. a. Infants and children are prone to breathing difficulties because they have small air passages that are easily occluded; they also rely heavily on their diaphragms and suffer frequent respiratory infections.

30. d. The normal respiratory rate for an infant is 40–60/min.

31. b. Snoring indicates that the tongue has relaxed into the upper airway, partially obstructing it.

32. c. Inadequate chest movement with breathing indicates that the tidal volume (the amount of air moved with each breath) may be inadequate.

33. a. There are 33 vertebrae in the human spinal column.

34. b. Gurgling is a sign that fluid is present in the airway; the correct procedure is to immediately open and suction the airway. An airway adjunct may be used to assist in maintaining airway patency once it is cleared.

35. d. The first step in treating a nonresponsive patient is to open the airway.

36. d. The 2005 American Heart Association guidelines for CPR state that rate of compression to breaths in adult CPR is 30:2.

37. c. Measure the diameter of the patient's little finger. An alternative method is to measure from the tip of the nose to the tip of the ear. The other choices will produce too small or too large of a measurement.

38. b. A child's head should be slightly hyperextended for ventilation in a position called the sniffing position. For infants, the correct position is the neutral position with padding placed below the shoulders and upper back. You should never flex the airway forward as this will close off the airway. The recovery position is used for spontaneously breathing patients to protect their airway.

39. a. If you are unsuccessful at clearing the airway after three attempts, transport immediately, continuing your attempts en route.

40. b. With convection, the more wind, the more heat loss. With a 20 mph wind, 10° Fahrenheit will feel like − 25°.

41. b. The patient should inhale deeply and hold her breath to absorb the medicine.

42. a. Agonal respirations are a sign that the patient is nearing death. Because he is also pulseless, begin CPR immediately.

43. b. Inhalers, also called bronchodilators, work by dilating the bronchioles and thus decreasing resistance inside the airways and increasing airflow.

44. c. Document all side effects of medication administration and report them to the receiving facility; besides increased pulse rate and nausea, other common side effects are tremors and nervousness.

45. a. The oropharyngeal airway cannot be used in conscious patients because of their gag reflex.

46. a. While **b** may seem correct, an AED cannot detect a pulse. It can only detect an organized rhythm that may produce a pulse.

47. d. The normal respiratory rate for an adult is 12–20 breaths per minute, and chest-wall motion should be regular and neither shallow nor very deep. Patient **a** is breathing too quickly for a 3-month-old (it should be around 40 at this age), and the use of accessory muscles in the neck shows some level of distress is present. Patient **b** has a slower than normal rate (it should be around 20), and the irregularity and diaphragmatic nature suggest a spinal cord injury may be present. Patient **c** is breathing much too fast (rate 12–20 for adults), and the shallow chest motions suggests insufficiency or distress.

48. b. Before attaching a regulator to an oxygen tank, always open and close the valve quickly to remove dirt or contamination from the opening so it does not clog the regulator.

49. b. See-saw breathing is the alternating use of chest muscles and abdominal muscles to breath. It is an extremely ominous sign of impending respiratory failure in pediatric patients.

50. d. The 2005 American Heart Association guidelines recommend two minutes of CPR prior to defibrillation for unwitnessed arrests to "prime the heart."

51. d. Adult defibrillators and pads can be used on patients over the age of eight unless specifically recommended by the manufacturer.

52. a. When using a rigid catheter to suction infants and small children, take care not to touch the back of the throat, since stimulation here can cause bradycardia due to stimulation of the vagus nerve. Touching the back of the throat or around the base of the tongue in any patient can trigger a gag, which could lead to vomiting, but the chance of this is not any greater in pediatric patients. The tongue cannot "fall into the airway"; however, in the absence of proper positioning, a flaccid tongue can relax into a position that could lead to obstruction of the airway.

53. c. The modified jaw thrust should be used to open the airway of patients with suspected spinal injuries.

54. c. The nasopharyngeal airway is preferable for responsive patients because it is less likely to stimulate the gag reflex than an oropharyngeal airway.

55. b. The white blood cells, which make up a part of the body's immune system, fight infections.

56. d. In angina, unlike a heart attack, the reduced blood flow to the heart does not result in permanent damage.

57. a. Do not administer nitroglycerin if the patient's systolic blood pressure is below 100 mm Hg.

58. d. Before assisting a patient to administer nitroglycerin, check for the right patient, the right route of administration, the right dose, and the expiration date.

59. b. The 2005 American Heart Association guidelines recommend two minutes of CPR between each shock.

60. b. "Coffee-grounds" vomit is digested blood and indicates the presence of internal bleeding, as do abdominal tenderness and signs and symptoms of shock. A ruptured appendix and fractured pelvis will not cause bleeding into the gastrointestinal (GI) tract. Ingested poisoning may or may not result in GI bleeding, but inhaled poisoning will result in respiratory problems.

61. c. The patient, complaining of chest heaviness, difficulty breathing, and vomiting is showing signs of a cardiac event and cardiac compromise.

62. a. The vena cava carries oxygen-poor blood from the body to the right atrium, so it can be transported to the right ventricle and from there to the lungs.

63. d. Oxygen-rich blood reaches the left atrium from the lungs via the pulmonary veins; then the left ventricle pumps it out to the rest of the body.

64. c. Central pulses may be palpated at the carotid artery in the neck and at the femoral artery in the groin. The brachial and radial pulses are peripheral pulses.

65. b. The diastolic blood pressure represents the pressure in the brachial artery when the ventricles are at rest (diastole).

66. c. Stridor, a harsh sound usually heard during inspiration, is a sign of upper-airway obstruction.

67. c. Assess onset by asking when the pain began and how long it took to reach its greatest severity.

68. b. A patient may take up to three doses of nitroglycerin, each dose three to five minutes apart. The blood pressure should be greater than 100, and the pulse rate should be greater than 60. Nitroglycerine use is contraindicated in children.

69. d. Headache is a possible side effect of nitroglycerin, as are decreased blood pressure and pulse rate, and a burning sensation on or under the tongue. Some patients experience reflex tachycardia following the administration of nitroglycerine due to the rapid drop in blood pressure.

70. a. Pelvic fractures carry danger of severe internal bleeding.

71. b. The back of an infant's head (occiput) is relatively larger compared with an adult's. Placing the infant on his or her back, without shoulder padding, may cause the head to tilt forward excessively, closing the airway.

72. c. Always manage the airway and breathing before controlling bleeding.

73. c. A barrel chest is associated with a long history of respiratory disease, such as bronchitis, emphysema, or COPD. Because the alveoli are not functioning properly, air trapping occurs in the lungs. The increased effort it takes to move air in and out of the lungs results in an overdevelopment of the chest muscles and in time, leads to the barrel-shaped appearance.

74. d. The absolute contraindication for the use of PASG (MAST) pants is pulmonary edema.

75. d. You auscultate (listen with a stethoscope) through the chest wall to determine if breath sounds are present and equal on both sides of the chest. As you are listening, you may also note the relative rate and quality of breathing, but those are secondary reasons for listening to the chest wall. If you are having trouble determining the respiratory rate when you are performing vital signs, you can listen to one side of the chest wall to determine the respiratory rate.

76. a. Before taking further action in this case, be sure you are applying concentrated direct pressure at the right location. Your next steps are **b** and **c**, in that order.

77. d. The proper order for controlling bleeding is direct pressure, elevation, pressure point, and lastly, a tourniquet.

78. b. An EMT-Basic may help a patient in respiratory difficulty to administer an inhaler if the inhaler was prescribed for that patient and medical direction is obtained. In some jurisdictions, you may have standing orders to assist the patient, which means medical direction is provided ahead of time in the standing order. It is important for you to determine how many doses she has already taken (choice **a**), but you must first determine if the medication she took was prescribed to her before you can assist her further. The standard dosing regimen for an EMT-Basic assisting with a prescribed inhaler is to provide a total of two doses, one every three minutes.

79. d. After helping a patient take prescribed nitroglycerin, reassess vital signs and chest pains; a second dose may be given three to five minutes later.

80. b. The AED can detect only the electrical activity within the patient's heart. It does not assess rate, mechanical activity (pumping action), or the degree of cardiac compromise.

81. d. If life-threatening conditions are present, you should focus on those injuries or begin to package the patient for rapid transport if you cannot manage her life-threatening problems.

82. d. COPD is unlikely to occur in pediatric patients. The other three choices may cause some level of respiratory distress in the pediatric patient.

83. a. A seesaw pattern is a sign of breathing difficulty in infants.

84. d. Orthopnea is the medical term indicating difficulty breathing when the patient lies down. It is usually an indicator of congestive heart failure.

85. b. As the body tries to compensate for a decrease in oxygen levels in the blood stream, the heart will try to beat more quickly to circulate blood to the cells more quickly. The skin will also turn pale and cool as the body shifts blood flow back to the critical organs. The patient will also breathe more quickly to draw in more oxygen and expel more carbon dioxide.

86. d. If a patient is immobilized to a long board, you can tilt the entire board to clear the airway.

87. c. Sudden onset of altered mental status strongly suggests diabetic emergency. Alcohol intoxication will have a slower onset. Poisoning may also cause altered mental status, but you should first rule out the possibility of a diabetic emergency as it is a more common occurrence. An allergic reaction will not cause the sudden onset of altered mental status.

88. d. The term rhythmic is not used when describing a patient's pulse.

89. b. Talk quietly with the patient to help her remain calm and persuade her to seek medical help. Be on guard for a violent outburst. Restraints and police backup are not necessary to manage this patient. Asking too many personal questions may agitate her.

90. a. This patient may be experiencing internal bleeding and possible signs of shock. High-flow oxygen is warranted.

91. b. Hot, red skin is not a sign of hypoxia. The skin is usually cool, pale, and moist.

92. b. In shock, the body attempts to preserve perfusion by shunting blood away from the skin, increasing heart rate and increasing respiratory rate.

93. a. The central nervous system consists of the brain and the spinal cord.

94. b. Even if the patient has extricated himself from the car, immobilize him to a long spine board if the mechanisms of injury lead you to suspect spine damage. A standing take-down will allow you to immobilize the patient from the standing position.

95. d. It is not generally expected to see diarrhea as a primary sign or symptom of shock. On the other hand, the remaining choices can be easily seen in shock.

96. c. A rapid heart rate, increased respirations, and falling blood pressure are all indicative of shock.

97. a. The other choices do not make sense as potential signs or symptoms of hypothermia. As blood flow to the brain diminishes, altered mental status may occur, causing confusion and eventually unconsciousness.

98. c. Indications for use of epinephrine are signs and symptoms of respiratory distress or hypoperfusion (shock). Glucose is indicated for diabetic patients. There are no medications (other than oxygen) indicated for use by EMTs in the treatment of cardiac arrest patients.

99. b. The other choices may either further injure the site or otherwise not be effective in managing a local cold injury like frostbite.

100. a. Elderly persons are especially prone to hypothermia, even when the temperature is not extremely cold.

101. c. In the late stages of hypothermia, the patient will have slow breathing, slow pulse, pale skin, and will no longer be shivering.

102. b. This patient is in late stages of respiratory distress. Simply providing oxygen without ventilation will be inadequate for this child's needs.

103. d. The most important principle of care for patients with severe hypothermia is to prevent further heat loss by removing the patient from the cold environment; active rewarming should be done in the hospital.

104. b. "Trending" in vital signs is observing several sets of vital signs to determine a trend that would indicate a possible medical condition.

105. d. In infants and children, who rely heavily on the diaphragm for breathing, abdominal breathing is normal in the absence of other signs of labored breathing, such as supraclavicular and intercostal retractions.

106. a. Because a child's tongue is large in relation to the size of the airway, it is likely to cause an obstruction.

107. b. Water or air in the stomach caused by involuntary swallowing during a drowning episode may cause the stomach to expand and press against the diaphragm, making it difficult to ventilate the lungs.

108. c. The correct rate of providing artificial ventilations to infants and children is 20 breaths per minute, or one breath every three seconds.

109. d. The other three choices are common medical reasons why patients can act in a bizarre manner. It is unlikely that an allergic reaction will produce a mental stuatus change without other noticeable signs.

110. d. Care for an unresponsive infant with a foreign-body airway obstruction includes a series of back blows, followed by chest thrusts, alternating with ventilation attempts.

111. a. Decreased heart rate and altered mental status are considered late signs of respiratory distress and most likely are really signs of respiratory failure. A breathing rate of 22 can be normal for a child.

112. b. Seizures, seen as body stiffness and/or shaking, are a common side effect of high fevers in infants and small children.

113. a. A dry diaper and absence of tears when the infant cries are signs of dehydration, a cause of hypovolemic shock.

114. d. A child that is making a high pitched noise (called *stridor*) is indicative of a severe airway obstruction.

115. a. Suspect shock (decreased tissue perfusion) whenever the distal pulse is weaker than the central pulse. Low blood pressure is a late sign of shock; do not wait to treat the patient for shock until the blood pressure drops.

116. d. The *sniffing position* refers to the placement of a child's head when you perform the head-tilt/chin-lift, with the face lying parallel to the surface he or she is lying on. It improves breathing by opening the airway further than hyperextending does.

117. b. Diastolic pressure is a measure of the force exerted against the walls of the blood vessels when the heart muscle relaxes; it is thus the lower of the two numbers that make up a blood pressure reading. Choice **d** describes the capillary refill test. The force of arterial circulation is not assessed in the prehospital setting as it requires very invasive procedures.

118. a. With the patient being altered in his mental status, it appears that he is not ventilating adequately. A nonrebreather mask will not be able to ventilate the child appropriately. There is no information to indicate a foreign-body obstruction.

119. a. To prevent the baby from being delivered too rapidly and to prevent the mother's perineum from tearing, exert gentle pressure on the baby's head and the mother's perineum.

120. b. The fontanels are the soft spots on the baby's head where the bony parts of the skull have not yet grown together, allowing the head to contract somewhat during delivery.

121. d. Oxygen-poor blood arrives in the right atrium and is pumped out through the right ventricle via the pulmonary arteries to the lungs.

122. a. The third stage of labor consists of the delivery of the placenta after the baby is delivered.

123. c. To stimulate a healthy newborn to breathe, rub his or her back, or flick the soles of his or her feet.

124. d. Meconium, or fetal stool, appears as yellow, brown, or green material in the amniotic fluid. When present, it is associated with an increased risk of fetal distress.

125. c. For a patient such as this one who is displaying signs and symptoms of cardiac compromise, use the SAMPLE survey to focus your questioning to determine if there is any past history of cardiac disease and if the patient has a prescription for nitroglycerin.

126. b. The APGAR score is done 1 minute post-birth and then at five minutes post-birth.

127. d. Bleeding that exceeds 500 cc's is considered excessive after childbirth.

128. a. Childbirth outside of the hospital is not a true emergency unless there are complications during childbirth.

129. d. Blood is shunted away from the skin early in children with shock, causing it to pale, become cool, and sweat.

130. b. Acting as a patient advocate means treating all patients as you would like to be treated yourself.

131. c. The earliest signs of shock are subtle changes in mental status, such as anxiety and restlessness, and tachycardia. Fatigue and depression are not common signs of shock. Cyanosis is not one of the earliest signs, and shallow respirations can occur any time during the shock process. Low blood pressure is a late sign of shock.

132. c. Effective stress-reduction techniques include balancing work and recreation, getting enough rest, eating a healthy diet, getting regular exercise, and seeking help if necessary.

133. d. Bilateral is the medical term for having, or related to, two sides.

134. b. Wear a mask and eye protection when there is a high probability of splattering, such as when suctioning a patient.

135. c. Because gloves protect both you and your patients, most protocols now call for EMTs to wear gloves for any patient contact. Remove gloves by pulling them off inside out, so you do not touch the soiled outer surface; change gloves for each new patient contact.

136. d. Implied consent means that, because your adult patient cannot give consent to treatment, you act without it.

137. c. The "recovery position" involves placing the patient on her side to prevent aspiration of vomit.

138. a. The Incident Command System was originally developed over 30 years ago to handle the large multi-agency responses of the California wildfires.

139. d. The patient's name should never be transmitted over the radio when calling in a report to the hospital because of patient confidentiality.

140. c. The EMT's report should not include a diagnosis, but rather a complete description of the patient's condition.

141. b. Always speak directly to the patient, and explain what you are doing in words he or she can understand. If the parent is present, explain your treatment to him or her as well.

142. a. Pregnancy is a contraindication of the use of PASG (MAST) pants.

143. d. This is a subjective statement. Statement **a** is inappropriate and unnecessary. Statements **b** and **c** are objective statements.

144. a. Apply indirect pressure (pressure point pressure) on the femoral artery by pressing on the left side of the groin. By pressing on the femoral artery, you will slow the flow of blood into the leg.

145. b. Internal bleeding caused by the rupture of an abdominal artery is an occasional emergency among elderly patients; symptoms are abdominal pain, tenderness, and rigidity. This patient is too old to be pregnant. A thoracic aneurysm will not cause abdominal distension.

146. b. Only the most critical care, such as opening the airway to assess respirations, is provided during triage. Unfortunately, CPR cannot be started by the individuals performing triage.

147. a. From the choices offered, the patient with multiple fractures, unless severe bleeding occurred, would be given lowest priority. Patient **b** would have the highest priority followed by patient **c** then **d**.

148. b. An emergency move is one required to remove the patient from imminent danger, such as a fire, or when you must move a patient to gain access to other critically wounded patients. You should stabilize the head and neck with your hands, and if possible, apply a cervical collar before moving the patient.

149. a. Posterior is the medical term for the back.

150. d. The skin is the largest organ in the body.

6 ▶ EMT-BASIC PRACTICE EXAM 3

CHAPTER SUMMARY
This is the third of four practice exams in this book based on the National Registry EMT-Basic cognitive exam. Use this test to identify which types of questions continue to give you problems.

Ystrong>ou should now be familiar with the format of the National Registry EMT-Basic exam. Your practice test-taking experience will help you most, however, if you have created a situation as close as possible to the real one.

For this third exam, simulate a real test. Find a quiet place where you will not be disturbed. Have two sharpened pencils and a good eraser. Complete the test in one sitting, setting a timer or a stopwatch. You should have plenty of time to answer all of the questions when you take the real exam, but be sure to practice maintaining your concentration and maintaining a steady pace.

As before, the answer sheet you should use appears next. Following the exam is an answer key, with all the answers explained. These explanations will help you see where you need to concentrate further study. When you've finished the exam and scored it, note your weaknesses so that you'll know which parts of your textbook to concentrate on before you take the fourth exam.

Practice Exam 3

1.	ⓐ	ⓑ	ⓒ	ⓓ	51.	ⓐ	ⓑ	ⓒ	ⓓ	101.	ⓐ	ⓑ	ⓒ	ⓓ
2.	ⓐ	ⓑ	ⓒ	ⓓ	52.	ⓐ	ⓑ	ⓒ	ⓓ	102.	ⓐ	ⓑ	ⓒ	ⓓ
3.	ⓐ	ⓑ	ⓒ	ⓓ	53.	ⓐ	ⓑ	ⓒ	ⓓ	103.	ⓐ	ⓑ	ⓒ	ⓓ
4.	ⓐ	ⓑ	ⓒ	ⓓ	54.	ⓐ	ⓑ	ⓒ	ⓓ	104.	ⓐ	ⓑ	ⓒ	ⓓ
5.	ⓐ	ⓑ	ⓒ	ⓓ	55.	ⓐ	ⓑ	ⓒ	ⓓ	105.	ⓐ	ⓑ	ⓒ	ⓓ
6.	ⓐ	ⓑ	ⓒ	ⓓ	56.	ⓐ	ⓑ	ⓒ	ⓓ	106.	ⓐ	ⓑ	ⓒ	ⓓ
7.	ⓐ	ⓑ	ⓒ	ⓓ	57.	ⓐ	ⓑ	ⓒ	ⓓ	107.	ⓐ	ⓑ	ⓒ	ⓓ
8.	ⓐ	ⓑ	ⓒ	ⓓ	58.	ⓐ	ⓑ	ⓒ	ⓓ	108.	ⓐ	ⓑ	ⓒ	ⓓ
9.	ⓐ	ⓑ	ⓒ	ⓓ	59.	ⓐ	ⓑ	ⓒ	ⓓ	109.	ⓐ	ⓑ	ⓒ	ⓓ
10.	ⓐ	ⓑ	ⓒ	ⓓ	60.	ⓐ	ⓑ	ⓒ	ⓓ	110.	ⓐ	ⓑ	ⓒ	ⓓ
11.	ⓐ	ⓑ	ⓒ	ⓓ	61.	ⓐ	ⓑ	ⓒ	ⓓ	111.	ⓐ	ⓑ	ⓒ	ⓓ
12.	ⓐ	ⓑ	ⓒ	ⓓ	62.	ⓐ	ⓑ	ⓒ	ⓓ	112.	ⓐ	ⓑ	ⓒ	ⓓ
13.	ⓐ	ⓑ	ⓒ	ⓓ	63.	ⓐ	ⓑ	ⓒ	ⓓ	113.	ⓐ	ⓑ	ⓒ	ⓓ
14.	ⓐ	ⓑ	ⓒ	ⓓ	64.	ⓐ	ⓑ	ⓒ	ⓓ	114.	ⓐ	ⓑ	ⓒ	ⓓ
15.	ⓐ	ⓑ	ⓒ	ⓓ	65.	ⓐ	ⓑ	ⓒ	ⓓ	115.	ⓐ	ⓑ	ⓒ	ⓓ
16.	ⓐ	ⓑ	ⓒ	ⓓ	66.	ⓐ	ⓑ	ⓒ	ⓓ	116.	ⓐ	ⓑ	ⓒ	ⓓ
17.	ⓐ	ⓑ	ⓒ	ⓓ	67.	ⓐ	ⓑ	ⓒ	ⓓ	117.	ⓐ	ⓑ	ⓒ	ⓓ
18.	ⓐ	ⓑ	ⓒ	ⓓ	68.	ⓐ	ⓑ	ⓒ	ⓓ	118.	ⓐ	ⓑ	ⓒ	ⓓ
19.	ⓐ	ⓑ	ⓒ	ⓓ	69.	ⓐ	ⓑ	ⓒ	ⓓ	119.	ⓐ	ⓑ	ⓒ	ⓓ
20.	ⓐ	ⓑ	ⓒ	ⓓ	70.	ⓐ	ⓑ	ⓒ	ⓓ	120.	ⓐ	ⓑ	ⓒ	ⓓ
21.	ⓐ	ⓑ	ⓒ	ⓓ	71.	ⓐ	ⓑ	ⓒ	ⓓ	121.	ⓐ	ⓑ	ⓒ	ⓓ
22.	ⓐ	ⓑ	ⓒ	ⓓ	72.	ⓐ	ⓑ	ⓒ	ⓓ	122.	ⓐ	ⓑ	ⓒ	ⓓ
23.	ⓐ	ⓑ	ⓒ	ⓓ	73.	ⓐ	ⓑ	ⓒ	ⓓ	123.	ⓐ	ⓑ	ⓒ	ⓓ
24.	ⓐ	ⓑ	ⓒ	ⓓ	74.	ⓐ	ⓑ	ⓒ	ⓓ	124.	ⓐ	ⓑ	ⓒ	ⓓ
25.	ⓐ	ⓑ	ⓒ	ⓓ	75.	ⓐ	ⓑ	ⓒ	ⓓ	125.	ⓐ	ⓑ	ⓒ	ⓓ
26.	ⓐ	ⓑ	ⓒ	ⓓ	76.	ⓐ	ⓑ	ⓒ	ⓓ	126.	ⓐ	ⓑ	ⓒ	ⓓ
27.	ⓐ	ⓑ	ⓒ	ⓓ	77.	ⓐ	ⓑ	ⓒ	ⓓ	127.	ⓐ	ⓑ	ⓒ	ⓓ
28.	ⓐ	ⓑ	ⓒ	ⓓ	78.	ⓐ	ⓑ	ⓒ	ⓓ	128.	ⓐ	ⓑ	ⓒ	ⓓ
29.	ⓐ	ⓑ	ⓒ	ⓓ	79.	ⓐ	ⓑ	ⓒ	ⓓ	129.	ⓐ	ⓑ	ⓒ	ⓓ
30.	ⓐ	ⓑ	ⓒ	ⓓ	80.	ⓐ	ⓑ	ⓒ	ⓓ	130.	ⓐ	ⓑ	ⓒ	ⓓ
31.	ⓐ	ⓑ	ⓒ	ⓓ	81.	ⓐ	ⓑ	ⓒ	ⓓ	131.	ⓐ	ⓑ	ⓒ	ⓓ
32.	ⓐ	ⓑ	ⓒ	ⓓ	82.	ⓐ	ⓑ	ⓒ	ⓓ	132.	ⓐ	ⓑ	ⓒ	ⓓ
33.	ⓐ	ⓑ	ⓒ	ⓓ	83.	ⓐ	ⓑ	ⓒ	ⓓ	133.	ⓐ	ⓑ	ⓒ	ⓓ
34.	ⓐ	ⓑ	ⓒ	ⓓ	84.	ⓐ	ⓑ	ⓒ	ⓓ	134.	ⓐ	ⓑ	ⓒ	ⓓ
35.	ⓐ	ⓑ	ⓒ	ⓓ	85.	ⓐ	ⓑ	ⓒ	ⓓ	135.	ⓐ	ⓑ	ⓒ	ⓓ
36.	ⓐ	ⓑ	ⓒ	ⓓ	86.	ⓐ	ⓑ	ⓒ	ⓓ	136.	ⓐ	ⓑ	ⓒ	ⓓ
37.	ⓐ	ⓑ	ⓒ	ⓓ	87.	ⓐ	ⓑ	ⓒ	ⓓ	137.	ⓐ	ⓑ	ⓒ	ⓓ
38.	ⓐ	ⓑ	ⓒ	ⓓ	88.	ⓐ	ⓑ	ⓒ	ⓓ	138.	ⓐ	ⓑ	ⓒ	ⓓ
39.	ⓐ	ⓑ	ⓒ	ⓓ	89.	ⓐ	ⓑ	ⓒ	ⓓ	139.	ⓐ	ⓑ	ⓒ	ⓓ
40.	ⓐ	ⓑ	ⓒ	ⓓ	90.	ⓐ	ⓑ	ⓒ	ⓓ	140.	ⓐ	ⓑ	ⓒ	ⓓ
41.	ⓐ	ⓑ	ⓒ	ⓓ	91.	ⓐ	ⓑ	ⓒ	ⓓ	141.	ⓐ	ⓑ	ⓒ	ⓓ
42.	ⓐ	ⓑ	ⓒ	ⓓ	92.	ⓐ	ⓑ	ⓒ	ⓓ	142.	ⓐ	ⓑ	ⓒ	ⓓ
43.	ⓐ	ⓑ	ⓒ	ⓓ	93.	ⓐ	ⓑ	ⓒ	ⓓ	143.	ⓐ	ⓑ	ⓒ	ⓓ
44.	ⓐ	ⓑ	ⓒ	ⓓ	94.	ⓐ	ⓑ	ⓒ	ⓓ	144.	ⓐ	ⓑ	ⓒ	ⓓ
45.	ⓐ	ⓑ	ⓒ	ⓓ	95.	ⓐ	ⓑ	ⓒ	ⓓ	145.	ⓐ	ⓑ	ⓒ	ⓓ
46.	ⓐ	ⓑ	ⓒ	ⓓ	96.	ⓐ	ⓑ	ⓒ	ⓓ	146.	ⓐ	ⓑ	ⓒ	ⓓ
47.	ⓐ	ⓑ	ⓒ	ⓓ	97.	ⓐ	ⓑ	ⓒ	ⓓ	147.	ⓐ	ⓑ	ⓒ	ⓓ
48.	ⓐ	ⓑ	ⓒ	ⓓ	98.	ⓐ	ⓑ	ⓒ	ⓓ	148.	ⓐ	ⓑ	ⓒ	ⓓ
49.	ⓐ	ⓑ	ⓒ	ⓓ	99.	ⓐ	ⓑ	ⓒ	ⓓ	149.	ⓐ	ⓑ	ⓒ	ⓓ
50.	ⓐ	ⓑ	ⓒ	ⓓ	100.	ⓐ	ⓑ	ⓒ	ⓓ	150.	ⓐ	ⓑ	ⓒ	ⓓ

EMT-Basic Practice Exam 3

1. The term *palmar* refers to which of the following?
   a. top of the head
   b. palm of the hand
   c. top of the foot
   d. the forearm

2. What does the "A" in SAMPLE stand for?
   a. airway
   b. assessment
   c. allergies
   d. activity

3. Your patient is a 23-year-old male who has sprained his ankle. He tells you that he is a marathon runner. When taking baseline vital signs, you find that his resting pulse is 48. You should
   a. treat the patient for signs and symptoms of shock.
   b. consult online medical direction for advice.
   c. administer oxygen and nitroglycerin, and transport.
   d. ask the patient what his normal pulse rate is.

4. You assess the color, temperature, and condition of a patient's skin to gather information about his or her
   a. capillary refill.
   b. heart rate.
   c. perfusion.
   d. respiration.

5. The reason for assessing a patient's pupils is to look for signs of
   a. shock.
   b. trauma.
   c. cardiac compromise.
   d. head injury.

6. Which statement about assessing blood pressure is correct?
   a. If you obtain one normal reading, it is not necessary to reassess blood pressure.
   b. A single reading is not as useful as multiple readings used to look for a trend.
   c. Variations of more than 5 mm Hg from normal is considered very significant.
   d. Assess blood pressure by palpation only when the patient is in a quiet place.

7. While evaluating your 56-year-old male patient with chest discomfort, he suddenly collapses and becomes unconscious. He is apneic and pulseless. Which of the following will most likely reverse this condition?
   a. Provide high-flow oxygen with a nonrebreather mask.
   b. Begin chest compressions at a rate of 80 beats per minute.
   c. Begin the process of defibrillating a patient with an AED.
   d. Ventilate the patient with a pocket mask and supplemental oxygen.

8. Your patient is a 67-year-old female whom you found in cardiac arrest. You have resuscitated her by using an AED and are now transporting her. If she again becomes pulseless, you should
   a. request online medical direction.
   b. stop the ambulance and use the AED.
   c. begin CPR and continue en route.
   d. defibrillate quickly while en route.

9. Which of the following is not a standard responsibility of 911 emergency medical dispatchers?
   a. determining the location of the call
   b. providing medical direction to the EMTs
   c. dispatching other units to assist the EMTs as needed
   d. providing basic medical directions to the caller (pre-arrival instructions)

10. A bystander is doing CPR on a patient in cardiac arrest. You size up the scene, practice body substance isolation, and begin your initial assessment by having the bystander
   a. verify pulselessness.
   b. continue CPR.
   c. stop CPR.
   d. provide a history of cardiac arrest.

11. How many bones are in the adult patient?
   a. 106
   b. 200
   c. 206
   d. 260

12. While transporting a 65-year-old female who is experiencing chest pain, she becomes unconscious, pulseless, and apneic. You and your partner should immediately
   a. contact medical control for direction.
   b. drive faster to the hospital.
   c. administer CPR for one minute, then apply AED pads to her chest.
   d. apply the AED pads to her chest while administering CPR.

13. The imaginary vertical line that divides the body in half is called the
   a. midline.
   b. mid-clavicular line.
   c. mid-axillary line.
   d. dividing line.

14. For which patient can you safely perform only a focused assessment, after taking vital signs and a SAMPLE history?
   a. 6-year-old male, who fell off his bicycle in the road
   b. 11-year-old male, who had a diving accident
   c. 25-year-old female, with cuts and bruises after a car crash
   d. 43-year-old female, who cut her finger in the kitchen

15. Which question would you ask to evaluate the T part of the OPQRST acronym?
   a. How long have you felt this pain?
   b. How bad is this pain today?
   c. Has the pain spread anywhere else?
   d. What makes the pain feel better?

16. You are treating a 39-year-old female who has been in a motor vehicle accident. She has a suspected broken arm and leg, moderate bleeding from the leg wound, and signs and symptoms of early shock. Vital signs are pulse, 96 and thready; respirations, 28 and shallow; BP, 110/78. Your treatment should focus on
   a. stabilizing the patient and transporting her to the hospital.
   b. carefully splinting and bandaging all the patient's injuries.
   c. performing a detailed trauma assessment in the field.
   d. opening the airway and monitoring vital signs every 15 minutes.

17. You are en route to the receiving facility with a 71-year-old male patient with a history of heart disease. The patient's distress has been relieved with nitroglycerin, and his vital signs are stable. How often should you reassess the patient's vital signs?
a. every five minutes or less
b. every 15 minutes
c. every 30 minutes
d. There is no need to reassess a stable patient.

18. The major purpose of the EMT's interactions with a patient during transport is to continuously evaluate the patient's
a. mental status and airway.
b. pulse and respirations.
c. anxiety and restlessness.
d. skin color and pupils.

19. Your patient is a 62-year-old female with chest pain. When assessing the P in the SAMPLE history, you might ask
a. do you have any pain right now?
b. are you allergic to any medications?
c. have you ever had this pain before?
d. what medications are you currently taking?

20. Your trauma patient has an amputated foot. How should you care for an amputated foot?
a. Wrap it in a sterile dressing, then in plastic, and keep it cool.
b. Immerse it in a tub of ice water and transport it with the patient.
c. Put it inside the PASG and inflate the other leg of the garment.
d. Put the foot back on the leg and then splint it in place.

21. If a patient's respiratory rate is irregular, you should count the respirations for how long?
a. 15 seconds and multiply by four
b. 30 seconds and multiply by two
c. one full minute
d. two full minutes

22. What should you assume when you hear wheezing during respiration?
a. The small airways are constricted.
b. The patient cannot keep the airway open.
c. There is liquid in the airway.
d. The patient is using accessory muscles.

23. Your ambulance responds to a traffic accident involving a small car and a tractor trailer. Which of the following is your first priority?
a. triaging the patients into green, yellow, and red categories
b. performing a rapid extrication of the patient
c. stabilizing the vehicle before entering it
d. assessing the scene for hazards including hazardous materials in the tractor trailer

24. Which statement about the assessment of a patient with cardiac compromise is correct?
a. You cannot determine the degree of cardiac damage in the field.
b. You should not ask patients about nitroglycerin or other drug use.
c. The purpose of the focused history is to determine whether to use the AED.
d. Patients usually describe cardiac pain as localized and moderately severe.

25. Which of the following is a priority patient who should be transported immediately?
   a. 27-year-old female: 40 weeks pregnant, crowning, no complications
   b. 67-year-old male: history of heart disease, pain leaves after taking nitroglycerin
   c. 32-year-old female: allergic reaction to bee sting, rapid pulse, difficulty breathing
   d. 15-year-old male: fell off bicycle, possible fractured wrist, cuts, and bruises

26. The main purpose of the detailed physical examination is to
   a. reveal hidden or less obvious injuries.
   b. detect changes in the patient's condition.
   c. obtain a complete medical history.
   d. check vital signs and breath sounds.

27. While performing a rapid trauma assessment of a patient who was injured in a motor vehicle accident, you note paradoxical motion. This indicates the presence of
   a. pelvic fracture.
   b. internal bleeding.
   c. chest injury.
   d. head injury.

28. The glottis is the
   a. soft tissue at the base of the tongue.
   b. nasopharynx and oropharynx.
   c. midaxillary intercostal muscles.
   d. opening between the pharynx and the trachea.

29. Which of the following is a sign of inadequate breathing?
   a. breathing through the mouth
   b. shallow breathing
   c. warm, dry skin
   d. bilateral breath sounds

30. Your patient is a 19-year-old male who has been in a motorcycle crash. Vital signs are pulse, 92 and weak; respirations, 24 and shallow; BP 116/80. He has a suspected spinal injury, as well as a painful, deformed, swollen right foot. Blood loss is not significant. What should your treatment plan focus on?
   a. immobilizing the injured foot in position of function
   b. immobilizing the patient and transporting him rapidly
   c. opening the airway and ventilating the patient
   d. applying the PASG and inflating all compartments

31. What is the general rule for administration of high-flow oxygen in the field?
   a. Administer high-flow oxygen only under specific online medical direction.
   b. Do not administer high-flow oxygen to children, elderly, or pregnant patients.
   c. Do not administer high-flow oxygen to patients with obvious signs of shock.
   d. Administer high-flow oxygen to all patients who are in respiratory distress.

32. The use of reasonable force when dealing with a patient with a behavioral disorder refers to
   a. the force necessary to incapacitate the patient.
   b. calling in police backup in a reasonable way.
   c. using soft restraints rather than handcuffs.
   d. the force necessary to restrain the patient.

33. What is the purpose of the jaw-thrust technique?
   a. to open the airway without moving the neck
   b. to reduce the possibility of a gag response
   c. to open the airway of infants and children
   d. to allow the insertion of an oropharyngeal airway

34. Rapid onset of altered mental status in a diabetic patient often results when the patient
   a. decreases her or his insulin dose.
   b. gets too little exercise.
   c. skips a meal.
   d. drinks alcohol.

35. When suctioning a patient, you would make sure that you did not insert the catheter too far by
   a. inserting it only until it reaches the glottis or trachea.
   b. using the epiglottis as a landmark for inserting the catheter.
   c. measuring the catheter before inserting it in the mouth or nose.
   d. inserting it only until the point where it meets resistance.

36. While suctioning, if you cannot clear a patient's mouth in 15 seconds, you should
   a. immediately suction the airway again.
   b. suction the nose along with the mouth.
   c. suction for 15 more seconds and reassess.
   d. logroll the patient to clear the mouth.

37. A 65-year-old female is complaining of chest pressure, difficulty breathing, and is pale. She presents supine in bed. What should you do before sitting her up?
   a. Check her blood pressure to make sure it is adequate.
   b. Do nothing; sit her up right away.
   c. Help the patient administer her own nitroglycerin tablets.
   d. Check her pupils to make sure they are reactive.

38. You are assessing a three-year-old who fell out of a chair at a restaurant. As you assess capillary refill you remember that adequate capillary refill time in children is less than
   a. one second.
   b. two seconds.
   c. three seconds.
   d. four seconds.

39. A 70-year-old male is complaining of chest pain and shortness of breath. He is alert with pale, cool, sweaty skin. His pulse is 100; BP, 136/64; and respirations, 24. Upon auscultation, you can hear crackles in the lung fields. Which of the following actions would be appropriate?
   a. Have the patient lie flat because he could be in shock.
   b. Provide oxygen at 2 L/min using a nasal cannula.
   c. Administer nitroglycerin that is prescribed to the patient's wife.
   d. Have the patient sit up to assist with his breathing effort.

40. Your patient is a 23-year-old male who has suffered possible spinal trauma while playing football. He is still wearing his sports helmet as you begin your initial assessment. When should you remove his helmet?
   a. when it is time to apply a cervical collar
   b. if it prevents you from assessing the airway
   c. before you position him on the long board
   d. when you assess his level of consciousness

41. The breathing process begins when the diaphragm contracts and
   a. the intercostal muscles relax.
   b. air is forced out of the mouth and nose.
   c. the size of the thoracic cavity increases.
   d. the lungs and bronchi contract.

42. You respond to a 30-year-old male who spilled hot grease on himself while cooking. You note that his skin is red and blistered. This type of burn would be best classified as
   a. superficial.
   b. medium thickness.
   c. partial thickness.
   d. full thickness.

43. Your patient, a 45-year-old female, is still seated in her car after a crash. She does not appear to be in a life-threatening situation. What technique should you use to immobilize her spine?
   a. Logroll her directly onto the ground; then apply a long spine board.
   b. Have her get out of the car; then immobilize her while standing.
   c. Apply a cervical collar before assisting her out of the car.
   d. Apply a short spine board and then transfer her to a long spine board.

44. Your patient is a 68-year-old female with chronic respiratory disease. She is experiencing difficulty breathing in spite of home oxygen delivery. You should
   a. increase the flow rate of her oxygen supply.
   b. replace her nasal cannula with a face mask.
   c. consult medical direction for instructions.
   d. treat the patient for the signs of shock.

45. In which situation should you assist a patient with using a prescribed inhaler?
   a. 47-year-old male: history of severe asthma; respirations, 28/min; wheezing, unresponsive
   b. 6-year-old female: history of upper-respiratory infection; respiratory rate, 24/min; coughing
   c. 69-year-old male: history of emphysema; difficulty breathing; inhaler was prescribed for his son
   d. 14-year-old female: history of asthma; respirations, 24/min; alert; used the inhaler one time yesterday

46. Your patient is showing signs of possible carbon monoxide poisoning. What should be your first concern on this call?
   a. Secure the safety of yourself, other people, and the patient.
   b. Open the airway and administer supplemental oxygen.
   c. Transport the patient rapidly to the closest facility.
   d. Obtain medical direction to administer activated charcoal.

47. A defusing session is often held after major events to discuss emotions that were experienced during the call. When should a defusing session be held?
   a. within a few hours of the call
   b. no sooner than 24 hours after the call to let crews have time to relax
   c. 1–2 weeks after the incident
   d. a defusing session should not be held as they have no benefit

48. Which patient's respiratory rate is normal?
   a. 4-year-old male: respirations, 38/min
   b. 11-year-old female: respirations, 12/min
   c. 27-year-old male: respirations, 14/min
   d. 82-year-old female: respirations, 10/min

49. Which of the following is a sign of normal respiration in infants and children?
   a. reliance on the diaphragm instead of the intercostal muscles for movements
   b. use of accessory muscles in the chest and neck to expand the chest
   c. nasal flaring noted during respiratory efforts when the infant is sleeping
   d. seesaw breathing pattern noted when the child or infant is at rest

50. Which of the following is not one of the classic signs of grief?
   a. denial
   b. anger
   c. hysteria
   d. acceptance

51. The leaf-shaped structure that protects the larynx and the trachea is the
   a. carina.
   b. epiglottis.
   c. uvula.
   d. adenoids.

52. Another name for insulin shock is
   a. hypoglycemia.
   b. hyperglycemia.
   c. hypokalemia.
   d. hyperkalemia.

53. Another name for diabetic coma is
   a. hypoglycemia.
   b. hyperglycemia.
   c. hypokalemia.
   d. hyperkalemia.

54. All of the following are signs of inadequate breathing EXCEPT
   a. slow rate of breathing.
   b. cool, clammy skin.
   c. respiratory rate of 12–20.
   d. shallow breathing.

55. Which of the following lists the correct order for cardiopulmonary circulation?
   a. vena cava, left atrium, left ventricle, pulmonary veins, lungs, pulmonary arteries, right atrium, right ventricle, aorta
   b. aorta, right ventricle, right atrium, pulmonary arteries, lungs, pulmonary veins, left ventricle, left atrium, vena cava
   c. aorta, right atrium, right ventricle, pulmonary veins, lungs, pulmonary arteries, left atrium, left ventricle, vena cava
   d. vena cava, right atrium, right ventricle, pulmonary arteries, lungs, pulmonary veins, left atrium, left ventricle, aorta

56. Where is the xyphoid process located in the body?
   a. it is located behind the ear
   b. it is one of the bones that make up the cheekbone
   c. it is below the kneecap
   d. it is the lower part of the sternum

57. The artery that can be palpated on the anterior surface of the foot is the
   a. femoral artery.
   b. brachial artery.
   c. anterior tibial artery.
   d. dorsalis pedis artery.

58. Your ambulance responds to a house fire where the fire department has just pulled a victim out. The patient has black, charred skin with exposed muscle. This burn would be classified as
   a. superficial.
   b. partial thickness.
   c. partial-full thickness.
   d. full thickness.

59. Your patient is a 35-year-old female who has been in an automobile accident. She has suspected injuries to the pelvis, right upper leg, and shoulder. Her vital signs are pulse, 96, weak; respirations, 28/min, shallow; BP, 120/80. After checking the airway and administering oxygen, the next thing you should do is
   a. splint the injured arm and the leg injury, and then package for transport.
   b. perform a detailed physical assessment for internal bleeding.
   c. treat for signs and symptoms of shock and transport rapidly.
   d. determine the exact mechanism of injury to find all injuries.

60. Which of the following is a fibrous tissue that connects muscle to bone?
   a. tendon
   b. ligament
   c. cartilage
   d. conjuctiva

61. Your patient is a 79-year-old male who is experiencing chest pain. Which question would you ask to investigate the O part of the OPQRST acronym?
   a. Have you ever felt this kind of pain before?
   b. What were you doing when the pain started?
   c. How long ago did the pain begin?
   d. What does the pain feel like?

62. All of the following may be signs and symptoms of cardiac compromise EXCEPT
   a. shivering.
   b. anxiety.
   c. irregular pulse rate.
   d. nausea or vomiting.

63. Your patient is a 67-year-old female with chest pains and a history of heart disease. After helping her take a dose of prescribed nitroglycerin, you find that her blood pressure is 96/68 and she is still in severe pain. Medical direction tells you to administer a second dose of nitroglycerin and transport. You should
   a. administer the medication and document the vital signs and the order.
   b. repeat the blood pressure reading and the order to medical direction.
   c. ask to speak to a senior physician.
   d. request advanced cardiac life support (ACLS) backup immediately.

64. The major differences between the airway of a child and that of an adult are that the child's airway is
   a. straighter and moister.
   b. longer and more extended.
   c. smaller and more flexible.
   d. weaker and wider.

65. Which of the following is the name of the imaginary vertical line that is drawn down the middle of the armpit?
   a. midline
   b. mid-axillary
   c. mid-clavicular
   d. mid-scapular

66. You should select the correct size oropharyngeal airway for a child by measuring from the
   a. angle of the jaw to the corner of the mouth.
   b. central incisor to the angle of the jaw.
   c. central incisor to the tragus of the ear.
   d. corner of the mouth to the cricoid cartilage.

67. Cool, clammy skin that is a sign of shock results from
    a. a rise in the patient's temperature.
    b. the body's attempt to increase the vascular space.
    c. decreased heart rate and blood pressure.
    d. diversion of blood flow to the vital organs.

68. Delayed capillary refill is a reliable test of peripheral circulation in
    a. elderly patients.
    b. infants and children.
    c. patients in early shock.
    d. pregnant women.

69. Your medical patient is experiencing clinical signs of shock. You should
    a. lay the patient flat on his stomach.
    b. lay the patient flat on his back.
    c. sit the patient up.
    d. lay the patient flat on his back with legs elevated.

70. The most important treatment intervention for shock is to maintain an open airway and to
    a. provide 100% oxygen.
    b. ventilate the patient with a bag-valve mask.
    c. provide 100 mL fluid every 15 minutes.
    d. splint and bandage all wounds.

71. Bleeding caused by a wound to one large artery or vein can usually be controlled by
    a. concentrated direct pressure.
    b. diffuse direct pressure.
    c. pressure points.
    d. extremity elevations.

72. The proper technique for applying the PASG to a patient with a suspected spinal injury is to
    a. immobilize the patient to a long spine board before applying the PASG.
    b. place the PASG on a long spine board and logroll the patient onto it.
    c. apply both the PASG and the long spine board while the patient is standing.
    d. elevate the patient's legs while applying the PASG, but don't move the pelvis.

73. Performing a rapid trauma assessment identifies
    a. all sites of bleeding.
    b. life-threatening conditions.
    c. all fracture sites.
    d. any threat that will require surgical intervention.

74. Your patient is a 27-year-old male who has been in a motorcycle accident. He is bleeding heavily from his nose. How should you position him?
    a. sitting up and leaning forward
    b. supine
    c. in shock position, with his feet elevated
    d. on a long spine board, tilted on one side

75. Your patient is a 43-year-old female pedestrian who was hit by a car. No spinal trauma is suspected, but the patient is showing signs of early shock and has a tender abdomen. You strongly suspect
    a. head injury.
    b. internal bleeding.
    c. evisceration.
    d. impaled objects.

76. A 14-year-old female is unconscious after a 15-foot fall off a ladder. When evaluating her chest during a rapid trauma assessment, you should assess for
   a. paradoxical motion.
   b. jugular vein distention.
   c. softness.
   d. distention.

77. Your patient is a 62-year-old male who has survived a serious car crash. He is unconscious, cyanotic, and bleeding profusely from a thigh wound. Breathing is rapid and shallow. Other injuries are suspected. In which order should you provide care?
   a. open the airway and provide oxygen, control bleeding, immobilize, transport
   b. immobilize, control bleeding, transport, open the airway and provide oxygen
   c. open the airway and provide oxygen, immobilize, control bleeding, transport
   d. control bleeding, open the airway and provide oxygen, immobilize, transport

78. For which type of wound should you use an occlusive dressing that is taped on only three sides?
   a. an impaled object
   b. a sucking chest wound
   c. an abdominal evisceration
   d. an amputation

79. Which patient has burns that would be considered critical?
   a. 30-year-old: partial-thickness burns covering 15% of the body
   b. 11-year-old: full-thickness burns covering 1% of the body
   c. 22-year-old: full-thickness burns covering 10% of the body
   d. 28-year-old: partial-thickness burns covering 35% of the body

80. What is your primary concern at a scene where a patient has been electrocuted?
   a. scene safety
   b. airway management
   c. rapid defibrillation
   d. burn care

81. A 36-year-old male is a restrained passenger in a car crash. He complains of pain to his right leg. While assessing his leg, you palpate for
   a. distention.
   b. deformity.
   c. defasciculation.
   d. debridement.

82. Your patient has a painful deformity of the right lower leg. The pulse in the right posterior tibial artery is missing. Before splinting the injured leg, you should
   a. use gentle traction to attempt to align the limb.
   b. apply a tourniquet to stop internal bleeding.
   c. check the right brachial pulse as well.
   d. place the right foot in the position of function.

83. Which symptoms are signs of a partial upper-airway obstruction due to the presence of a foreign body?
   a. increased work of breathing during expiration with a wheezy cough
   b. gasping respiratory efforts, and the patient is unable to cough or speak
   c. no effort of breathing, absent chest-wall movement, unable to cough or speak
   d. stridor during inspiration, inability to speak, and dyspnea

84. A 23-year-old male has suffered a penetrating head wound that is bleeding profusely and a cervical spine injury. During your rapid trauma assessment, you should
   a. treat the head wound and continue your rapid assessment.
   b. stop your exam and provide appropriate care for both injuries.
   c. manage the cervical spine injury and continue your rapid assessment.
   d. make a mental note of both injuries and continue the assessment.

85. What should you do if you do not have the right size cervical collar to fit a patient with a suspected spinal injury?
   a. use the next larger or smaller size collar
   b. use rolled towels secured with tape
   c. leave the neck unsecured and tape the head
   d. place the patient on a backboard without a collar

86. Whiplash injuries commonly occur when
   a. a pedestrian is hit by a moving vehicle and dragged along the ground.
   b. a patient's neck is not properly stabilized before the patient is transported.
   c. the neck of a passenger in a car is snapped back and forth by a rear impact.
   d. a person falls greater than ten meters and dislocates his or her neck during the fall.

87. Your patient is a 35-year-old female who is conscious and alert after a serious car accident. She has multiple injuries that suggest spinal trauma. To help determine the extent of her spinal injury, you should ask her to
   a. move her fingers and toes.
   b. turn her head from side to side.
   c. lift both legs together.
   d. wiggle her hips.

88. A 12-year-old female fell while skating. She did not strike her head and is alert, complaining of pain to the left wrist. How should you assess this patient?
   a. Assess just the areas that the patient tells you are painful.
   b. Assess every body part from head to toe.
   c. Focus on just the patient's airway and cervical spine.
   d. Complete only the initial and ongoing assessment.

89. Which statement by a patient is most likely to suggest that the patient's thinking is psychotic?
   a. "I've never felt this bad before."
   b. "I know you can't help me."
   c. "Am I going to die now?"
   d. "They sent you to lock me up."

90. Your patient is agitated and confused and seems to be displaying symptoms of drug use. The best way to prevent the situation from becoming dangerous to the patient, yourself, or others is to
   a. restrain the patient as soon as possible.
   b. speak calmly and quietly to the patient.
   c. refuse to treat the patient until he calms down.
   d. inform the patient of your self-defense techniques.

91. A 20-year-old female complains of leg and hip pain after falling off a 20-foot ladder. You should conduct
   a. a focused physical exam.
   b. a rapid trauma assessment.
   c. an OPQRST on the pain only.
   d. a detailed physical exam.

92. Which of the following patients is showing signs and symptoms of imminent respiratory arrest?
   a. 2-year-old male: respirations, 60/min; severe retractions; cyanosis
   b. 3-year-old female: respirations, 50/min; nasal flaring; wheezing
   c. 4-year-old male; respirations, 8/min; unresponsive; limp muscle tone
   d. 3-year-old female: respirations, 10/min; cyanosis; decreased muscle tone

93. A patient in a postictal state is one who has
   a. stopped breathing but not yet died.
   b. demonstrated the early signs of shock.
   c. had a seizure and is now unresponsive.
   d. just given birth but not yet delivered the placenta.

94. When caring for a patient whose baby is delivering in a breech presentation, you should do all of the following EXCEPT
   a. position the mother with her knees flexed, drawn up, and widely separated.
   b. administer high-flow oxygen to the mother and begin transport quickly.
   c. pull gently on the infant's trunk or legs if delivery of the head is delayed.
   d. allow the delivery to occur spontaneously until the trunk is delivered.

95. You are assessing an awake, alert patient complaining of abdominal pain. He denies any trauma. When conducting a focused history and physical exam, what should you do first?
   a. conduct a rapid physical exam
   b. obtain baseline vital signs
   c. gather the history of the present illness
   d. question the patient about past medical problems

96. The correct way to stimulate a newborn to breathe is to
   a. rub his or her back or flick the soles of his or her feet.
   b. position him or her with the head higher than the body.
   c. suction his or her nose and then the mouth.
   d. smack him or her gently on the buttocks.

97. During your focused history and physical exam of an unresponsive patient, you should first
   a. obtain vital signs, and then gather OPQRST from the patient.
   b. conduct a rapid physical assessment, and then obtain vital signs.
   c. gather a SAMPLE history, and then OPQRST from the family.
   d. request ALS and begin a detailed head-to-toe exam.

98. To help determine what poison a patient has ingested, you should be alert for chemical burns around the mouth as well as
   a. burns on the hands.
   b. red-colored vomitus.
   c. moist or dry skin.
   d. unusual breath odors.

99. What does the "T" in DCAP-BTLS stand for?
    a. trauma
    b. tenderness
    c. tactical stimulation
    d. turgor

100. Your ambulance responds to a chemical exposure at a local industrial plant. On the scene a worker has had acid spilled in his eyes. Which of the following is the most appropriate treatment?
    a. neutralize the acid with a base (such as baking powder)
    b. cover both of his eyes with a wet cloth
    c. flush his eyes with copious amounts of water
    d. neutralize the acid with a normalizing agent after talking to Poison Control

101. You just completed a rapid physical exam on an unresponsive 65-year-old female. Your next action should be to
    a. take a history of the present illness.
    b. gather a SAMPLE history.
    c. perform a focused physical exam.
    d. obtain baseline vital signs.

102. You are assisting with childbirth in the field. As the infant's head is delivered, you should immediately check to see if the
    a. infant is spontaneously breathing.
    b. cord is wrapped around the neck.
    c. mouth and nose need suctioning.
    d. amniotic sac has broken open.

103. Your patient is a 14-year-old male who struck his head on a diving board and nearly drowned. Your first reaction should be to
    a. remove the patient from the water and warm him.
    b. release gastric distention and provide artificial ventilation.
    c. administer oxygen and provide artificial ventilation.
    d. immobilize the patient while still in the water.

104. You are caring for a 52-year-old male with a history of hepatitis. His skin is yellow in color. This is called
    a. pallor.
    b. flushing.
    c. cyanosis.
    d. jaundice.

105. Which statement about suctioning infants and children is correct?
    a. Insert the suction catheter until it touches the back of the throat.
    b. Administer oxygen immediately before and after suctioning.
    c. Never suction for longer than 30 seconds at a time.
    d. The vacuum pump should be set no higher than 200 mm Hg.

106. You are caring for a victim of a motor vehicle accident who is approximately seven months pregnant. The mechanism of injury strongly suggests spinal trauma. How should you position the patient during transport?
   a. immobilized on a long backboard that is then tilted to the left
   b. immobilized and transported supine on a long backboard
   c. immobilized in whatever position she is most comfortable
   d. seated upright with her torso immobilized in a short spine device

107. In order to determine whether an infant is responsive to verbal stimuli, you would
   a. say the child's name.
   b. ask the child to say his or her name.
   c. make a sudden loud noise.
   d. have a parent speak to the child.

108. The correct procedure for inserting an oral airway in an infant or child is to
   a. use the tongue depressor to move the tongue forward, and insert the airway right side up.
   b. tip the head back and open the mouth wide, and then rotate the airway on insertion.
   c. lubricate the tip of the airway with sterile saline, and insert it until you feel resistance.
   d. insert the airway with the bevel toward the base of the throat, pushing gently if you feel resistance.

109. When caring for a rape victim, it is important to discourage the patient from
   a. bathing or douching.
   b. reporting the crime.
   c. talking about feelings.
   d. naming the assailant.

110. In order to care for a child who has a partial upper-airway obstruction, you should
   a. use a combination of back blows and chest thrusts.
   b. open the airway and attempt to ventilate the child.
   c. provide oxygen, position the child, and transport rapidly.
   d. use back blows and finger sweeps to remove the obstruction.

111. The landmarks for abdominal thrusts in a child are the
   a. diaphragm and intercostal muscles.
   b. cricoid cartilage and diaphragm.
   c. carotid artery and umbilicus.
   d. umbilicus and xiphoid process.

112. In which of the following circumstances should you suspect the possibility of child abuse?
   a. A parent tells you the 4-month-old infant's injuries were caused by rolling off the bed.
   b. A distraught parent promptly reports and requests treatment for a seriously injured child.
   c. A parent tells you that the child walked into a door at school, but the teacher disagrees.
   d. The child and parent both give you an identical account of how an injury occurred.

113. You should suspect the possibility of shock in a child who has a recent history of
   a. vomiting and diarrhea.
   b. cardiac arrest.
   c. epileptic seizures.
   d. upper-respiratory disease.

114. Your patient, a 27-year-old-female who is pregnant with her second child, tells you, "My water broke an hour ago." This should alert you that the patient
   a. has signs and symptoms of shock.
   b. is pregnant with twins.
   c. will have her baby fairly soon.
   d. is having a miscarriage.

115. You should place your hand on a pregnant woman's abdomen during contractions to determine
   a. the strength of the contractions.
   b. the duration of the contractions.
   c. the size of the fetus.
   d. the fetal heart rate.

116. When assisting at a delivery in the field, you should clamp, tie, and cut the umbilical cord
   a. right after the head is delivered.
   b. after the pulsations have stopped.
   c. after the placenta has delivered.
   d. before suctioning the newborn's mouth and nose.

117. You are assisting with a delivery in the field. As the baby's head is born, you find that the cord is wrapped tightly around the infant's neck and cannot be dislodged. You should
   a. transport the mother immediately in the knee/chest position.
   b. clamp the cord in two places and cut it between the clamps.
   c. pull hard on the cord to force the placenta to deliver immediately.
   d. exert gentle pressure on the baby's head to slow the delivery.

118. Right after her baby is delivered, a mother tells you that she feels contractions starting up again. You should
   a. contact medical direction.
   b. prepare to deliver the placenta.
   c. expect the birth of a second infant.
   d. treat the mother for shock.

119. When is it normal for the baby's head to rotate from the facedown position to the side?
   a. during crowning
   b. right before the head delivers
   c. right after the head delivers
   d. as the body delivers

120. You are assessing a newborn who has a pink body but blue extremities, a pulse rate of 98/min, no response to suctioning, moderate flexion of the extremities, and a respiratory rate of 38/min. What is the APGAR score for this infant?
   a. 2
   b. 4
   c. 6
   d. 8

121. When should you expect an infant to start to breathe spontaneously?
   a. one to five seconds after birth
   b. 10–15 seconds after birth
   c. 20–30 seconds after birth
   d. one minute after birth

122. A prolapsed cord is an emergency situation in which the umbilical cord is
   a. the first, or presenting, part of the delivery.
   b. wrapped around the infant's neck.
   c. collapsed and unable to deliver oxygen.
   d. accidentally torn during the delivery.

123. Which of these situations is a true emergency that cannot be managed in the field?
   a. breech presentation
   b. meconium in the amniotic fluid
   c. multiple births
   d. limb presentation

124. According to the Centers for Disease Control, which of the following is the most effective method to prevent the spread of infectious disease?
   a. wearing gloves on all medical calls
   b. using an antibiotic, waterless hand cleaner
   c. immunizations such as Hep-B, and TB
   d. hand washing after each patient contact

125. All of the following are examples of indirect medical direction EXCEPT
   a. continuing education classes taught by physicians.
   b. contact between physicians and EMTs in the field.
   c. design of EMS systems by physicians.
   d. quality-improvement efforts by physicians.

126. You should allow family members to remain with a patient EXCEPT when
   a. the patient is in the process of dying.
   b. the patient has gruesome injuries.
   c. they want to reassure the patient.
   d. they interfere with patient care.

127. Appropriate stress-management techniques include maintaining a healthy lifestyle, striking a balance between work and leisure activities, and, if necessary
   a. getting counseling.
   b. taking sick leave.
   c. using sedatives to sleep.
   d. moving to a different home.

128. If a newborn infant's respiratory effort is inadequate, your first intervention should be to
   a. provide artificial ventilations at a rate of 120/min.
   b. provide positive pressure ventilations at a rate of 60/min.
   c. administer high-flow oxygen via the blow-by method.
   d. transport immediately to a hospital with a newborn intensive care unit.

129. In which situation would you be treating a patient under an assumption of implied consent?
   a. 4-year-old male, with broken leg, parent gives permission for treatment
   b. 19-year-old female, with seizure, who refuses treatment or transport
   c. 47-year-old male, with chest pain, requests transport to the hospital
   d. 80-year-old female, unconscious, no friends or family members present

130. A standard of care is the
   a. highest level of care an EMT can legally provide.
   b. list of skills EMTs are required to perform in your state.
   c. national description of all procedures the EMTs may perform.
   d. minimum level of care that is normally provided in your locality.

131. Which of the following is not one of the four criteria to establish simple negligence?
   a. duty to act
   b. failure to perform to the standard of care
   c. abandonment of the patient
   d. harm occurred

132. Which situation might constitute legal abandonment of a patient?
   a. You leave your patient because the fire in an adjacent building reaches the room you are in.
   b. You begin CPR on a patient and ask a bystander to continue while you assess another patient.
   c. Your patient states that he or she does not want treatment and signs a statement to that effect.
   d. You transport a patient to the hospital and leave him or her in the care of a nurse who signed your patient-care report.

133. Your patient is an adult male who was found in a state of collapse. He has no identification, and no one else is nearby. When you care for this patient, you are acting under the legal doctrine of
   a. expressed consent.
   b. eminent domain.
   c. advance directives.
   d. implied consent.

134. Your patient is a 25-year-old male who has had two seizures within the last hour. He shows no signs of drug or alcohol use. He now states that he feels fine and refuses both transport and further treatment. You should
   a. carefully document every attempt you make to provide care.
   b. obtain an order for tranquilizers from the medical direction physician.
   c. call for police backup to help you restrain the patient.
   d. leave the patient immediately to avoid being sued for battery.

135. Most states mandate that EMTs report suspected child abuse. Which of the following is not one of the parties to which suspected abuse must be reported?
   a. local police
   b. emergency department nurses and physician
   c. child's pediatrician
   d. social services

136. Ambulance run reports can be used for all of the following EXCEPT
   a. evidence in court.
   b. quality improvement.
   c. statistical data collection.
   d. press releases.

137. Which of the following devices would be most appropriate for packaging a patient with a suspected hip fracture?
   a. Stokes basket
   b. Reeves stretcher
   c. scoop stretcher
   d. stair chair

138. You respond to a high school football game where a player has a suspected spinal injury. You have decided to remove the patient's helmet to care for his airway. Which of the following people would be most beneficial in assisting with removal of the helmet?
   a. athletic trainer
   b. a physician in the crowd
   c. the patient's parents
   d. the referee

139. Which of the following statements regarding lifting is correct?
   a. Pull rather than push whenever possible.
   b. Do not lock your back.
   c. Avoid twisting while reaching.
   d. Keep your hands close together (less than five inches) when lifting.

140. Which patient should be placed in the recovery position?
   a. pregnant woman who has been in a car accident
   b. conscious cardiac patient complaining of shortness of breath
   c. unresponsive patient who has a suspected spine injury
   d. child in respiratory distress with a rate of 6/min

141. The increased pressure on arterial walls produced when the left ventricle contracts is the
   a. systolic pressure.
   b. arterial pressure.
   c. diastolic pressure.
   d. residual pressure.

142. You are called to the scene of a car crash. The rescue crew tells you that the patient, who is still trapped inside the car, is not breathing. An emergency move is not possible at this time, as the patient is pinned. After determining that the scene is safe to enter, you should
   a. assist the rescue crew in extricating the patient.
   b. open the airway while extrication is going on.
   c. call for further backup to the scene.
   d. perform a complete physical exam immediately.

143. Which of the following is an example of an effective way to communicate with an elderly patient?
   a. "Sir, I'm going to try to make you comfortable until we get to the hospital."
   b. "You just sit down here on this nice, comfortable chair and don't worry."
   c. "I will try to talk very slowly so you can understand me."
   d. "Sir, I'll make sure I explain everything I'm doing to your son."

144. When healthcare professionals speak of trending, they are referring to
   a. new styles and methods of care delivery.
   b. the tendency of depressed patients to refuse treatment.
   c. a general change in the nation's health status.
   d. a comparison of a patient's present and past condition.

145. The bladder of a blood pressure cuff should be centered over the
   a. carotid artery.
   b. radial artery.
   c. brachial artery.
   d. femoral artery.

146. An example of a generic name of a medication used by EMTs includes which of the following?
   a. nitroglycerin
   b. Nitro-Bid
   c. 1,3-dinitrooxypropan-2-yl nitrate
   d. Nitrostat

147. Epinephrine is given to patients with severe allergic (anaphylactic reactions) for which of the following reasons?
   a. Epinephrine will constrict the bronchioles, making breathing easier.
   b. Epinephrine will dilate the coronary arteries, increasing blood flow to the heart.
   c. Epinephrine will constrict the vessels, improving blood pressure.
   d. Epinephrine will increase histamine response to fight the allergen.

148. Which of the following is not a medication that EMTs are normally allowed to use?
   a. oral glucose
   b. Albuterol
   c. Epinephrine 1:1,000
   d. Valium

149. A contraindication to a medicine
   a. increases the effectiveness of the medicine.
   b. is an accepted reason why the medicine is given.
   c. is a reason why the medicine should not be given.
   d. is a side effect of the medication.

150. Albuterol is given during asthma attacks for which of the following reasons?
   a. it will increase heart rate
   b. it dilates constricted bronchioles
   c. it constricts a dilated airway
   d. it stops mucous from being produced in the lungs

Answers

1. b. The term *palmar* refers to the palm of the hand.

2. c. The "A" in SAMPLE stands for allergies.

3. d. This low resting pulse may be normal for a healthy athlete. To be sure, ask the patient if he knows what his normal resting pulse rate is.

4. c. The color, temperature, and condition of the skin allows you to form an indirect assessment of the patient's perfusion, or circulatory status.

5. d. You assess the size and reactivity of a patient's pupils to determine if there is a possibility of head injury.

6. b. A single blood pressure reading, unless it is extremely high or extremely low, is not in itself significant. Blood pressure readings are most useful in establishing a trend that can signal changes in the patient status. Blood pressure varies constantly during the day by 20 mm Hg or more during sleep, work, and relaxation activities. Assessment of BP by palpation is useful when the patient is in a very noisy environment, making auscultation difficult.

7. c. Chances are, this patient is experiencing sudden ventricular fibrillation that may be most likely reversed with defibrillation attempt.

8. b. For a pulseless patient, defibrillation takes precedence over either administering oxygen or performing CPR, but always stop the ambulance before using the AED. Do not analyze a heart rhythm in a moving vehicle.

9. b. Emergency medical dispatchers are not responsible for providing medical direction to EMTs. This is the responsibility of medical control.

10. c. In order to accurately assess the patient's airway, breathing, and circulation status, all external compressions or ventilations must be stopped.

11. c. There are 206 bones in the adult body.

12. d. It is critical to support life functions immediately and defibrillate a heart in ventricular fibrillation as soon as possible.

13. a. The midline is the imaginary line that divides the body in half.

14. d. This patient has no significant mechanism of injury. If vital signs and a SAMPLE history disclose no abnormal findings, you need only perform a focused assessment. If you are ever unsure, however, you should perform a very thorough assessment, like a rapid trauma assessment, to look for hidden injuries.

15. a. The T in the OPQRST acronym stands for time, or the duration of the problem.

16. a. Although you should quickly splint the patient's wounds and stop major bleeding, treatment of a patient in shock should focus on rapidly transporting her to the hospital. You can continue to stabilize and treat her injuries while you are transporting her. Perform any other examinations while en route to the hospital. Monitor and assess her vital signs every five minutes.

17. b. Reassess a stable patient every 15 minutes while en route to the receiving facility.

18. a. Although interacting with the patient continuously will keep you informed about his or her level of anxiety and allow you to observe skin color and pupils, the main purpose is to assess changes in mental status and patency of airway.

19. c. The P in the SAMPLE history stands for pertinent past medical history, so you would ask the patient about previous episodes of chest pain.

20. a. Always transport an amputated part along with the patient, wrapped in sterile dressings and then in plastic. Keep the amputated part cool, but do not put the foot directly in contact with ice or ice water because the ice can cause further tissue damage, which may result in the inability to reimplant the amputated part.

21. c. If a patient's respiratory rate is irregular, count for one full minute; otherwise, count for 30 seconds and multiply by two to obtain the respiratory rate.

22. a. Wheezing indicates that smaller airways and bronchioles are constricted, usually because of infection or allergy. Fluid is only one of the possible reasons; bronchial constriction is another cause.

23. d. Scene size-up and assessment of hazards is always the first priority at any scene. This is especially important at vehicle accidents involving trucks that could be carrying hazardous materials.

24. a. It is impossible to determine the actual degree of tissue damage in the field, so the purpose of the focused assessment is to gather information for the receiving facility. You should always ask about medications; it is the M of SAMPLE. The focused history has nothing to do with AED use. Cardiac pain has all sorts of presentations, making it difficult to differentiate from other conditions.

25. c. Patients who are having difficulty breathing are priority patients, as are patients who are unstable or who give a poor general impression, are having complications of childbirth, or who have signs and symptoms of shock.

26. a. The purpose of the detailed physical examination, which is performed while en route to the hospital on all trauma patients as well as unresponsive medical patients, is to reveal hidden injuries.

27. c. Paradoxical motion, the movement of one portion of the chest wall in the opposite direction from the rest of the chest during respirations, indicates serious injury to the chest wall.

28. d. The glottis is the opening between the pharynx and the trachea.

29. b. Shallow breathing, or inadequate tidal volume, is a sign of inadequate breathing, as are difficulty breathing, shortness of breath, irregular rhythm, cyanosis, and change in breathing rate.

30. b. For a patient who is showing signs of shock as well as possible spinal injury, care focuses on immobilization and rapid transport, rather than on caring for isolated extremity injuries. This patient already has an open airway, and ventilation is not necessary, although oxygen should be administered by a nonrebreather mask and his respiratory status should be closely monitored as his respiratory rate is a little fast and his effort is shallow.

31. d. EMTs should administer high-flow oxygen to all patients who show signs and symptoms of respiratory distress.

32. d. *Reasonable force* refers to the amount of force necessary to prevent injury to the patient or anyone else, including the rescuers. It is sometimes necessary to use force to restrain a patient with a behavioral disorder. Reasonable force does not define the type of restraints needed.

33. a. The jaw thrust is performed instead of the head-tilt/chin-lift on patients with suspected spinal trauma, since it allows you to open the airway without moving the patient's neck.

34. c. Rapid onset of altered mental status in diabetic patients is associated with hypoglycemia, or low blood sugar. This most commonly occurs when patients take their normal dose of insulin but skip a meal. Excessive exercise can also bring on a hypoglycemic state.

35. c. Before inserting the catheter, measure the distance between the corner of the patient's mouth and the earlobe, and keep your fingers at that spot on the catheter; insert only to the point where your fingers are.

36. d. If you cannot clear the patient's mouth of secretions, logroll the patient so the secretions can drain out. Never suction for longer than 15 seconds at a time, and oxygenate the patient between suction attempts.

37. a. The position of comfort for most people having trouble breathing is sitting; however, this patient may have low blood pressure, possibly due to a cardiac emergency. In this case, it would be important to ensure that her blood pressure is adequate to support a sudden change in body position.

38. b. Adequate capillary refill in children is less than two seconds.

39. d. This patient's blood pressure is adequate to support a sitting patient. This patient also requires high-flow oxygen via nonrebreather as part of the treatment plan.

40. b. Leave a helmet in place if it fits well, does not interfere with assessment or administration of oxygen, and the patient is not in cardiac arrest. Leave the shoulder pads in place along with the helmet. You do not need to apply a cervical collar to this patient, but you should immobilize his body and head to a long spine board. You can assess his level of consciousness without moving the helmet.

41. c. Inhalation is an active process that begins when the diaphragm and intercostal muscles contract, increasing the size of the thoracic cavity and pulling air into the lungs.

42. c. Burns that are red and blistered are classified as partial thickness.

43. d. Immobilize the patient to a short spine board like the Kendrick Extrication Device or other commercial device while she is still seated; then transfer her to a long spine board. If you suspected she was in shock or was unstable, you would perform a rapid extrication by applying a cervical collar and quickly removing her from the vehicle with the assistance of several rescuers while trying to maintain a neutral alignment to her spine.

44. c. Consult medical direction when you encounter a patient who is having difficulty breathing in spite of home administration of oxygen.

45. d. You can help a patient to use a prescribed inhaler if the patient has signs and symptoms of respiratory emergency, if the inhaler was prescribed for that patient, and if the patient is responsive. Be sure and determine if the patient has used the inhaler already and if it helped lessen the distress.

46. a. In cases of inhalation poisoning when the toxin may still be present, your first concern should be to ensure your own safety and that of other people in the area. Move the patient to your ambulance, then begin your assessment and treatment. Activated charcoal is administered in the case of ingested (swallowed) poisons, not inhaled poisons.

47. a. A defusing session is held within a couple of hours of a major call to allow the responders to discuss their feelings.

48. c. The normal breathing rate for an adult is between 12–20 breaths per minute.

49. a. Reliance on the diaphragm, rather than the intercostal muscles, to expand the chest during inspiration is normal in infants and children.

50. c. The five classic signs of grief are denial, anger, bargaining, depression, and acceptance.

51. b. The epiglottis is a leaf-shaped structure that protects the trachea from liquids and solids.

52. a. Hypoglycemia is another name for insulin shock.

53. b. Hyperglycemia is another name for diabetic coma.

54. c. A respiratory rate of 12–20 breaths per minute is normal; signs of inadequate breathing include cyanosis, increased or decreased breathing rate, shortness of breath, and irregular rhythm.

55. d. This is the correct order for cardiopulmonary circulation.

56. d. The xyphoid process is located at the bottom of the sternum.

57. d. The dorsalis pedis artery, which can be palpated on the anterior surface of the foot, is used to check peripheral pulses.

58. d. Burns with black, charred skin and exposed muscle are classified as full thickness.

59. c. The patient's pulse and breathing rate indicate that she is in shock; therefore, the first priority is to treat her for shock and transport her to a hospital.

60. a. Tendons connect muscle to bone, whereas ligaments connect muscle to muscle.

61. c. O stands for onset, or when the pain began.

62. a. Signs and symptoms of cardiac compromise include pressure or pain that starts in the chest and radiates, sweating, difficulty breathing, anxiety, irregular pulse rate, abnormal blood pressure, and nausea or vomiting.

63. b. Nitroglycerin is not administered to a patient whose systolic blood pressure is lower than 100. Repeat the blood pressure reading and the order and request that the physician confirm it.

64. c. In comparison with an adult's airway, a child's airway is smaller, narrower, and more flexible; therefore, there is danger of occluding the airway by hyperextending the neck.

65. b. The mid-axillary line is the name of the imaginary line drawn down the armpit.

66. a. Select the correct size oral airway for a child by measuring from the angle of the jaw to the corner of the mouth.

67. d. In early shock, the body diverts blood flow away from the skin and toward the body's vital organs, resulting in decreased peripheral circulation and cool, clammy skin.

68. b. Capillary refill time is used to determine peripheral perfusion in infants and children only.

69. d. If no traumatic injury mechanism is suspected, keeping the patient flat with legs elevated will promote blood circulation back to the critical organs.

70. a. The most important intervention for shock is to provide a high concentration of oxygen; this helps prevent cells from dying due to lack of oxygen.

71. a. Bleeding from a single site can usually be controlled by concentrated direct applied pressure to that site. Diffuse pressure is reserved for circumstances when concentrated direct pressure is unadvisable, like when controlling bleeding from an open skull fracture. Pressure point pressure and elevation are steps to take if direct pressure is ineffective.

72. b. Because most patients for whom PASG is appropriate also have suspected spinal injury, place the PASG on the long spine board and logroll the patient onto the PASG and the board together.

73. b. The purpose of performing a rapid trauma assessment is to identify major injuries sustained in the kill zone areas of the body, such as the head, neck, chest, and abdomen.

74. d. Because the mechanism of injury strongly suggests spinal trauma, you should immobilize the patient on a long spine board, but tilt the board to one side to allow blood to drain. Suction may also be needed to keep the airway clear.

75. b. This mechanism of injury, plus the tender abdomen and signs of shock, strongly suggests that the patient has internal bleeding.

76. a. Paradoxical motion of the chest may indicate broken ribs or flail chest. Softness and distention during assessment generally refers to the abdomen.

77. a. Always open the airway first, regardless of other priorities. Since the patient is bleeding profusely, the second priority is to control the bleeding from the leg wound. Since the patient is showing signs and symptoms of shock, the next priorities are to immobilize the spine and transport rapidly.

78. b. For a sucking chest wound, apply an occlusive dressing that is taped on only three sides. This will allow air to escape from the chest cavity.

79. d. In an adult, full-thickness burns covering more than 10% of the body or partial-thickness burns covering more than 30% of the body are considered critical.

80. a. Scene safety is the primary concern at a scene where a patient has been electrocuted.

81. b. In DCAP-BTLS, the D stands for deformity. Distention may be found on palpation and visualization of the abdomen.

82. a. When a pulse is missing distal to an injury, attempt to align the limb with gentle traction. Bringing the limb into alignment may relieve pressure on the blood vessels and restore circulation.

83. d. Partial upper-airway obstruction due to a foreign body is differentiated from complete obstruction by the patient's ability to breathe or speak. Stridor indicates upper-airway obstruction. A wheezing sound (patient **a**) indicates a lower-airway obstruction. Patients **b** and **c** have a total airway obstruction.

84. b. Both life-threatening injuries to the patient must be treated as quickly as possible.

85. b. If the mechanism of injury of the patient's signs and symptoms suggest spinal injury, you must immobilize the neck and spine. Use rolled-up towels if you do not have a cervical collar that fits properly.

86. c. Whiplash injuries result when a passenger in a car that is hit from the rear has his or her neck snapped backward and then forward as a result of the impact.

87. a. To help determine the extent of injuries, ask a patient with suspected spinal trauma to move her fingers and toes; otherwise, the patient should remain immobile.

88. a. Without a serious mechanism of injury being reported, a focused physical assessment of the patient's injuries is appropriate.

89. d. This statement reflects paranoia, a psychotic state in which people imagine that other people are conspiring to harm them.

90. b. You can frequently prevent situations from becoming dangerous by maintaining a calm, professional manner and speaking quietly to a distraught patient.

91. b. The mechanism of injury suggests that you should look through the kill zone areas to make sure there are no other underlying injuries.

92. c. Signs of imminent respiratory arrest are a breathing rate of less than 10/min, limp muscle tone, slow or absent heart rate, and weak or absent distal pulses; the patient will also be unresponsive. These patients need artificial ventilation and chest compression. Patients **a**, **b**, and **d** are in respiratory insufficiency and the early stages of respiratory failure, which, if uncorrected, will lead to respiratory arrest.

93. c. A patient who is in a postictal state has just had a seizure and appears to be asleep.

94. c. Do not pull on the infant's trunk or legs to assist delivery. If the baby's head is not delivered spontaneously, place your hand inside the birth canal to hold the cord and walls of the vagina away from the baby's face, and transport immediately.

95. c. Conducting an OPQRST on the pain and finding out the SAMPLE history will gather a lot of information about the patient's complaint.

96. a. If necessary, stimulate a newborn to breathe by gently rubbing his or her back or flicking the soles of his or her feet. You should always suction the mouth first and then the nose because infants are obligate nasal breathers, and if you suction the nose first, it may stimulate them to take a breath, inhaling any amniotic fluid remaining in the oropharynx into the lungs.

97. b. Since the patient is unresponsive, the most effective method of obtaining information about the patient's condition is through a rapid physical assessment.

98. d. Some poisons can be identified by the unusual breath odors they cause; for example, cyanide causes an odor of bitter almonds. Choice **a** is incorrect because some substances may burn mucous membranes of the mouth but may not burn the skin. Choice **b** is incorrect because, depending upon the substance ingested, vomit may or may not be discolored or bloody. Choice **c** is incorrect because the toxin may or may not cause changes in skin temperature or color; it will depend upon the action of the poison and if it causes shock.

99. b. The "T" in DCAP-BTLS stands for tenderness.

100. c. All chemical burns to the eyes should be treated by flushing the eyes with copious amounts of water. Responders should never attempt to neutralize chemical burns with another chemical.

101. d. Since the patient is unresponsive, it will not be possible to elicit a medical history directly. An early set of vital signs may help determine the underlying cause of the patient's condition.

102. b. As the head is delivered, make sure that the cord is not wrapped around the infant's neck. All newborns are suctioned at this point. You should check for spontaneous respirations after the infant is completely emerged from the birth canal, and if necessary, break the amniotic sac just as the head appears. You will note the presence of the amniotic sac during the time the infant is crowning.

103. d. Because of the great risk of spinal injury with this type of trauma, the EMT's first action should be to immobilize the patient while still in the water; the second step is to attend to the airway.

104. d. Jaundice is the medical term for yellowing of the skin, most often caused by liver failure.

105. b. When suctioning infants and children, be sure not to stimulate the back of the throat, which can lead to bradycardia. Administer oxygen before and after suctioning, suction for no more than 10–15 seconds at a time, and set the vacuum pump at 80–120 mm Hg.

106. a. The patient should be immobilized on a long backboard, but the entire board should be tilted to the left side with padding to reduce the pressure of the fetus on her circulatory systems. This condition is called supine hypotension syndrome.

107. d. An infant who is responsive to voice, or to verbal stimuli, would turn in the direction of the parent's voice.

108. a. When inserting an airway in an infant or child, use a tongue depressor and avoid rotating the airway.

109. a. The rape victim should be discouraged from bathing, douching, urinating, or cleaning any wounds, since these activities may destroy evidence.

110. c. Back blows, chest thrusts, and ventilation are performed on infants with complete airway obstructions; care for a child with partial obstruction consists of placing the child in a position of comfort and transporting rapidly.

111. d. To perform abdominal thrusts on a child, place one fist between the umbilicus and the xiphoid process, place the other fist on top of the first, and give five inward, upward thrusts.

112. c. In cases of child abuse, different people frequently give different accounts of the same accident, or parents may appear unconcerned.

113. a. Shock in children is most frequently associated with fluid loss due to vomiting and diarrhea or to blood loss.

114. c. It is normal for the amniotic sac to rupture and the fluid it contains to drain out of the woman's vagina before delivery.

115. a. If the mother's abdomen feels hard during the contractions, they are strong, and birth is more likely to happen quickly.

116. b. The EMT who is caring for the mother should clamp, tie, and cut the umbilical cord after its pulsations have stopped; a second EMT will simultaneously be caring for the infant.

117. b. If the cord is wrapped around the infant's neck and it cannot be placed back over the head, the infant is in danger of suffocation. Immediately clamp the cord in two places and carefully cut between the clamps. Never pull on the umbilical cord as this can cause uterine inversion, which is a life-threatening emergency.

118. b. The mother will feel contractions before the placenta delivers. Prepare to wrap it in a towel and place it in a plastic bag for delivery to the hospital along with the mother and infant.

119. c. The baby's head is usually born facedown in the vertex position, and the head rotates just after it emerges from the birth canal.

120. b. This infant would receive one point for skin color (appearance), one point for pulse rate, zero for grimace, one point for activity, and one point for respirations.

121. c. An infant normally starts breathing independently within about 20–30 seconds after birth; if it does not, provide tactile stimulations.

122. a. A prolapsed cord is an emergency condition in which the umbilical cord is the presenting part; in this position, the cord can be compressed by the baby's head, preventing it from supplying oxygen to the infant during delivery. If the infant is still inside the mother, transport her immediately in either the kneeling, knee-chest position, or Trendelenburg position with the hips elevated. Keep the cord warm by wrapping it in sterile saline-soaked dressings. A gloved hand can be placed into the vagina to lift the head off the umbilical cord.

123. d. A limb presentation, in which an arm or leg is the presenting part, is a true emergency situation that cannot be managed in the field. Place the mother with her pelvis elevated, exert gentle pressure on the baby's body, and transport the mother in this position. Breech, meconium, and multiple births can all be handled in the field. Call for ALS assistance for each of these emergencies and expect fetal distress in the newborn(s).

124. d. According to the CDC, frequent hand washing is the most effective way to minimize the spread of disease.

125. b. Indirect medical direction includes all involvement by physicians with EMS systems except direct supervision of EMTs in the field.

126. d. Always allow family members to stay with a patient except if their presence interferes with necessary care.

127. a. Effective stress-management techniques include making various lifestyle changes that promote health, seeking a healthy balance between work and recreation, changing one's work schedule if necessary, and seeking professional counseling help.

128. b. If, on initial assessment, the newborn's respirations are slow, shallow, or absent, you should provide positive pressure ventilations with a bag-valve mask at the rate of 60/min. After about 30 seconds of this intervention, you should reassess the patient to determine if you need to continue with the bag-valve-mask ventilation.

129. d. Implied consent is applicable in cases where the patient is unable to consent; you provide treatment under the assumption that any rational person would want to receive treatment under the circumstances.

130. d. A standard of care for any locality is the minimum acceptable level of care normally provided there. All care providers, including EMTs, are legally held to this standard.

131. c. The four criteria to establish simple negligence are duty to act, inappropriate care given, harm caused, proximate causation. Abandonment is not part of a simple negligence suit.

132. b. Abandonment may occur if you stop caring for a patient without his or her consent, and without transferring care to personnel of the same or higher level. For patient **a**, personal safety takes priority over patient care. If a conscious capable adult patient has signed a refusal (and he or she heard about risks/benefits first), you have not committed abandonment, ruling out case **c**. To avoid abandonment when dealing with hospitals, hospital personnel must assume care of patient before you can leave, and this occurred in case **d**.

133. d. Implied consent means that you assume that any rational person would consent to care under the circumstances.

134. a. Refusal of treatment requires that the patient be fully aware of the consequences of refusing care. Document all attempts made to change the patient's mind by you and other caregivers.

135. c. A child's pediatrician is not required to be notified of suspected child abuse cases.

136. d. Ambulance run reports are used for evidence in court, quality improvement, and statistical data collection. They are not available for press releases.

137. c. A scoop stretcher is most appropriate for a patient with a suspected hip fracture because of the ability to separate the halves of the stretcher.

138. a. An athletic trainer is familiar with the equipment used by players, and is usually the best person to help remove the helmet.

139. d. To reduce the risk of back injury, do not twist while lifting.

140. c. Use the recovery position for a patient who is breathing spontaneously but who is unresponsive or likely to vomit and aspirate material into the airway. You should not use it for a spinal injured patient until he or she is properly immobilized. Patient **a** should be placed in the left lateral recumbent position once she is immobilized. Patient **b** should be assisted into the position of comfort with the recovery position used if the mental status decreases (and he or she is still breathing adequately). Patient **d** needs bag-valve-mask ventilation.

141. c. The diastolic pressure is the resting pressure in the artery when the left ventricle is relaxed.

142. b. Always perform critical care, such as opening the patient's airway, while extrication is occurring.

143. a. Speak to elderly patients respectfully, directly, and clearly, and do not assume that they can't understand the situation.

144. d. *Trending* refers to a comparison of a patient's past and present condition. Trending is always more significant than a single set of vital signs.

145. c. The blood pressure cuff, when inflated, squeezes the brachial artery until it squeezes shut. As air is released from the bladder, at some point, the pressure in the artery exceeds the pressure in the cuff, causing blood to squirt past the cuff. In order for this to be accurate, the bladder should be as closely centered over the brachial artery as possible.

146. a. Nitroglycerin is an example of a generic name. Nitro-Bid® and Nitrostat® are trade names, and 1,3-dinitrooxypropane-2-yk nitrate is a chemical name.

147. c. Epinephrine constricts blood vessels and dilates bronchioles.

148. d. Valium is not a medication that EMTs are normally allowed to use.

149. c. A contraindication to medicine is a reason why the medication should not be given.

150. b. Albuterol is given to asthmatics because it dilates constricted bronchioles.

7 ▶ EMT-BASIC PRACTICE EXAM 4

CHAPTER SUMMARY
This is the last of four practice exams in this book based on the National Registry EMT-Basic cognitive exam. Using all the experience and strategies you gained from the other three, take this exam to see how far you have come since taking the first test.

Multiple-choice exams are efficient and have become a common method of testing. It has been argued that fill-in or free-response testing is more challenging and provides a superior evaluation of a person's knowledge. Why not take advantage of both methods? The questions in this exam represent each of the modules found in the U.S. Department of Transportation's Emergency Medical Technician-Basic National Standard Curriculum. The results can be used to guide your study. If necessary, use the open book technique and refer to your EMT training text as you go. Take your time—there is more to this exam than simply getting the answer correct; you must also understand the concept.

EMT-Basic Practice Exam 4

1. Describe the difference between online and offline medical direction.

_____

_____

_____

_____

2. True or false: The safety of your patient and bystanders is your primary responsibility on an EMS scene.

_____

_____

_____

3. Leaving your patient with another qualified individual is called

_____

_____

_____

4. An EMT should speak up for a patient and make sure the patient's needs are addressed. This is called

_____

_____

_____

_____

5. The government department responsible for creating the EMT curriculum is

_____

_____

_____

_____

6. The process consisting of continuous self-review with the purpose of identifying aspects that require improvement is called

_____

_____

_____

_____

7. The person who assumes ultimate responsibility for the oversight of the patient care is called

_____

_____

_____

8. Describe the difference between a Do Not Resuscitate order and a Living Will.

_____

_____

_____

9. A policy or protocol issued by a medical director that authorizes EMT and others to perform certain skills is called

_____

_____

_____

10. Organisms that cause infection such as viruses and bacteria are called

_____

_____

_____

11. The processes and procedures designed to protect you from infection are known as

_____

_____

_____

12. The equipment used to protect you from all possible routes of contamination are collectively known as

_____

_____

_____

13. A patient has a productive cough. What potentially fatal lung disease should an EMT be concerned about with respect to personal safety and that of his or her crew?

_____

_____

_____

_____

14. As blood flows through the heart it passes through four valves. List these valves in order.

_____

_____

_____

_____

15. The U.S. Congress act that establishes procedures by which emergency response workers may find out if they have been exposed to life-threatening infectious diseases is called

_____

_____

_____

_____

16. EMTs and other EMS workers are routinely given a test called a PPD test. What does PPD mean, and what can the test detect?

_____

_____

_____

_____

17. What is the difference between eustress and distress?

_____

_____

_____

_____

18. When a patient finds out he or she is dying, it is common to go through various emotional stages such as denial. Name some others.

_____

_____

_____

_____

19. List at least five signs of a myocardial infarction

_____

_____

_____

_____

20. Explain the difference between expressed consent and implied consent.

_____

_____

_____

_____

21. In order for a patient to refuse care or transport, several conditions must be fulfilled. List as many of these conditions as possible.

_____

_____

_____

22. Provide an example of an advance directive.

_____

_____

_____

23. Name two of the most significant causes of lawsuits against EMTs.

_____

_____

_____

_____

24. List the four criteria that must be present in a simple negligence lawsuit.

_____

_____

_____

_____

25. List what the acronym DCAP-BTLS stands for.

_____

_____

_____

_____

26. The anatomical term for the front of the body is

_____

_____

_____

27. The anatomical term for the rear of the body is

_____

_____

_____

28. The anatomical term to describe a position closer to the torso is

_____

_____

_____

29. The anatomical term to describe a position farther from the torso is

_____

_____

_____

30. The anatomical term for an imaginary line drawn down the center of the body passing between the eyes and past the umbilicus is

_____

_____

_____

31. Provide the positional term for the following patients (e.g., a patient lying on his or her back is in the supine position).
A patient lying on his or her abdomen
A patient sitting
A patient lying with the head slightly lower than the feet

_____

_____

_____

_____

32. What is the name of the bone of the lower jaw?

_____

_____

_____

33. What is the name of the bone found at the base of the sternum?

_____

_____

_____

34. The spinal column is made up of individual bones called vertebrae. How many vertebrae are there in the human spine?

_____

_____

_____

35. Name the five divisions of the spine and state the number of vertebrae in each division.

_____

_____

_____

_____

36. Tarsals and metatarsals are found where?

_____

_____

_____

37. The bone that sits anterior to the knee joint is known as

_____

_____

_____

38. Describe the difference between voluntary and involuntary muscles. Give at least one example of each.

_____

_____

_____

_____

39. A leaf-shaped structure that closes to prevent food and other objects from entering the trachea is known as

_____

_____

_____

_____

40. Small sacs within the lungs where gas exchange takes place with the bloodstream are called

_____

_____

_____

_____

41. The component of blood primarily instrumental in the formation of blood clots is called

_____

_____

_____

_____

42. What is a key function of the white blood cells?

_____

_____

_____

_____

43. What is perfusion?

_____

_____

_____

_____

44. The division of the nervous system that controls involuntary motor function and affects such things as digestion and heart rate is the

_____

_____

_____

_____

45. Epinephrine is sometimes called

_____

_____

_____

_____

46. During the initial assessment, how do you determine signs of adequate breathing?

_____

_____

_____

_____

47. Your patient presents with skin that appears blue or gray. This condition is called

_____

_____

_____

_____

48. Describe what a hypoxic drive is, and what type and percentage of patients may have this condition.

_____

_____

_____

_____

49. List as many signs of inadequate breathing as you can.

_____

_____

_____

_____

50. What is the normal breathing rate for an adult?

_____

_____

_____

51. The technique used to provide the maximum opening of a patient's airway is

_____

_____

_____

52. The technique used to open the airway of a patient with a head, neck, or spine injury is

_____

_____

_____

_____

53. What is the best method to ensure adequate ventilation of a patient when using a bag-valve mask?

_____

_____

_____

_____

54. What percentage of oxygen will a bag-valve mask with a reservoir deliver?

_____

_____

_____

55. Based on American Heart Association guidelines, how much air should be delivered to a patient using an adult bag-valve mask?

_____

_____

_____

_____

56. What is the best method to size an oropharyngeal airway (OPA)?

_____

_____

_____

_____

57. What does the term *contraindication* mean?

_____

_____

_____

_____

58. What is the best method to size a nasopharyngeal airway (NPA)?

_____

_____

_____

_____

59. Describe supine hypotensive syndrome.

_____

_____

_____

_____

60. Never suction a patient for more than _____ seconds at a time.

61. The atmosphere contains approximately _____% oxygen.

62. A portable oxygen cylinder, when filled, is pressurized to approximately _____ pounds per square inch (psi).

63. Oxygen should not be allowed to empty below a safe residual pressure. The safe residual pressure for a portable cylinder is

_____

_____

_____

_____

64. List five signs and symptoms of meningitis.

65. You are the first on the scene of a motor vehicle accident (MVA). List a number of priorities to consider during your scene size-up.

_____

_____

_____

_____

66. On the scene of the same MVA, you have determined that you have one patient. As part of your initial assessment, your primary objectives will be

_____

_____

_____

_____

67. What does the acronym AVPU stand for, and when would it be used?

_____

_____

_____

_____

68. What type of injury patterns are likely in a head-on motor vehicle collision?

_____

_____

_____

_____

69. What type of vehicle damage would be noteworthy when making a determination of the mechanism of injury?

_____

_____

_____

_____

70. Textbooks often describe three collisions in a motor vehicle crash. List them.

_____

_____

_____

71. Falls from greater than _____ feet, or _____ times the height of the patient, are usually considered severe.

72. List examples of low-velocity weapons.

_____

_____

_____

_____

73. Describe a coup-contra coup injury.

_____

_____

_____

_____

74. Define compensated shock.

_____

_____

_____

75. Is decreasing blood pressure an early or late sign of shock?

_____

_____

_____

76. What would the pulse rate of a patient be if he or she was described as tachycardic?

_____

_____

_____

_____

77. List possible reasons for an elevated pulse rate.

_____

_____

_____

_____

78. List possible reasons for a slow pulse rate.

_____

_____

_____

_____

79. In addition to the rate, what other assessment should be made with respect to the pulse?

_____

_____

_____

_____

80. In patients under 1 year of age, the
_____ pulse should be assessed.

81. Why shouldn't you use your thumb when
assessing a patient's pulse?

_____

_____

_____

_____

82. Provide a possible cause and an appropriate
intervention for each of the following respiratory sounds: snoring, wheezing, gurgling.

_____

_____

_____

_____

83. The memory aid HEENT can be used during
patient assessment. What do the letters mean?

_____

_____

_____

_____

84. What is crepitation?

_____

_____

_____

_____

85. What would be the normal pulse rate for a
child between ages 1–3 years?

_____

_____

_____

_____

86. How should a correction be made on a patient-
care report?

_____

_____

_____

_____

87. When would an NPA be contraindicated?

_____

_____

_____

_____

88. What is a medication side effect?

_____

_____

_____

_____

89. What are the three layers of the skin from outside to inside?

_____

_____

_____

90. What medication route would you use to administer sublingual nitroglycerin tablets to your patient complaining of chest pain?

_____

_____

_____

91. What do the letters *COPD* mean?

_____

_____

_____

92. List some contraindications for the use of a medication inhaler.

_____

_____

_____

_____

93. What is the largest artery in the cardiovascular system?

_____

_____

_____

_____

94. After the use of the AED, your patient is awake. While on the stretcher, your patient becomes unresponsive again. An assessment reveals no breathing and no pulse. What is your next action?

_____

_____

_____

_____

95. You have delivered one shock to your patient who is in cardiac arrest. What is the next action you should take?

_____

_____

_____

_____

96. Your patient complains of shortness of breath and a feeling of heavy pressure in his chest. His respirations are 38, shallow. His pulse is 56 and irregular, and he reports a history of angina. Do you have enough information to assist the patient with his prescribed nitroglycerin?

_____

_____

_____

_____

97. What distinctive lung sounds would you expect to hear if your patient has pulmonary edema?

_____

_____

_____

98. What type of medication is often taken by a patient who has a history of congestive heart failure (CHF)?

_____

_____

_____

_____

99. What types of medications are described as clot busters?

_____

_____

_____

_____

100. Which organ produces insulin?

_____

_____

_____

101. What does the term _hypoglycemia_ mean?

_____

_____

_____

_____

102. Your patient's family member reports that the patient accidentally took too much insulin. Would you expect to find the blood sugar too low or too high?

_____

_____

_____

103. What can cause low blood sugar in a diabetic patient?

_____

_____

_____

104. What are common findings in a patient with low blood sugar?

_____

_____

_____

105. Describe an ectopic pregnancy.

_____

_____

_____

106. What is the most common cause of seizures in children?

_____

_____

_____

107. What type of information should you report on a seizure patient?

_____

_____

_____

108. What is the term to describe two or more seizures without regaining full consciousness?

_____

_____

_____

109. Describe the difference between a transient ischemic attack and a stroke.

_____

_____

_____

110. What are the two main causes of a stroke?

_____

_____

_____

111. What are the three items of assessment used in the Cincinnati Prehospital Stroke scale?

_____

_____

_____

112. Describe how arm drift is assessed in a suspected stroke patient.

_____

_____

_____

113. What is the term used to describe a severe, life-threatening allergic reaction?

_____

_____

_____

114. What signs and symptoms would you expect to find in order to distinguish between anaphylaxis and a mild allergic reaction?

_____

_____

_____

_____

115. Describe considerations that should be taken when parking your ambulance at a motor vehicle collision.

_____

_____

_____

_____

116. What are the contraindications to consider before using a prescribed epinephrine autoinjector on a patient presenting signs of severe allergic reaction, including difficulty breathing?

_____

_____

_____

_____

117. What is the dose contained in an adult epinephrine autoinjector?

_____

_____

_____

_____

118. Describe the difference in appearance between an arterial bleed and a venous bleed.

_____

_____

_____

_____

119. List the information that should be gathered for a patient suspected of poison inhalation.

_____

_____

_____

_____

120. What is the most commonly inhaled poison that is characterized by its lack of odor, color, and taste?

_____

_____

_____

_____

121. List some common signs and symptoms of carbon monoxide poisoning.

_____

_____

_____

_____

122. List four types of "upper" drugs.

_____

_____

_____

123. What is the term for the severe reaction to alcohol withdrawal characterized by sweating, trembling, anxiety, and hallucinations?

_____

_____

_____

124. List the four ways a poison can enter the body.

_____

_____

_____

_____

125. Do most poisons have an antidote?

_____

_____

_____

126. Conduction is one way the body loses heat. What are the other possible methods?

_____

_____

_____

127. A condition in which the body temperature drops below that required for normal bodily functions is known as

_____

_____

_____

_____

128. Describe the treatment for an impaled object in the eye.

_____

_____

_____

_____

129. What are the likely changes that may be observed in the condition of the skin of a person in the early stages of frostbite?

_____

_____

_____

_____

130. Describe heat exhaustion.

_____

_____

_____

_____

131. What causes decompression sickness?

_____

_____

_____

132. In the interest of personal safety, what rescue methods should be considered before going into the water and swimming to a patient?

_____

_____

_____

_____

133. List four common causes of altered mental status.

_____

_____

_____

_____

134. What does the term _afterbirth_ describe?

_____

_____

_____

_____

135. What type of personal protection equipment should be part of an obstetrical kit?

_____

_____

_____

_____

136. What is meconium staining?

_____

_____

_____

_____

137. What are the signs and symptoms of preeclampsia?

_____

_____

_____

_____

138. How would you define a premature infant?

_____

_____

_____

_____

139. What happens during the third stage of labor?

_____

_____

_____

_____

140. In what position should a third-trimester pregnant patient be transported and why?

_____

_____

_____

_____

141. What are the names of the pressure points used to stop excessive bleeding from the arm or the leg?

_____

_____

_____

_____

142. Name three major types of shock.

_____

_____

_____

_____

143. What would be the typical skin condition of a patient in shock?

_____

_____

_____

_____

144. Define *compensated shock*.

_____

_____

_____

_____

145. You transport your patient to the hospital. While waiting to give your report, you receive another call. You move your patient over to a bed, and leave without giving your report. Is this appropriate?

_____

_____

_____

_____

146. What type of shock would be a contraindication for the use of PASGs?

_____

_____

_____

_____

147. Describe the difference between the platinum ten minutes and the golden hour.

_____

_____

_____

_____

148. A collection of blood under the skin at an injury site describes what?

_____

_____

_____

149. What are the signs of a tension pneumothorax?

_____

_____

_____

_____

150. Your adult patient has moderate burns to the chest and the entire right arm. Using the rule of nine formula, what is the body surface area involved?

_____

_____

_____

_____

151. A helicopter landing zone should be at least how big?

_____

_____

_____

152. How much blood loss can be expected from a broken femur?

_____

_____

_____

153. Describe the difference between ligaments and tendons.

_____

_____

_____

_____

154. What is the purpose of splinting a broken bone?

_____

_____

_____

_____

155. Your patient opens his eyes at the sound of your voice. He can speak but uses inappropriate words and pushes your hand away when you pinch his arm. What is the patient's Glasgow Coma Scale (GCS)?

_____

_____

_____

156. Other than trauma, what is the most likely cause of cardiac arrest in a child?

_____

_____

_____

157. If a child is afraid of an oxygen mask, what technique can be used?

_____

_____

_____

158. What would be considered delayed capillary refill in a child under 5 years of age?

_____

_____

_____

159. The paramedic you are working with is attempting to intubate the patient and is asking you to perform the Sellick maneuver. Describe how you would perform this maneuver.

_____

_____

_____

_____

160. List four times when it is appropriate to remove a patient's helmet (such as motorcycle helmet, or sporting helmet).

_____

_____

_____

_____

Answers

1. Online medical direction is talking to a physician over the radio or phone, while offline medical direction is protocols or standing orders.

2. This is false. Your personal safety comes first. It is not possible for you to help a patient if you are injured first.

3. This describes transfer of care. You must never leave your patient until proper transfer has taken place.

4. Sticking up for a patient and making sure the patient's needs are met is called patient advocacy. Among other things, you must make sure the hospital personnel have all the information that you have learned about your patient.

5. The U.S. Department of Transportation created the EMT curriculum.

6. A quality-improvement committee is often formed to carry out consistent review of operations and personnel performance.

7. The medical director assumes responsibility for the oversight of the patient care. This is a physician who also oversees training and the development of protocols.

8. A Do Not Resuscitate order is for patients with a terminal illness and describes the resuscitation care that they desire. A Living Will describes the care that a patient desires in the event that they cannot make decisions for themselves.

9. This policy or protocol is called standing orders. Additional orders can also be issued by telephone while the patient is in the care of the EMT.

10. These organisms are called pathogens. Blood-borne pathogens can be found in blood and other body fluids. Airborne pathogens are spread by tiny droplets sprayed during breathing, coughing, etc.

11. The processes and procedures designed to protect you from infection are known as body substance isolation precautions (BSI).

12. This equipment is called personal protective equipment (PPE). Such equipment would include masks, eye protection, gowns, etc.

13. The patient may have TB. EMS workers can become infected even without direct contact. It is impossible to determine why a patient has a productive cough. Assume the worst for safety reasons.

14. The four valves are tricuspid, pulmonic, mitral, and aortic.

15. This act is called the Ryan White CARE Act. It was named in honor of Ryan White, an Indiana teenager who contracted AIDS through a tainted hemophilia treatment in 1984 and was expelled from school because of the disease.

16. PPD means purified protein derivative. The test can detect exposure to TB. There are currently no immunizations against TB.

17. *Eustress* is defined as stress that is healthy or gives one a feeling of fulfillment. This type can help people work under pressure. *Distress* can occur when a situation becomes overwhelming. Distressed EMTs will not be as effective.

18. In addition to denial, other emotions may include anger ("Why me?"), bargaining ("OK, but first let me . . ."), depression ("But I haven't had a chance to . . ."), and acceptance ("I am not afraid").

19. Signs of a myocardial infarction are: chest pain; chest pressure; shortness of breath; palpitations; sweating; pain in the back; shoulders, or jaw; dizziness; nausea and vomiting.

20. Expressed consent is given by adults who are of legal age and are mentally competent to make a rational decision. Implied consent assumes that a patient would give consent if he or she were conscious.

21. The patient must be legally able to consent (legal age or emancipated minor), mentally competent and oriented, and fully informed. The patient must sign a release form.

22. A common advance directive found in EMS is a do not resuscitate order (DNR). Other advance directives can direct specific care and treatment.

23. Patient refusal of care and/or transport and ambulance collisions are the two most common reasons for legal action against EMTs.

24. The four criteria that must be present in a simple negligence lawsuit are: 1) duty to act; 2) harm caused; 3) inappropriate care given; and 4) the actions caused the harm (proximate cause).

25. DCAP-BTLS stands for Deformity, Contusion, Abrasion, Penetration/Puncture, Burns, Tenderness, Lacerations, and Swelling.

26. The anatomical term for the front of the body is anterior.

27. The anatomical term for the rear of the body is posterior.

28. The anatomical term to describe a position closer to the torso is proximal.

29. The anatomical term to describe a position farther from the torso is distal.

30. Midline describes the imaginary line drawn down the center of the body.

31. A patient lying on his or her abdomen is prone. A patient sitting is in Fowler's position. A patient lying with the head slightly lower than the feet is in Trendelenburg position.

32. Mandible is the lower jawbone. (The fused bones of the upper jaw are called the maxillae.)

33. Xiphoid process is at the base of the sternum. Hand placement during CPR is important to avoid breaking this bone.

34. There are 33 vertebrae in the human spine.

35. The five divisions of the spine are the cervical (neck), with 7 vertebrae; thoracic (thorax, ribs, upper back), with 12; lumbar (lower back), with 5; sacral (back wall of pelvis), with 5; and coccyx (tailbone), with 4.

36. Tarsals and metatarsals are found in the ankle and foot, respectively.

37. This bone is the patella, or kneecap.

38. Voluntary muscle, or skeletal muscle, is under conscious control of the brain. Examples would include any muscle used to do things like walk, reach, or pick something up. Involuntary muscle, or smooth muscle, responds automatically to orders from the brain; there is no conscious thought in their operation. Examples are found in the digestive and respiratory systems.

39. The epiglottis prevents food from entering the trachea.

40. Alveoli are small sacs within the lungs where gas exchange with the blood stream takes place.

41. Platelets are instrumental in the formation of blood clots.

42. White blood cells, also known as leukocytes, are involved in the destruction of germs and the production of antibodies.

43. Perfusion is the adequate supply of oxygen and nutrients to the organs and tissues of the body with the removal of waste products.

44. The autonomic nervous system controls involuntary muscle function. Other divisions include the central and peripheral nervous systems.

45. Epinephrine is also called adrenaline.

46. Look for equal chest expansion in inhalation. Listen for air exchange at the nose or mouth. Feel for air movement at the nose or mouth.

47. A patient with skin that appears to be blue or gray has cyanosis. This could be an indication of hypoxia.

48. A hypoxic drive indicates that a patient's urge to breathe is because of low oxygen levels, and not high carbon dioxide levels. This is seen in about 15% of patients with COPD.

49. Signs of inadequate breathing are uneven, minimal, or absent chest rise; breathing effort limited to abdominal motion; no air can be felt or heard; breath sound diminished or absent, and the patient makes noises such as wheezing, crowing, stridor, snoring, and gurgling; rate of breathing too rapid or too slow; breathing very shallow, deep, or labored; there is prolonged inspiration or expiration; the patient is unable to speak in full sentences, and there is nasal flaring.

50. The normal adult breathing rate is 12–20 breaths per minute.

51. The head-tilt/chin-lift maneuver provides the maximum opening of a patient's airway.

52. The jaw-thrust maneuver opens the airway of a patient with a head, neck, or spine injury.

53. Observe the patient's chest rise and fall with ventilations.

54. It should deliver nearly 100% oxygen.

55. An adult bag-valve mask should deliver 800 mL of air.

56. Place the OPA to the side of the patient's face, and make sure that it extends from the center of the mouth to the angle of the jaw, or from the corner of the patient's mouth to the top of the earlobe.

57. Contraindications are specific signs, symptoms, or circumstances under which the administration of a drug would not be advisable.

58. Measure from the patient's nostril to the earlobe or angle of the jaw.

59. Supine hypotensive syndrome occurs when the third trimester fetus compresses the vena cava of the mother when she is lying flat. By placing the mother in the left lateral recumbent position, the pressure of the fetus will be removed, generating normal blood flow.

60. Never suction a patient for more than 15 seconds. If the patient requires additional suctioning, ventilate for two minutes and then suction for an additional 15 seconds. This sequence may be repeated. Consider obtaining medical direction in this situation.

61. The atmosphere contains 21% oxygen. The remainder is made up of approximately 78% nitrogen, 0.93% argon, 0.038% carbon dioxide, and trace amounts of other gases and water vapor.

62. A portable oxygen cylinder is pressurized to 2,000–2,200 psi when filled.

63. The cylinder should be changed before the pressure drops to 200 psi to ensure proper oxygen delivery to the patient.

64. Signs of symptoms of meningitis include high fever, lethargy, irritability, headache, stiff neck, sensitivity to light, bulging fontanelles in infants, pain on movement, rash, and seizures.

65. Ensure safety for yourself and your crew, consider the mechanism of injury, account for all people who are potentially injured, consider additional resources (haz-mat, heavy rescue, additional ambulances, etc.), and determine best access for other responders.

66. Maintain manual spine stabilization; form a general impression of the patient; determine responsiveness; look for life-threatening conditions with emphasis on airway, breathing, and circulation; and make a transport decision.

67. AVPU stands for Alert, Verbal, Painful, and Unresponsive and it is used to determine level of consciousness.

68. Two types are likely. If the patient went up and over the steering wheel, head, neck, chest, and abdomen injuries should be suspected. If the patient followed a down-and-under pathway, one may find injuries to the knees, legs, and hips.

69. Noteworthy vehicle damage would be evidence of rollover; spidered windshield; bent steering wheel; damage to dashboard, seats, or floor; damage intrusion into passenger compartment; and broken axle or other major component.

70. The three collisions in a motor vehicle crash are when the vehicle strikes an object, when the body strikes the interior of the car, and when the internal organs strike the interior surface of the body.

71. Falls from greater than 15 feet or three times the height of the patient are usually considered severe.

72. Low-velocity weapons are those propelled by hand such as knives, clubs, etc.

73. A coup-contra coup injury occurs when the head is struck causing bruising to the brain (coup). The brain then bounces in the skull, causing a bruise on the opposite side of the brain (contra coup).

74. Compensated shock occurs when the body is developing shock, but the body is able to compensate to maintain perfusion. This compensation occurs in the form of increased heart rate, increased respiratory rate, peripheral shunting of blood, and constriction of peripheral circulation.

75. Low blood pressure is a late sign of shock indicating that the body is unable to compensate for the blood loss.

76. A pulse rate of a tachycardic patient would be greater than 100 beats per minute.

77. Reasons for an elevated heart rate include exertion, fright, fever, blood loss, shock, drugs, and cardiac-related conditions.

78. Reasons for a slow heart rate include head injury, drugs, some poisons, and cardiac-related conditions.

79. Rhythm and quality are other assessments that should be made in respect to the pulse. For example, in addition to the number of beats per minute, an EMT should report the regularity and the feel of the force. "The pulse is 84 regular and full."

80. The brachial pulse, which is found in the upper arm, should be assessed.

81. Your thumb has its own pulse and may cause you to measure your own pulse instead of the patient's.

82. Snoring might be caused by a blocked airway. To treat, open the airway and clear as necessary. Wheezing might be caused by medical problems such as asthma. To treat, assist with prescribed meds and administer meds as allowed by local protocols. Gurgling might be caused by fluids in the airway. To treat, suction airway, provide oxygen, and transport promptly.

83. HEENT stands for head, ears, eyes, nose, and throat.

84. Crepitation describes the sound of grating bones rubbing together, often indicating a fracture.

85. The normal pulse rate for a child between ages 1–3 years is 80–130 beats per minute at rest.

86. A single line may be drawn through the error, the correct information written beside it, and then initialed. The erroneous information should not be obliterated.

87. An NPA should be contraindicated anytime there is a suspicion of facial or skull fractures.

88. A side effect is the action of a drug other than the desired action.

89. The three layers of the skin from outside to inside are the epidermis, dermis, and subcutaneous tissue.

90. Sublingual means under the tongue. In this case, you would place the tablets under the tongue and allow them to dissolve.

91. COPD stands for chronic obstructive pulmonary disease. Emphysema, chronic bronchitis, black lung, and other undetermined respiratory illnesses fall into this category.

92. The patient is not alert and not able to use the device, the inhaler is not prescribed to the patient, use has been denied by medical control, or the patient has already taken maximum prescribed dose.

93. The aorta carries blood from the left ventricle to the systemic circulation.

94. Reanalyze using the AED and shock if indicated.

95. Perform two minutes of CPR. You are unlikely to find a pulse immediately after a shock even if the shock successfully converted the rhythm. CPR is required to maintain perfusion in the meantime.

96. You need a blood pressure before you can safely administer nitroglycerin. Hypotension is a contraindication for its use.

97. Crackling or bubbling lung sounds can often be heard as air passes through the fluid that has accumulated in the lungs. These sounds are called rales.

98. Diuretics, also known as water pills, are often prescribed to these patients. A common example of this type of medication is Lasix (furosemide).

99. Thrombolytics are used to dissolve blood clots that block the coronary arteries. To be used effectively, these medications must be used early in the process.

100. The pancreas produces insulin.

101. Hypoglycemia means low blood sugar.

102. Too much insulin would cause more sugar to be put into the cells, leaving too little in the blood. A low blood sugar reading would be expected.

103. Low blood sugar can be caused by the patient taking too much insulin, not eating, overexercising, or vomiting a meal.

104. Altered mental status and possible unconsciousness are typical in a patient with low blood sugar.

105. An ectopic pregnancy occurs when the fertilized egg is implanted somewhere other than the uterus. This frequently occurs in the fallopian tube, cervix, or abdominopelvic cavity.

106. High fever is the most common cause of seizures in children. These are called febrile seizures.

107. You should note what the patient was doing before the seizure, description of the seizure activity, loss of bowel or bladder control, how long the seizure lasted, and how the patient's mental status was after the seizure.

108. Status epilepticus is the term. This is a high-priority call. Rapid, safe transport and support of airway are the priorities.

109. A transient ischemic attack presents similarly to a stroke. However, the symptoms resolve within 24 hours without treatment. If symptoms persist, this is a likely indication of a stroke.

110. A stoke, or CVA, can be caused by a blockage of an artery that supplies blood to part of the brain. This is also known as an ischemic stoke. Another cause would be bleeding in the brain, known as hemorrhagic stroke.

111. Three items of assessment are facial droop, arm drift, and speech difficulties.

112. Ask the patient to close his or her eyes and extend his or her arms out in front for ten seconds. A normal response would be for the patient to move both arms at the same time. An abnormal response would be if the patient could not move an arm or one arm drifts down.

113. Anaphylaxis, or anaphylactic shock, describes a severe, life-threatening allergic reaction.

114. Respiratory distress and signs or symptoms of shock are indicators of a severe allergic reaction (anaphylaxis).

115. The ambulance should be parked uphill and upwind from the scene, as well as behind the accident, to warn other motorists. The ambulance's red lights should be left on, but white lights should be turned off—they could blind oncoming vehicles.

116. There are no contraindications when used in a life-threatening situation.

117. The dose is 0.3 mg.

118. An arterial bleed will present with bright red spurting blood, whereas a venous bleed will have dark red, oozing blood.

119. Find out the name of the substance involved, when the exposure occurred, how long the exposure lasted, interventions taken, and effects on the patient.

120. The most commonly inhaled poison that is characterized by its lack of color, odor, and taste is carbon monoxide.

121. Common signs and symptoms of carbon monoxide poisoning are headache, dizziness, breathing difficulty, nausea, cyanosis, altered mental status, unconsciousness, and death. Note: Despite commonly accepted ideas, cherry red skin is not a common finding.

122. Amphetamine, biphetamine, cocaine, dextro-amphetamine, methamphetamine, methyl-phenidate, and preludin are all types of "uppers."

123. This describes delirium tremens (DTs).

124. The four ways poison can enter the body are ingestion, inhalation, injection, and absorption.

125. Although many people think there is an antidote for many poisons, there are, in fact, very few true antidotes.

126. Convection, radiation, evaporation, and respiration are ways the body loses heat.

127. This condition is called hypothermia. The body can be significantly affected with a drop of one or two degrees.

128. An object that is impaled in the eye should be carefully secured with a rigid stabilizer to prevent further movement, and the other eye should be covered to prevent sympathetic eye movement. The patient should be reassured and treated for shock.

129. A person in the early stages of frostbite often presents white, waxy skin; blotchy skin; loss of skin texture; and discoloration, including grays, yellows, and blues.

130. Heat exhaustion is a form of shock. An active, healthy individual can lose as much as a liter of fluid per hour through perspiration.

131. A diver ascending quickly from a dive is the most common cause of decompression sickness. Any sudden decrease in pressure can be a cause.

132. First try to reach with your arm; then consider throwing a floating object or rope and towing the victim out. Rowing to the victim would be next. Remember: reach, throw, tow, row. Swim only if you are a good swimmer and trained to do so.

133. Common causes of altered mental status include: low blood sugar, hypoxia, strokes, head trauma, drugs, hypothermia, and hyperthermia.

134. The afterbirth describes the placenta, the membranes that are normally expelled after the birth of the baby.

135. Personal protection should include gloves, face mask, eye shield, and gown.

136. Meconium staining refers to the discoloration of the amniotic fluid. It is an indication of fetal distress during labor.

137. Symptoms of preeclampsia include high blood pressure, fluid retention, headache, and seizures.

138. A premature infant is generally described as weighing less than 5.5 pounds or born within 37 weeks of pregnancy.

139. The placenta is delivered during the third stage of labor.

140. The patient should be transported on the left side to avoid supine hypotensive syndrome.

141. The brachial pressure point is found in the arm and the femoral pressure point is found in the leg.

142. Three major types of shock are hypovolemic shock, cardiogenic shock, and neurogenic shock.

143. Cool, pale, and sweaty skin is a typical presentation of a patient in shock.

144. Compensated shock is when the body senses a decrease in perfusion and compensates by raising the heart rate and concentrating blood flow to critical organs.

145. Failing to give report about your patient and transfer care is considered abandonment. EMTs can be held criminally and/or civilly liable.

146. Cardiogenic shock would be a contraindication for the use of PASG.

147. The platinum ten minutes describes the maximum amount of time that should be spent on the scene of a trauma call. The golden hour represents the time of injury to surgical intervention.

148. A collection of blood under the skin is called hematoma. As much as a liter of blood can be lost in a hematoma.

149. Signs of a tension pneumothorax include difficulty breathing, signs of shock, distended neck veins, tracheal deviation, and diminished breath sounds on the affected side.

150. The body surface area is 13.5%, per the rule of nines: chest (9) + 1 arm (4.5) = 13.5%.

151. Helicopter landing zones should be at least 100 feet by 100 feet on ground that has less than an eight degree slope and is free of any obstacles.

152. Approximately 1,000 cc can be lost from a broken femur.

153. Ligaments connect bone to bone, while tendons connect muscle to bone.

154. Splinting a broken bone minimizes movement; decreases pain; helps prevent additional injury to nerves, arteries, veins, muscle, etc.; and minimize blood loss.

155. The GCS is 11, per the equation: eye opening to voice (3) + inappropriate words (3) + localizes pain (5) = 11.

156. Respiratory problems are likely to be the cause of cardiac arrest in children. Adult cardiac arrest is more likely to originate from a heart problem.

157. Provide blow-by oxygen. Have a parent or trusted person hold the oxygen tubing close to the child's face.

158. More than two seconds would be considered delayed capillary refill in a child under 5.

159. The Sellick maneuver, also known as cricoid pressure, is performed by pressing your thumb and index finger on either side of the cricoid cartilage.

160. The four indications for removing a patient's helmet are: 1) it interferes with ability to assess and manage the airway and breathing; 2) it is improperly fitted, allowing excessive head movement; 3) it interferes with immobilization; and 4) cardiac arrest.

EMT-BASIC PRACTICAL SKILLS EXAM

CHAPTER SUMMARY
This chapter presents the National Registry's EMT-Basic practical skills examination, which is used by many states and forms the basis for the practical exam in many other states. Being familiar with what will be expected of you—and knowing how the practical exam is scored—will help your self-confidence when you take the practical exam.

During your EMT-Basic training, you practiced various techniques and skills under a variety of conditions. But during a practical examination for certification, conditions have to be standardized as much as possible. The procedural guidelines that your examiners will be following will be sequential and often stringent. You have to do things in a particular order, just as you are told. This means that testing can be stressful. Proper preparation can help you overcome this stress.

The National Registry of Emergency Medical Technicians (NREMT) requires successful completion of a state-approved practical examination that meets the NREMT's minimum standards. The following 13 skills are tested because they are directly related to the potential loss of life or limb.

1. Patient Assessment/Management–Trauma
2. Patient Assessment/Management–Medical
3. Cardiac Arrest Management
4. Airway, Oxygen, Ventilation Skills/Bag-Valve Mask–Apneic with Pulse
5. Spinal Immobilization–Supine Patient

6. Spinal Immobilization–Seated Patient
7. Immobilization Skills–Long Bone
8. Immobilization Skills–Joint Injury
9. Immobilization Skills–Traction Splinting
10. Bleeding Control/Shock Management
11. Airway, Oxygen, Ventilation Skills/Upper-Airway Adjuncts and Suction
12. Airway, Oxygen, Ventilation Skills/Mouth-to-Mask with Supplemental Oxygen
13. Airway, Oxygen, Ventilation Skills/Supplemental Oxygen Administration

The National Registry developed a sample practical examination to help states develop their EMT-Basic practical exam. Many states have adopted this sample exam as their skills certification examination. Whether your state uses the NREMT exam or has developed its own EMT-Basic skills exam, the NREMT exam that follows will help you prepare for your practical examination. *However, you should become familiar with your state's examination, local scope of practice, and treatment protocols before you take the exam.*

The skills examination consists of six stations. Five of these stations are mandatory stations, and one is a random skill station. The stations and time limits are listed in the table on this page.

NREMT PRACTICAL SKILLS EXAM		
STATION	SKILLS TESTED	TIME
Station 1	Patient Assessment/Management–Trauma	10 min.
Station 2	Patient Assessment/Management–Medical	10 min.
Station 3	Cardiac Arrest Management/AED	15 min.
Station 4	Bag-Valve Mask–Apneic with Pulse	10 min.
Station 5	Spinal Immobilization–Supine or Seated	10 min.
Station 6	Random Skill:	
	Long Bone Immobilization Skills	5 min.
	Joint Injury Immobilization Skills	5 min.
	Traction Splinting Immobilization Skills	10 min.
	Bleeding Control/Shock Management	10 min.
	Upper-Airway Adjuncts and Suction	5 min.
	Mouth-to-Mask with Supplemental Oxygen	5 min.
	Supplemental Oxygen Administration	5 min.

You will not be told which random skill you will be tested on before the examination. Many examiners will have you blindly select from skills listed on separate cards, or the coordinator may select one skill to administer to all candidates.

This chapter contains the NREMT sample practical examination and the instruction to the candidates. Generally, you can fail up to three skills and retest those skills on the same day. Retests are proctored by a different examiner. Please refer to Candidate General Instructions on page 168 for more detailed information.

It may be helpful to the examiner during the examination process if you talk aloud while performing each skill. The examiner can then not only see what you are doing, but he or she can also hear what you are thinking as you go through the process. This might also help you stay on track during the skills exam, as it might jog your memory of a missing or out-of-sequence step.

Instructions for each station are listed with the skill-assessment sheet, along with the minimum score for each station. In addition, failure to perform critical criteria, listed at the bottom of each skill-assessment sheet, constitutes failure of that station. All the necessary equipment will be provided for you at each station. You must follow proper body substance isolation procedures for every skill.

Before you begin each station, ask any questions that you have; you will not be permitted to ask questions during the assessment. Remember, good communication and critical-thinking skills are vital to successfully completing any practical examination.

Remember this: "Practice makes perfect" applies perfectly to the skills exam portion of any EMT-Basic testing process. The more times you can rehearse these skills, the more comfortable you will be when performing them in front of an examiner. This translates directly to the field setting, where you can be confident that your skills will be competent when the patient needs them the most!

EMT-Basic Practical Exam

Candidate General Instructions

Welcome to the EMT-Basic practical examination. I'm *name and title*. By successfully completing this examination process and receiving subsequent certification, you will have proven to yourself and the medical community that you have achieved the level of competency assuring the public receives quality prehospital care.

I will now read the roster, for attendance purposes, before we begin the orientation. Please identify yourself when your name is called.

The skill station examiners utilized today were selected because of their expertise in the particular skill station. Skill station examiners observe and record your expected appropriate actions. They record your performance in relationship to the criteria listed on the evaluation instrument.

The skill station examiner will call you into the station when it is prepared for testing. No candidate, at any time, is permitted to remain in the testing area while waiting for his or her next station. You must wait outside the testing area until the station is open and you are called. You are not permitted to take any books, pamphlets, brochures, or other study materials into the station. You are not permitted to make any copies or recordings of any station. The skill station examiner will greet you as you enter the skill station. The examiner will ask your name. Please assist him or her in spelling your name so that your results may be reported accurately. Each skill station examiner will then read aloud "Instructions to the Candidate" exactly as printed on the instruction provided to him or her by the examination coordinator. The information is read to each candidate in the same manner to ensure consistency and fairness.

Please pay close attention to the instructions, as they correspond to dispatch information you might receive on a similar emergency call and give you valuable information on what will be expected of you during the skill station. The skill station examiner will offer to repeat the instructions and will ask you if the instructions were understood. Do not ask for additional information. Candidates sometimes complain that skill station examiners are abrupt, cold, or appear unfriendly. No one is here to add to the stress and anxiety you may already feel. It is important to understand that the examiners have been told they must avoid casual conversation with candidates. This is necessary to assure fair and equal treatment of all candidates throughout the examination. We have instructed the skill station examiners not to indicate to you, in any way, a judgment regarding your performance in the skill station. Do not interpret any of the examiner's remarks as an indication of your overall performance. Please recognize the skill station examiner's attitude as professional and objective, and simply perform the skills to the best of your ability.

Each skill station is supplied with several types of equipment for your selection. You will be given time at the beginning of the skill station to survey and select the equipment necessary for the appropriate management of the patient. Do not feel obligated to use all the equipment. If you brought any of your own equipment, I must inspect and approve it before you can enter the skill station.

As you progress through the practical examination, each skill station examiner will be observing and recording your performance. Do not let his or her documentation practices influence your performance in the station.

If the station has an overall time limit, the examiner will inform you of this when reading the instructions. When you reach the time limit, the skill station examiner will instruct you to stop your performance. However, if you complete the station before the allotted time, inform the examiner that you are finished. You may be asked to remove equipment from the patient before leaving the skill station.

You are not permitted to discuss any specific details of any station with each other at any time. Please be courteous to the candidates who are testing by keeping all excess noise to a minimum. Be prompt in reporting to each station so that we may complete this examination within a reasonable time period.

Failure of three or less skill stations entitles you to a same-day retest of those skills failed. Failure of four or more skill stations constitutes a failure of the entire practical examination, requiring a retest of the entire practical examination. Failure of a same-day retest entitles you to a retest of those skills failed. This retest must be accomplished at a different site with a different examiner. Failure of the retest at the different site constitutes a complete failure of the practical examination, and you will be required to retest the entire practical examination.

The results of the examination are reported as pass/fail of the skill station. You will not receive a detailed critique of your performance on any skill. Please remember that today's examination is a formal verification process and was not designed to assist with teaching or learning. The purpose of this examination is to verify achievement of the minimal DOT competencies after the educational component has been completed. Identifying errors would be contrary to the principle of this type of examination, and could result in the candidate "learning" the examination while still not being competent in the necessary skill. It is recommended that you contact your teaching institution for remedial training if you are unsuccessful in a skill station.

If you feel you have a complaint concerning the practical examination, a formal complaint procedure does exist. You must initiate any complaint with me today. Complaints will not be valid after today and will not be accepted if they are issued after you learn of your results or leave this site. You may file a complaint for only two reasons:

1. You feel you have been discriminated against. Any situation that can be documented in which you feel an unfair evaluation of your abilities occurred may be considered discriminatory.
2. There was an equipment problem or malfunction in your station.

If you feel either occurred, you must contact me immediately to initiate the complaint process. You must submit the complaint in writing. The examination coordinator and the medical director will review your concerns.

I am here today to assure that fair, objective, and impartial evaluations occur in accordance with the guidelines contained in this guide. If you have any concerns, notify me immediately to discuss your concerns. I will be visiting all skill stations throughout the examination to verify adherence to these guidelines. Please remember that if you do not voice your concerns or complaints today before you leave this site or before I inform you of your results, your complaints will not be accepted.

The skill station examiner does not know or play a role in the establishment of pass/fail criteria, but he or she is merely an observer and recorder of your actions in the skill station. This is an examination experience, not a teaching or learning experience.

Does anyone have any questions concerning the practical examination at this time?

Points to Remember

1. Follow instructions from the staff.
2. During the examination, move only to areas directed by the staff.
3. Give your name as you arrive at each station.
4. Listen carefully as the testing scenario is explained at each station.
5. Ask questions if the instructions are not clear.
6. During the examination, do not talk about the examination with anyone other than the skill station examiner, programmed patient, and when applicable, the EMT assistant.
7. Be aware of the time limit, but do not sacrifice quality performance for speed.
8. Equipment will be provided. Select and use only what is necessary to care for your patient adequately.

Patient Assessment/ Management—Trauma

Instructions to the Candidate

Minimum Score: 30

This station is designed to test your ability to perform a patient assessment of a victim of multisystems trauma and "voice" treat all conditions and injuries discovered. You must conduct your assessment as you would in the field, including communicating with your patient. You may remove the patient's clothing down to shorts or swimsuit if you feel it is necessary. As you conduct your assessment, you should state everything you are assessing. Clinical information not obtainable by visual or physical inspection will be given to you after you demonstrate how you would normally gain that information. You may assume that you have two EMTs working with you and that they are correctly carrying out the verbal treatments you indicate. You have ten minutes to complete this skill station. Do you have any questions?

Sample Trauma Scenario

The following is an example of an acceptable scenario for this station. It is not intended to be the only possible scenario for this station. Variations of the scenario are possible and should be used to reduce the possibility of future candidates knowing the scenario before entering the station. If the scenario is changed, the following four guidelines must be used.

1. A clearly defined mechanism of injury must be included. The mechanism of injury must indicate the need for the candidate to perform a rapid trauma assessment.
2. There must be a minimum of an airway, breathing, and circulatory problem.
3. There must be an additional associated soft-tissue or musculoskeletal injury.
4. Vital signs must be given for the initial check and one recheck.

Trauma Situation #1: Patient Assessment/Management
Mechanism of Injury

You are called to the scene of a motor vehicle crash, where you find a victim who was thrown from a car. You find severe damage to the front end of the car. The victim is found lying in a field 30 feet from the upright car.

Injuries

The patient will present with the following injuries. All injuries will be moulaged. Each examiner should program the patient to respond appropriately throughout the assessment and assure the victim has read the "Instructions to Simulated Trauma Victim" that have been provided.

1. unresponsive
2. left side flail chest
3. decreased breath sounds, left side
4. cool, clammy skin; no distal pulses
5. distended abdomen
6. pupils equal
7. neck veins flat
8. pelvis stable
9. open injury of the left femur with capillary bleeding

Vital Signs

1. Initial vital signs—BP, 72/60; P, 140; RR, 28
2. Upon recheck—if appropriate treatment: BP, 86/74; P, 120; RR, 22
3. Upon recheck—if inappropriate treatment: BP, 64/48; P, 138; RR, 44

Patient Assessment/Management—Trauma

Start Time: _____

Stop Time: _____   **Date:** _____

Candidate's Name: _____

Evaluator's Name: _____

		Points Possible	Points Awarded
Takes, or verbalizes, body substance isolation precautions		1	
SCENE SIZE-UP			
Determines the scene is safe		1	
Determines the mechanism of injury		1	
Determines the number of patients		1	
Requests additional help if necessary		1	
Considers stabilization of spine		1	
INITIAL ASSESSMENT			
Verbalizes general impression of the patient		1	
Determines responsiveness/level of consciousness		1	
Determines chief complaint/apparent life threats		1	
Assesses airway and breathing	Assessment	1	
	Initiates appropriate oxygen therapy	1	
	Assures adequate ventilation	1	
	Injury management	1	
Assesses circulation	Assess/controls major bleeding	1	
	Assesses pulse	1	
	Assesses skin (color, temperature, and condition)	1	
Identifies priority patients/makes transport decision		1	
FOCUSED HISTORY AND PHYSICAL EXAMINATION/RAPID TRAUMA ASSESSMENT			
Selects appropriate assessment *(focused or rapid assessment)*		1	
Obtains, or directs assistance to obtain, baseline vital signs		1	
Obtains SAMPLE history		1	
DETAILED PHYSICAL EXAMINATION			
Assesses the head	Inspects and palpates the scalp and ears	1	
	Assesses the eyes	1	
	Assesses the facial areas, including oral and nasal areas	1	
Assesses the neck	Inspects and palpates the neck	1	
	Assesses for JVD	1	
	Assesses for trachael deviation	1	
Assesses the chest	Inspects	1	
	Palpates	1	
	Auscultates	1	
Assesses the abdomen/pelvis	Assesses the abdomen	1	
	Assesses the pelvis	1	
	Verbalizes assessment of genitalia/perineum as needed	1	
Assesses the extremities	1 point for each extremity includes inspection, palpation, and assessment of motor, sensory, and circulatory function	4	
Assesses the posterior	Assesses thorax	1	
	Assesses lumbar	1	
Manages secondary injuries and wounds appropriately **1 point for appropriate management of the secondary injury/wound**		1	
Verbalizes reassessment of the vital signs		1	

Critical Criteria   **Total:** 40

____ Did not take, or verbalize, body substance isolation precautions

____ Did not determine scene safety

____ Did not assess for spinal protection

____ Did not provide for spinal protection when indicated

____ Did not provide high concentration of oxygen

____ Did not find, or manage, problems associated with airway, breathing, hemorrhage, or shock (hypoperfusion)

____ Did not differentiate patient's need for transportation versus continued assessment at the scene

____ Did other detailed physical examination before assessing the airway, breathing, and circulation

____ Did not transport patient within (10) minute time limit

Patient Assessment/Management— Medical

Instructions to the Candidate

Minimum Score: 22

This station is designed to test your ability to perform a patient assessment of a patient with a chief complaint of a medical nature and "voice" treat all conditions discovered. You must conduct your assessment as you would in the field, including communicating with your patient. You may remove the patient's clothing down to shorts or swimsuit if you feel it is necessary. As you conduct your assessment, you should state everything you are assessing. Clinical information not obtainable by visual or physical inspection will be given to you after you demonstrate how you would normally gain that information. You may assume that you have two EMTs working with you and that they are correctly carrying out the verbal treatments you indicate. You have ten minutes to complete this skill station. Do you have any questions?

When assessing the signs and symptoms of the patient, the candidate must gather the appropriate information by asking the questions listed on the skill sheet. The number of questions required to be asked differs based on the scenario and the chief complaint. The point for *"Signs and symptoms (Assess history of present illness)"* is awarded based on the following criteria:

Respiratory	five or more questions asked, award one point four or less questions asked, award no point
Cardiac	five or more questions asked, award one point four or less questions asked, award no point
Altered Mental Status	six or more questions asked, award one point five or less questions asked, award no point
Allergic Reaction	four or more questions asked, award one point three or less questions asked, award no point
Poisoning/Overdose	five or more questions asked, award one point four or less questions asked, award no point
Environmental Emergency	four or more questions asked, award one point three or less questions asked, award no point
Obstetrics	five or more questions asked, award one point four or less questions asked, award no point
Behavioral	four or more questions asked, award one point three or less questions asked, award no point

Each candidate is required to complete a full patient assessment. The candidate choosing to transport the victim immediately after the initial assessment must be instructed to continue the focused history and physical examination and ongoing assessment en route to the hospital.

NOTE: The preferred method to evaluate a candidate is to write the exact sequence the candidate follows during the station as it is performed. You may then use this documentation to fill out the evaluation instrument after the candidate completes the station. This documentation may then be used to validate the score on the evaluation instrument if questions arise later.

Patient Assessment/Management—Medical

Start Time: _____

Stop Time: _____   Date: _____

Candidate's Name: _____

Evaluator's Name: _____

	Points Possible	Points Awarded
Takes, or verbalizes, body substance isolation precautions	1	

SCENE SIZE-UP

	Points Possible	Points Awarded
Determines the scene is safe	1	
Determines the mechanism of inquiry/nature of illness	1	
Determines the number of patients	1	
Requests additional help if necessary	1	
Considers stabilization of spine	1	

INITIAL ASSESSMENT

		Points Possible	Points Awarded
Verbalizes general impression of the patient		1	
Determines responsiveness/level of consciousness		1	
Determines chief complaint/apparent life threats		1	
Assesses airway and breathing	Assessment	1	
	Initiates appropriate oxygen therapy	1	
	Assures adequate ventilation	1	
Assesses circulation	Assesses/controls major bleeding	1	
	Assesses pulse	1	
	Assesses skin (color, temperature, and condition)	1	
Identifies priority patients/makes transport decision		1	

FOCUSED HISTORY AND PHYSICAL EXAMINATION/RAPID ASSESSMENT

								Points Possible
Signs and symptoms (*Assess history of present illness*)								1

Respiratory	Cardiac	Altered Mental Status	Allergic Reaction	Poisoning/ Overdose	Environmental Emergency	Obstetrics	Behavioral
*Onset?	*Onset?	*Description of the episode?	*History of allergies?	*Substance?	*Source?	*Are you pregnant?	*How do you feel?
*Provokes?	*Provokes?	*Onset?	*What were you exposed to?	*When did you ingest/become exposed?	*Environment?	*How long have you been pregnant?	*Determine suicidal tendencies.
*Quality?	*Quality?	*Duration?	*How were you exposed?	*How much did you ingest?	*Duration?	*Pain or contractions?	*Is the patient a threat to self or others?
*Radiates?	*Radiates?	*Associated symptoms?	*Effects?	*Over what time period?	*Loss of consciousness?	*Bleeding or discharge?	*Is there a medical problem?
*Severity?	*Severity?	*Evidence of trauma?	*Progression?	*Interventions?	*Effects— general or local?	*Do you feel the need to push?	*Interventions?
*Time?	*Time?	*Interventions?	*Interventions?	*Estimated weight?		*Last menstrual period?	
*Interventions?	*Interventions?	*Seizures?					
		*Fever?					

	Points Possible	Points Awarded
Allergies	1	
Medications	1	
Past pertinent history	1	
Last oral intake	1	
Event leading to present illness (rule out trauma)	1	
Performs focused physical examination (*assesses affected body part/system or, if indicated, completes rapid assessment*)	1	
Vitals (*obtains baseline vital signs*)	1	
Interventions (*obtains medical direction or verbalizes standing order for medication interventions and verbalizes proper additional intervention/treatment*)	1	
Transport (re-evaluates the transport decision)	1	
Verbalizes the consideration for completing a detailed physical examination	1	

ONGOING ASSESSMENT (VERBALIZED)

	Points Possible	Points Awarded
Repeats initial assessment	1	
Repeats vital signs	1	
Repeats focused assessment regarding patient complaint or injuries	1	

Critical Criteria   Total: 30

_____ Did not take, or verbalize, body substance isolation precautions when necessary

_____ Did not determine scene safety

_____ Did not obtain medical direction or verbalize standing orders for medical interventions

_____ Did not provide high concentration of oxygen

_____ Did not find or manage problems associated with airway, breathing, hemorrhage, or shock (hypoperfusion)

_____ Did not differentiate patient's need for transportation versus continued assessment at the scene

_____ Did detailed or focused history/physical examination before assessing the airway, breathing, and circulation

_____ Did not ask questions about the present illness

_____ Administered a dangerous or inappropriate intervention

Sample Medical Scenarios

Altered Mental Status

When you arrive on the scene, you meet a 37-year-old male who says his wife is a diabetic and isn't acting normal.

Initial Assessment

Chief Complaint:	"My wife just isn't acting right. I can't get her to stay awake. She only opens her eyes, then goes right back to sleep."
Apparent Life Threats:	Depressed central nervous system, respiratory compromise
Level of Responsiveness:	Opens eyes in response to being shaken
Airway:	Patent
Breathing:	14 and shallow
Circulation:	120 and weak
Transport Decision:	Immediate

Focused History and Physical Examination

Description of Episode:	"My wife took her insulin this morning like any other morning, but she has had the flu and has been vomiting."
Onset:	"It happened so quickly. She was just talking to me and then she just went to sleep. I haven't really been able to wake her up since."
Duration:	"She's been this way for about 15 minutes now. I called you right away. I was really scared."
Associated Symptoms:	"The only thing that I can think of is that she was vomiting last night and this morning."
Evidence of Trauma:	"She didn't fall. She was just sitting on the couch and fell asleep. I haven't tried to move her."

Interventions:	"I haven't done anything but call you guys. I know she took her insulin this morning."
Seizures:	None
Fever:	Low-grade fever
Allergies:	Penicillin
Medications:	Insulin
Past Medical History:	Insulin-dependent diabetic since 21 years of age
Last Meal:	"My wife ate breakfast this morning."
Events Leading to Illness:	"My wife has had the flu and been vomiting for the past 24 hours."
Focused Physical Examination:	Complete a rapid assessment to rule out trauma.
Vitals:	RR, 14; P, 120; BP, 110/72

Allergic Reaction

You arrive to find a 37-year-old male who reports eating cookies he purchased at a bake sale. He has audible wheezing and is scratching red, blotchy areas on his abdomen, chest, and arms.

Initial Assessment

Chief Complaint:	"I'm having an allergic reaction to those cookies I ate."
Apparent Life Threats:	Respiratory and circulatory compromise
Level of Responsiveness:	Awake, very anxious, and restless
Airway:	Patent
Breathing:	26, wheezing, and deep
Circulation:	No bleeding, pulse 120 and weak, cold and clammy skin
Transport Decision:	Immediate transport

Focused History and Physical Examination

History of Allergies:	"Yes. I'm allergic to peanuts."
When Ingested:	"I ate cookies about 20 minutes ago and began itching all over about five minutes later."
How Much Ingested:	"I ate only two cookies."
Effects:	"I'm having trouble breathing, and I feel lightheaded and dizzy."
Progression:	"My wheezing is worse. Now I'm sweating really badly."
Interventions:	"I have my epi-pen upstairs, but I'm afraid to stick myself."
Allergies:	Peanuts and penicillin
Medications:	None
Past Medical History:	"I had to spend two days in the hospital the last time this happened."
Last Meal:	"The last thing I ate were those cookies."
Events Leading to Illness:	"None, except I ate those cookies."
Focused Physical Examination:	Not indicated (award point)
Vitals:	RR, 26; P, 120; BP, 90/60

Poisoning/Overdose

You arrive on the scene where a 3-year-old female is sitting on her mother's lap. The child appears very sleepy and doesn't look at you as you approach.

Initial Assessment

Chief Complaint:	"I think my baby has swallowed some of my sleeping pills. Please don't let her die!"
Apparent Life Threats:	Depressed central nervous system and respiratory compromise
Level of Responsiveness:	Responds slowly to verbal commands
Airway:	Patent
Breathing:	18 and deep
Circulation:	120 and strong
Transport Decision:	Immediate

Focused History and Physical Examination

Substance:	"My baby took sleeping pills. I don't know what kind they are. They just help me sleep at night."
When Ingested:	"I think she must have got them about an hour ago when I was in the shower. Her older sister was supposed to be watching her."
How Much Ingested:	"My prescription was almost empty. There couldn't have been more than four or five pills left. Now they're all gone. Please do something."
Effects:	"She just isn't acting like herself. She's usually running around and getting into everything."
Allergies:	None
Medications:	None
Past Medical History:	None
Last Meal:	"She ate breakfast this morning."
Events Leading to Illness:	"She just swallowed the pills."
Focused Physical Examination:	Complete a rapid trauma assessment to rule out trauma.
Vitals:	RR, 18; P, 120; BP, 90/64

Environmental Emergencies

You arrive on the scene as rescuers are pulling a 16-year-old female from an ice-covered creek. The teenager has been moved out of the creek onto dry land, is completely soaked, and appears drowsy.

Initial Assessment

Chief Complaint:	"I saw something in the water below the ice. When I tried to get it out, the ice broke."
Apparent Life Threats:	Generalized hypothermia
Level of Responsiveness:	Responsive, but slow to speak
Airway:	Patent
Breathing:	26 and shallow
Circulation:	No bleeding; pulse, 110 and strong; pale, wet skin still covered in wet clothing
Transport Decision:	Immediate transport

Focused History and Physical Examination

Source:	"I fell in the creek when the ice broke. I tried to get out, but the current was too strong."
Environment:	"The water was up to my neck. I could stand up, but I couldn't get out of the water."
Duration:	"I think I was in the water for ten minutes before they pulled me out. It felt like an hour."
Loss of Consciousness:	"I feel sick, but I never passed out."
Effects:	Lowered body temperature, slow speech patterns, "I can't stop shivering."
Allergies:	None
Medications:	None
Past Medical History:	None
Last Meal:	"I ate lunch at school three hours ago."
Events Leading to Illness:	"I thought the ice would hold me."
Focused Physical Examination:	Complete a rapid assessment to rule out trauma.
Vitals:	RR, 26; P, 110 and strong; BP, 120/80

Obstetrics

You arrive on the scene where a 26-year-old female is lying on the couch saying, "The baby is coming and the pain is killing me!"

Initial Assessment

Chief Complaint:	"I'm nine months pregnant and the baby is coming soon."
Apparent Life Threats:	None
Level of Responsiveness:	Awake and alert
Airway:	Patent
Breathing:	Panting, rapid breathing during contractions
Circulation:	No bleeding, pulse 120, skin is pale
Transport Decision:	Unknown

Focused History and Physical Examination

Are You Pregnant:	See chief complaint (award point if mentioned in general impression).
How Long Pregnant:	See chief complaint (award point if mentioned in general impression).

Pain or Contractions:	"My pain is every 2–3 minutes, and it lasts 2–3 minutes."
Bleeding or Discharge:	None
Do You Feel the Need to Push:	"Yes, every time the pain begins."
Crowning:	Present (award point if identified in focused physical exam)
Allergies:	None
Medications:	None
Past Medical History:	"This is my third baby."
Last Meal:	"I ate breakfast today."
Events Leading to Illness:	"The contractions started a few hours ago and have not stopped."
Focused Physical Examination:	Assess for crowning, bleeding, and discharge.
Vitals:	RR, 40 during contractions; P, 120; BP, 140/80

Behavioral

You arrive on the scene, where you find a 45-year-old male in the custody of the police. He is unable to stand and smells of beer. He appears to be dirty, and you notice numerous rips and tears in his clothes.

Initial Assessment

Chief Complaint:	"Nothing is wrong with me except these cops won't leave me alone. I only drank two beers."
Apparent Life Threats:	None
Level of Responsiveness:	Responds slowly with slurred speech to verbal questions
Airway:	Patent
Breathing:	16 and effortless

Circulation:	No bleeding, pulse 100, warm skin, and red nose
Transport Decision:	Delayed

Focused History and Physical Examination

How Do You Feel:	"I'm a little sick, otherwise, I just want to go to sleep."
Suicidal Tendencies:	"No, I ain't going to kill myself."
Threat to Others:	"Hey man, I ain't never hurt anyone in my life."
Is There a Medical Problem:	"My wife says I'm an alcoholic, but what does she know?"
Interventions:	"Yeah, I took three aspirins because I know I'm going to have one heck of a headache in the morning."
Allergies:	None
Medications:	None
Past Medical History:	"I've been in the hospital four time with those DTs."
Last Meal:	"Man, I haven't eaten since yesterday."
Events Leading to Illness:	"I don't care what these cops say, I didn't fall down. I was just taking a nap before going home."
Focused Physical Examination:	Complete a rapid assessment to rule out trauma.
Vitals:	RR, 16; P, 100; BP, 90/60

Cardiac Arrest Management

Instructions to the Candidate

Minimum Score: 15

This station is designed to test your ability to manage a prehospital cardiac arrest by integrating CPR skills, defibrillation, airway adjuncts, and patient/scene management skills. There will be an EMT assistant in this station. The EMT assistant will only do as you instruct him or her. As you arrive on the scene, you will encounter a patient in cardiac arrest. A first responder will be present performing single-rescuer CPR. You must immediately establish control of the scene and begin resuscitation of the patient with an AED. At the appropriate time, the patient's airway must be controlled, and you must ventilate or direct the ventilation of the patient using adjunctive equipment. You may use any of the supplies available in this room. You have 15 minutes to complete this skill station. Do you have any questions?

Cardiac Arrest Management

Start Time: _____

Stop Time: _____   **Date:** _____

Candidate's Name: _____

Evaluator's Name: _____

	Points Possible	Points Awarded
ASSESSMENT		
Takes, or verbalizes, body substance isolation precautions	1	
Briefly questions the rescuer about arrest events	1	
Directs rescuer to stop CPR	1	
Verifies absence of spontaneous pulse **(skill station examiner states "no pulse")**		1
Directs resumption of CPR	1	
Turns on defibrillator power	1	
Attaches automated defibrillator to the patient	1	
Directs rescuer to stop CPR and ensures all individuals are clear of the patient	1	
Initiates analysis of the rhythm	1	
Delivers shock (up to three successive shocks)	1	
Verifies absence of spontaneous pulse **(skill station examiner states "no pulse")**		1
TRANSITION		
Directs resumption of CPR	1	
Gathers additional information about arrest event	1	
Confirms effectiveness of CPR (ventilation and compressions)	1	
INTEGRATION		
Verbalizes or directs insertion of a simple airway adjunct (oral/nasal airway)	1	
Ventilates, or directs ventilation of, the patient	1	
Assures high concentration of oxygen is delivered to the patient	1	
Assures CPR continues without unnecessary/prolonged interruption	1	
Re-evaluates patient/CPR in approximately one minute	1	
Repeats defibrillator sequence	1	
TRANSPORTATION		
Verbalizes transportation of patient	1	
Total:	**21**	

Critical Criteria

_____ Did not take, or verbalize, body substance isolation precautions

_____ Did not evaluate the need for immediate use of the AED

_____ Did not direct initiation/resumption of ventilation/compressions at appropriate times

_____ Did not assure all individuals were clear of patient before delivering each shock

_____ Did not operate the AED properly (inability to deliver shock)

_____ Prevented the defibrillator from delivering indicated stacked shocks

Airway, Oxygen, Ventilation Skills/Bag-Valve Mask— Apneic with Pulse

Instructions to the Candidate

Minimum Score: 8

This station is designed to test your ability to ventilate a patient using a bag-valve mask. As you enter the station, you will find an apneic patient with a palpable central pulse. There are no bystanders, and artificial ventilation has not been initiated. The only patient management required is airway management and ventilatory support. You must initially ventilate the patient for a minimum of 30 seconds. You will be evaluated on the appropriateness of ventilator volumes. I will then inform you that a second rescuer has arrived and will instruct you that you must control the airway and the mask seal while the second rescuer provides ventilation. You may use only the equipment available in this room. You have five minutes to complete this station. Do you have any questions?

Airway, Oxygen, Ventilation Skills/Bag-Valve Mask—Apneic Patient

Start Time: _____

Stop Time: _____   **Date:** _____

Candidate's Name: _____

Evaluator's Name: _____

	Points Possible	Points Awarded
Takes, or verbalizes, body substance isolation precautions	1	
Voices opening the airway	1	
Voices inserting an airway adjunct	1	
Selects appropriately sized mask	1	
Creates a proper mask-to-face seal	1	
Ventilates patient at no less than 800 mL volume **(The examiner must witness for at least 30 seconds)**	1	
Connects reservoir and oxygen	1	
Adjusts liter flow to 15 L/min or greater	1	
The examiner indicates arrival of a second EMT. The second EMT is instructed to ventilate the patient while the candidate controls the mask and the airway.		
Voices re-opening the airway	1	
Creates a proper mask-to-face seal	1	
Instructs assistant to resume ventilation at proper volume per breath **(The examiner must witness for at least 30 seconds)**	1	
Total:	**11**	

Critical Criteria

____ Did not take, or verbalize, body substance isolation precautions

____ Did not immediately ventilate the patient

____ Interrupted ventilations for more than 20 seconds

____ Did not provide high concentration of oxygen

____ Did not provide, or direct assistant to provide, proper volume/breath (more than two ventilations per minute are below 800 mL)

____ Did not allow adequate exhalation

Spinal Immobilization— Supine Patient

Instructions to the Candidate

Minimum Score: 10

This station is designed to test your ability to provide spinal immobilization on a patient using a long spine immobilization device. You arrive on the scene with an EMT assistant. The assistant EMT has completed the scene size-up as well as the initial assessment, and no critical condition was found that would require intervention. For the purpose of this testing station, the patient's vital signs remain stable. You are required to treat the specific problem of an unstable spine using a long spine immobilization device. When moving the patient to the device, you should use the help of the assistant EMT and the evaluator. The assistant EMT should control the head and cervical spine of the patient while you and the evaluator move the patient to the immobilization device. You are responsible for the direction and subsequent action of the EMT assistant. You may use any equipment available in this room. You have ten minutes to complete this skill station. Do you have any questions?

Spinal Immobilization
Supine Patient

Start Time: _____

Stop Time: _____   Date: _____

Candidate's Name: _____

Evaluator's Name: _____

	Points Possible	Points Awarded
Takes, or verbalizes, body substance isolation precautions	1	
Directs assistant to place/maintain head in the neutral in-line position	1	
Directs assistant to maintain manual immobilization of the head	1	
Reassesses motor, sensory, and circulatory function in each extremity	1	
Applies appropriately sized extrication collar	1	
Positions the immobilization device appropriately	1	
Directs movement of the patient onto the device without compromising the integrity of the spine	1	
Applies padding to voids between the torso and the board as necessary	1	
Immobilizes the patient's torso to the device	1	
Evaluates and pads behind the patient's head as necessary	1	
Immobilizes the patient's head to the device	1	
Secures the patient's legs to the device	1	
Secures the patient's arms to the device	1	
Reassesses motor, sensory, and circulatory function in each extremity	1	
Total:	**14**	

Critical Criteria

_____ Did not immediately direct, or take, manual immobilization of the head

_____ Released, or ordered release of, manual immobilization before it was maintained mechanically

_____ Patient manipulated, or moved excessively, causing potential spinal compromise

_____ Patient moves excessively up, down, left, or right on the patient's torso

_____ Head immobilization allows for excessive movement

_____ Upon completion of immobilization, head is not in the neutral position

_____ Did not assess motor, sensory, and circulatory function in each extremity after immobilization to the device

_____ Immobilized head to the board before securing the torso

Spinal Immobilization– Seated Patient

Instructions to the Candidate

Minimum Score: 9

This station is designed to test your ability to provide spinal immobilization of a patient using a half-spine immobilization device. You and an EMT assistant arrive on the scene of an automobile crash. The scene is safe, and there is only one patient. The assistant EMT has completed the initial assessment, and no critical condition requiring intervention was found. For the purpose of this station, the patient's vital signs remain stable. You are required to treat the specific, isolated problem of an unstable spine using a half-spine immobilization device. You are responsible for the direction and subsequent actions of the EMT assistant. Transferring and immobilizing the patient to the long spine board should be accomplished verbally. You have ten minutes to complete this skill station. Do you have any questions?

Spinal Immobilization
Seated Patient

Start Time: _____

Stop Time: _____   **Date:** _____

Candidate's Name: _____

Evaluator's Name: _____

	Points Possible	Points Awarded
Takes, or verbalizes, body substance isolation precautions	1	
Directs assistant to place/maintain head in the neutral in-line position	1	
Directs assistant to maintain manual immobilization of the head	1	
Reassesses motor, sensory, and circulatory function in each extremity	1	
Applies appropriately sized extrication collar	1	
Positions the immobilization device behind the patient	1	
Secures the device to the patient's torso	1	
Evaluates torso fixation and adjusts as necessary	1	
Evaluates and pads behind the patient's head as necessary	1	
Secures the patient's head to the device	1	
Verbalizes moving the patient to a long spine board	1	
Reassesses motor, sensory, and circulatory function in each extremity	1	
Total:	**12**	

Critical Criteria

_____ Did not immediately direct, or take, manual immobilization of the head

_____ Released, or ordered release of, manual immobilization before it was maintained mechanically

_____ Patient manipulated, or moved excessively, causing potential spinal compromise

_____ Device moved excessively up, down, left, or right on the patient's torso

_____ Head immobilization allows for excessive movement

_____ Torso fixation inhibits chest rise, resulting in respiratory compromise

_____ Upon completion of immobilization, head is not in the neutral position

_____ Did not assess motor, sensory, and circulatory function in each extremity after voicing immobilization to the long board

_____ Immobilized head to the board before securing the torso

Immobilization Skills— Long Bone

Instructions to the Candidate

Minimum Score: 7

This station is designed to test your ability to properly immobilize a closed, nonangulated long bone injury. You are required to treat only the specific, isolated injury to the extremity. The scene size-up and initial assessment have been completed, and during the focused assessment, a closed, nonangulated injury of the _____ (radius, ulna, tibia, fibula) was detected. Ongoing assessment of the patient's airway, breathing, and central circulation is not necessary. You may use any equipment available in this room. You have five minutes to complete this skill station. Do you have any questions?

Immobilization Skills
Long Bone

Start Time: _____

Stop Time: _____   **Date:** _____

Candidate's Name: _____

Evaluator's Name: _____

	Points Possible	Points Awarded
Takes, or verbalizes, body substance isolation precautions	1	
Directs application of manual stabilization of the injury	1	
Assesses motor, sensory, and circulatory function in the injured extremity	1	
Note: The examiner acknowledges "motor, sensory, and circulatory function are present and normal."		
Measures the splint	1	
Applies the splint	1	
Immobilizes the joint above the injury site	1	
Immobilizes the joint below the injury site	1	
Secures the entire injured extremity	1	
Immobilizes the hand/foot in the position of function	1	
Reassesses motor, sensory, and circulatory function in the injured extremity	1	
Note: The examiner acknowledges "motor, sensory, and circulatory function are present and normal."		
Total:	**10**	

Critical Criteria

____ Grossly moves the injured extremity

____ Did not immobilize the joint above and the joint below the injury site

____ Did not reassess motor, sensory, and circulatory function in the injured extremity before and after splinting

Immobilization Skills– Joint Injury

Instructions to the Candidate

Minimum Score: 6

This station is designed to test your ability to properly immobilize a noncomplicated shoulder injury. You are required to treat only the specific, isolated injury to the shoulder. The scene size-up and initial assessment have been accomplished on the victim, and during the focused assessment, a shoulder injury was detected. Ongoing assessment of the patient's airway, breathing, and central circulation is not necessary. You may use any equipment available in this room. You have five minutes to complete this skill station. Do you have any questions?

Immobilization Skills
Joint Injury

Start Time: _____

Stop Time: _____　　　**Date:** _____

Candidate's Name: _____

Evaluator's Name: _____

	Points Possible	Points Awarded
Takes, or verbalizes, body substance isolation precautions	1	
Directs application of manual stabilization of the shoulder injury	1	
Assesses motor, sensory, and circulatory function in the injured extremity	1	
Note: The examiner acknowledges "motor, sensory, and circulatory function are present and normal."		
Selects the proper splinting material	1	
Immobilizes the site of the injury	1	
Immobilizes the bone above the injured joint	1	
Immobilizes the bone below the injured joint	1	
Reassesses motor, sensory, and circulatory function in the injured extremity	1	
Note: The examiner acknowledges "motor, sensory, and circulatory function are present and normal."		
Total:	**8**	

Critical Criteria

_____ Did not support the joint so that the joint did not bear distal weight

_____ Did not immobilize the bone above and below the injured site

_____ Did not reassess motor, sensory, and circulatory function in the injured extremity before and after splinting

Immobilization Skills– Traction Splinting

Instructions to Candidate

Minimum Score: 10

This station is designed to test your ability to properly immobilize a mid-shaft femur injury with a traction splint. You will have an EMT assistant to help you in the application of the device by applying manual traction when directed to do so. You are required to treat only the specific, isolated injury to the femur. The scene size-up and initial assessment have been accomplished on the victim, and during the focused assessment, a mid-shaft femur deformity was detected. Ongoing assessment of the patient's airway, breathing, and central circulation is not necessary. You may use any equipment available in this room. You have ten minutes to complete this skill station. Do you have any questions?

Immobilization Skills
Traction Splinting

Start Time: _____

Stop Time: _____   Date: _____

Candidate's Name: _____

Evaluator's Name: _____

	Points Possible	Points Awarded
Takes, or verbalizes, body substance isolation precautions	1	
Directs application of manual stabilization of the injured leg	1	
Directs the application of manual traction	1	
Assesses motor, sensory, and circulatory function in the injured extremity	1	
Note: The examiner acknowledges "motor, sensory, and circulatory function are present and normal."		
Prepares/adjusts splint to the proper length	1	
Positions the splint next to the injured leg	1	
Applies the proximal securing device (e.g . . . ischial strap)	1	
Applies the distal securing device (e.g . . . ankle hitch)	1	
Applies mechanical traction	1	
Positions/secures the support straps	1	
Re-evaluates the proximal/distal securing devices	1	
Reassesses motor, sensory, and circulatory function in the injured extremity	1	
Note: The examiner acknowledges "motor, sensory, and circulatory function are present and normal."		
Note: The examiner must ask the candidate how he or she would prepare the patient for transportation.		
Verbalizes securing the torso to the long board to immobilize the hip	1	
Verbalizes securing the splint to the long board to prevent movement of the splint	1	
Total:	**14**	

Critical Criteria

_____ Loss of traction at any point after it was applied

_____ Did not reassess motor, sensory, and circulatory function in the injured extremity before and after splinting

_____ The foot was excessively rotated or extended after splint was applied

_____ Did not secure the ischial strap before taking traction

_____ Final immobilization failed to support the femur or prevent rotation of the injured leg

_____ Secured the leg to the splint before applying mechanical traction

Note: If the Sagar splint or the Kendrick Traction Device is used without elevating the patient's leg, application of annual traction is not necessary. The candidate should be awarded one (1) point as if manual traction were applied.

Bleeding Control/Shock Management

Instructions to the Candidate

Minimum Score: 7

This station is designed to test your ability to control hemorrhage. This is a scenario-based testing station. As you progress throughout the scenario, you will be given various signs and symptoms appropriate for the patient's condition. You will be required to manage the patient based on these signs and symptoms. A scenario will be read aloud to you, and you will be given an opportunity to ask clarifying questions about the scenario; however, you will not receive answers to any questions about the actual steps of the procedures to be performed. You may use any of the supplies and equipment available in this room. You have ten minutes to complete this skill station. Do you have any questions?

Scenario (Sample) Bleeding Control/ Shock Management

You respond to a stabbing and find a 25-year-old male victim. Upon examination, you find a two-inch stab wound to the inside of the right arm at the anterior elbow crease (antecubital fascia). Bright-red blood is spurting from the wound. The scene is safe, and the patient is responsive and alert. His airway is open, and he is breathing adequately. Do you have any questions?

Bleeding Control/Shock Management

Start Time: _____

Stop Time: _____   Date: _____

Candidate's Name: _____

Evaluator's Name: _____

	Points Possible	Points Awarded
Takes, or verbalizes, body substance isolation precautions	1	
Applies direct pressure to the wound	1	
Elevates the extremity	1	
Note: The examiner must now inform the candidate that the wound continues to bleed.		
Applies an additional dressing to the wound	1	
Note: The examiner must now inform the candidate that the wound still continues to bleed. The second dressing does not control the bleeding.		
Locates and applies pressure to appropriate arterial pressure point	1	
Note: The examiner must now inform the candidate that the bleeding is controlled.		
Bandages the wound	1	
Note: The examiner must now inform the candidate the patient is now showing signs and symptoms indicative of hypoperfusion.		
Properly positions the patient	1	
Applies high-concentration oxygen	1	
Initiates steps to prevent heat loss from the patient	1	
Indicates the need for immediate transportation	1	
Total:	**10**	

Critical Criteria

_____ Did not take, or verbalize, body substance isolation precautions

_____ Did not apply high-concentration oxygen

_____ Applied a tourniquet before attempting other methods of bleeding control

_____ Did not control hemorrhage in a timely manner

_____ Did not indicate a need for immediate transportation

Airway, Oxygen, Ventilation Skills/Upper-Airway Adjuncts and Suction

Instructions to the Candidate

Minimum Score: 9

This station is designed to test your ability to properly measure, insert, and remove an oropharyngeal and a nasopharyngeal airway, as well as suction a patient's upper airway. This is an isolated skills test comprised of three separate skills. You may use any equipment available in this room. You have five minutes to complete this station. Do you have any questions?

Airway, Oxygen, and Ventilation Skills/Upper-Airway Adjuncts and Suction

Start Time: _____

Stop Time: _____   Date: _____

Candidate's Name: _____

Evaluator's Name: _____

OROPHARYNGEAL AIRWAY	Points Possible	Points Awarded
Takes, or verbalizes, body substance isolation precautions	1	
Selects appropriately sized airway	1	
Measures airway	1	
Inserts airway without pushing the tongue posteriorly	1	
Note: The examiner must advise the candidate that the patient is gagging and becoming conscious.		
Removes the oropharyngeal airway	1	

SUCTION

	Points Possible	Points Awarded
Note: The examiner must advise the candidate to suction the patient's airway.		
Turns on/prepares suction device	1	
Assures presence of mechanical suction	1	
Inserts the suction tip without suction	1	
Applies suction to the oropharynx/nasopharynx	1	

NASOPHARYNGEAL AIRWAY

	Points Possible	Points Awarded
Note: The examiner must advise the candidate to insert a nasopharyngeal airway.		
Selects appropriately sized airway	1	
Measures airway	1	
Verbalizes lubrication of the nasal airway	1	
Fully inserts the airway with the bevel facing toward the septum	1	
Total:	**13**	

Critical Criteria

____ Did not take, or verbalize, body substance isolation precautions

____ Did not obtain a patent airway with the oropharyngeal airway

____ Did not obtain a patent airway with the nasopharyngeal airway

____ Did not demonstrate an acceptable suction technique

____ Inserted any adjunct in a manner dangerous to the patient

Airway, Oxygen, Ventilation Skills/Mouth-to-Mask with Supplemental Oxygen

Instructions to the Candidate

Minimum Score: 6

This station is designed to test your ability to ventilate a patient with supplemental oxygen using a mouth-to-mask technique. This is an isolated skills test. You may assume that mouth-to-barrier device ventilation is in progress and that the patient has a central pulse. The only patient management required is ventilator support using a mouth-to-mask technique with supplemental oxygen. You must ventilate the patient for at least 30 seconds. You will be evaluated on the appropriateness of ventilatory volumes. You may use any equipment available in this room. You have five minutes to complete this station. Do you have any questions?

Airway, Oxygen, Ventilation Skills/Mouth-to-Mask with Supplemental Oxygen

Start Time: _____

Stop Time: _____   **Date:** _____

Candidate's Name: _____

Evaluator's Name: _____

	Points Possible	Points Awarded
Takes, or verbalizes, body substance isolation precautions	1	
Connects one-way valve to mask	1	
Opens patient's airway or confirms patient's airway is open (manually or with adjunct)		1
Establishes and maintains a proper mask-to-face seal	1	
Ventilates the patient at the proper volume and rate (800–1,200 mL per breath/10–20 breaths per minute)	1	
Connects the mask to high concentration of oxygen	1	
Adjusts flow rate to at least 15 L/min	1	
Continues ventilation of the patient at the proper volume and rate (800–1,200 mL per breath/10–20 breaths per minute)	1	
Note: The examiner must witness ventilations for at least 30 seconds.		
Total:	8	

Critical Criteria

_____ Did not take, or verbalize, body substance isolation precautions

_____ Did not adjust liter flow to at least 15 L/min

_____ Did not provide proper volume per breath (more than two ventilations per minute were below 800 mL)

_____ Did not ventilate the patient at a rate of 10–20 breaths per minute

_____ Did not allow for complete exhalation

Airway, Oxygen, Ventilation Skills/Supplemental Oxygen Administration

Instructions to the Candidate

Minimum Score: 11

This station is designed to test your ability to correctly assemble the equipment needed to administer supplemental oxygen in the prehospital setting. This is an isolated skills test. You will be required to assemble an oxygen tank and a regulator and administer oxygen to a patient using a nonrebreather mask. At this point, you will be instructed to discontinue oxygen administration by the nonrebreather mask and start oxygen administration using a nasal cannula because the patient cannot tolerate the mask. Once you have initiated oxygen administration using a nasal cannula, you will be instructed to discontinue oxygen administration completely. You may use only the equipment available in this room. You have five minutes to complete this station. Do you have any questions?

Airway, Oxygen, Ventilation Skills/Supplemental Oxygen Administration

Start Time: _____

Stop Time: _____   Date: _____

Candidate's Name: _____

Evaluator's Name: _____

	Points Possible	Points Awarded
Takes, or verbalizes, body substance isolation precautions	1	
Assembles the regulator to the tank	1	
Opens the tank	1	
Checks for leaks	1	
Checks tank pressure	1	
Attaches nonrebreather mask to oxygen	1	
Prefills reservoir	1	
Adjusts liter flow to 12 L/min or greater	1	
Applies and adjusts the mask to the patient's face	1	
Note: The examiner must advise the candidate that the patient is not tolerating the nonrebreather mask. The medical director has ordered you to apply a nasal cannula to the patient.		
Attaches nasal cannula to oxygen	1	
Adjusts liter flow to 6 L/min or less	1	
Applies nasal cannula to the patient	1	
Note: The examiner must advise the candidate to discontinue oxygen therapy.		
Removes the nasal cannula from the patient	1	
Shuts off the regulator	1	
Relieves the pressure within the regulator	1	
Total:	**15**	

Critical Criteria

_____ Did not take, or verbalize, body substance isolation precautions

_____ Did not assemble the tank and regulator without leaks

_____ Did not prefill the reservoir bag

_____ Did not adjust the device to the correct liter flow for the nonrebreather mask (*12 L/min or greater*)

_____ Did not adjust the device to the correct liter flow for the nasal cannula (*6 L/min or less*)

STATE CERTIFICATION REQUIREMENTS

CHAPTER 9

CHAPTER SUMMARY
This chapter outlines EMT-Basic certification requirements for all 50 states, the District of Columbia, Puerto Rico, and the U.S. Virgin Islands. It also lists state EMT agencies you can contact for more information about certification requirements.

The table on pages 202–204 shows some of the minimum requirements you must meet to be certified as an EMT-Basic in the 50 states, the District of Columbia, Puerto Rico, and the U.S. Virgin Islands. The next few paragraphs explain the entries on the table. After the table is a state-by-state list of EMT agencies that you can contact for more specific information.

You should know that some minimum requirements are pretty standard and so are not listed on the table. For instance, you must be physically, mentally, and emotionally able to perform all the tasks of an EMT. Usually, you are required to have a high school diploma or GED before you begin training. You must have a clean criminal record. And, of course, you must successfully complete an EMT-Basic training program that meets the standards set by the U.S. Department of Transportation.

The minimum age for most states is 18 years old; however, you should check age specifications with the EMT agency in your state. Some states allow you to begin a training program before you reach this minimum age, often requiring a parent or guardian's permission.

The first entry, Minimum Hours of Training, lists the number of hours this state or territory considers sufficient for EMT-Basic training. Courses that meet the requirements will typically cover both the DOT/NHTSA-approved curriculum and locality-specific protocols. Be sure to check with the licensing agency in the area where you intend to work to make sure your course meets the requirements. Note that in some states, such as California, the locality-specific requirements are just that: The requirements for EMT-Basic certification in Los Angeles differ from the requirements in San Diego and Santa Clara. You should also check with your licensing agency to see how much time you have between finishing your training course and fulfilling all the other requirements for certification—including passing the written and practical exams.

States use their own written and practical skills exams, exams from the National Registry of EMTs, or a combination of both. The entry under Training Accepted will be "State," meaning the state has its own exam; "NREMT" for National Registry; or an entry indicating a combination of both exams. Even when the state has its own exam, you'll find it's pretty similar to the National Registry exam, and therefore to the exams in this book (except for state- or locality-specific scopes of practice and protocols). After all, the federal government mandates the curriculum of EMT courses nationwide. You can expect exams based on similar curricula to be similar.

Some states' exams will require you to go through *their* certification process; others will accept the National Registry Exams, if you are already certified by the NREMT. Similarly, some states will accept your certification from out of state, some will accept it if you take their exam, and some will require that you be certified through the National Registry if you are transferring in from out-of-state. In most cases, a state that accepts out-of-state certification will insist that your training program and your exam meet or exceed its standards, so sometimes, it will come down to whether the state you're coming from is deemed to have done so. Some states have additional certification requirements for transferring EMTs, such as background investigation, being a state resident, being employed with an EMS agency in that state, or taking a refresher course. If you are certified in another state, you will need to show proof of certification when applying in a different state. Some states have what is known as "legal recognition," which means they will recognize and accept your training for a limited time period, often one year. This is similar to a temporary certification. During this period of legal recognition, you apply for official certification and fulfill the necessary requirements. Once the process is complete, your certification will be good for as long as that state allows. You should check with the appropriate state's EMS office for more detail.

The last column, Recertification, indicates the number of years from your initial certification to the time when you will have to be recertified. Recertification usually requires a given number of hours of continuing education, demonstration of your continuing ability to perform the necessary skills, or both—but you'll find out all about that once you're certified in the first place.

STATE	MINIMUM HOURS OF TRAINING	TRAINING ACCEPTED	RECERTIFICATION
Alabama	172	NREMT	2 years
Alaska	128	State	2 years
Arizona	115	NREMT	2 years
Arkansas	120	State and NREMT	2 years
California	110	State or NREMT	4 years
Colorado	110	State	3 years

STATE	MINIMUM HOURS OF TRAINING	TRAINING ACCEPTED	RECERTIFICATION
Connecticut	120	NREMT	2 years
Delaware	110	NREMT	1 year
District of Columbia	140	State	2 years
Florida	110	State or NREMT	2 years
Georgia	N/A	State	2 years
Hawaii	315	NREMT	2 years
Idaho	110	NREMT	3 years
Illinois	110	State	4 years
Indiana	144.5	State	2 years
Iowa	128	State	2 years
Kansas	150	State	1 year
Kentucky	120	State and NREMT	2 years
Louisiana	140	State and NREMT	2 years
Maine	111	State	3 years
Maryland	131	State	3 years
Massachusetts	110	State	2 years
Michigan	194	State	3 years
Minnesota	130	NREMT	2 years
Mississippi	110	NREMT	2 years
Missouri	110	State	5 years
Montana	110	NREMT	2 years
Nebraska	110	NREMT	3 years
Nevada	110	State	2 years
New Hampshire	110	State and NREMT	2 years
New Jersey	120	State	3 years
New Mexico	120	State	2 years
New York	130	State	3 years

STATE	MINIMUM HOURS OF TRAINING	TRAINING ACCEPTED	RECERTIFICATION
North Carolina	148	State	4 years
North Dakota	110	NREMT	2 years
Ohio	130	NREMT	3 years
Oklahoma	148	NREMT	2 years
Oregon	140	NREMT	2 years
Pennsylvania	123.5	State	3 years
Rhode Island	122	State and NREMT	3 years
South Carolina	139	State	3 years
South Dakota	110	NREMT	2 years
Tennessee	150	NREMT	2 years
Texas	140	State	4 years
Utah	120	State	3 years
Vermont	110	State and NREMT	2 years
Virginia	120	State	4 years
Washington	110	State	3 years
West Virginia	110	NREMT	3 years
Wisconsin	120	NREMT	2 years
Wyoming	120	NREMT	2 years
Puerto Rico	110	State	2 years
U.S. Virgin Islands	140	NREMT	2 years

State EMT Agencies

The following is a list of the agencies that control EMT certification in each state, with their addresses and phone numbers. You can contact those offices for more information on their certification requirements. Visit the NREMT website (www.nremt.org/EMTServices/emt_cand_state_offices.asp) for up-to-date links to state EMS websites.

ALABAMA

Emergency Medical Services
Department of Public Health
201 Monroe Street
Montgomery, AL 36104
Telephone: 334-206-5293

ALASKA

Department of Health and Social Services
Division of Public Health
Community Health and EMS Section
PO Box 110616
Juneau, AK 99811-0616
Telephone: 907-465-3027

ARIZONA

Bureau of EMS
150 North 18th Avenue, Suite 540
Phoenix, AZ 85007-3248
Telephone: 602-364-3150

ARKANSAS

Division of Health Section of EMS and Trauma Systems
5800 West 10th Street, Suite 800
Little Rock, AR 72204
Telephone: 501-661-2262

CALIFORNIA

EMS Authority, State of California
1930 9th Street, Suite 100
Sacramento, CA 95814
Telephone: 916-322-4336

COLORADO

Colorado Department of Public Health & Environment,
  EMS Division
4300 Cherry Creek Drive South
Denver, CO 80246-1530
Telephone: 303-692-2980

CONNECTICUT

Office of Emergency Medical Services
PO Box 340308, 410 Capitol Avenue
Hartford, CT 06134-0308
Telephone: 860-509-7975

DELAWARE

Division of Public Health,
  Department of Health and Social Services
Office of EMS, Blue Hen Corporate Center
655 Bay Road, Suite 4-H
Dover, DE 19901
Telephone: 302-739-6637

DISTRICT OF COLUMBIA

Emergency Health and Medical Services
864 New York Northeast, Suite 5000
Washington, D.C. 20001
Telephone: 202-671-4222

FLORIDA

Certification Office for EMT/Paramedic and
  Radiological Technology
4052 Bald Cypress Way, Bin C85
Tallahassee, FL 32399-3285
Telephone: 850-245-4910

GEORGIA

Office of EMS/Trauma
2600 Skyland Drive, Lower Level
Atlanta, GA 30319
Telephone: 404-679-0547

HAWAII

State Department of Health,
  Emergency Medical Services
3627 Kilauea Avenue, Room 102
Honolulu, HI 96816
Telephone: 808-733-9210

IDAHO
Idaho EMS Bureau
590 West Washington Street
Boise, ID 83720-0036
Telephone: 208-334-4000

ILLINOIS
Division of EMS and Highway Safety, State
    Department of Public Health
525 West Jefferson Street
Springfield, IL 62761
Telephone: 217-785-2080

INDIANA
State EMS Commission
302 West Washington Street, Room E208, IGCS
Indianapolis, IN 46204-2258
Telephone: 317-233-0208

IOWA
Bureau of EMS
Lucas State Office Building
321 East 12th Street
Des Moines, IA 50319
Telephone: 800-728-3367

KANSAS
Board of EMS
LSOB, Suite 1031, 900 Southwest Jackson
Topeka, KS 66612
Telephone: 785-296-7296

KENTUCKY
Kentucky Board of EMS,
    Commonwealth of Kentucky
2545 Lawrenceburg Road
Frankfort, KY 40601
Telephone: 859-256-3565

LOUISIANA
DHH–OPH, Bureau of EMS
8919 World Ministry Avenue
    Main Administration Building, Suite A
Baton Rouge, LA 70810
Telephone: 225-763-5700

MAINE
Mailing address:
Maine Emergency Medical Services
Department of Public Safety
152 State House Station
Augusta, ME 04333
Telephone: 207-626-3860

Office located at:
Central Maine Commerce Center
45 Commerce Drive, Suite 1
Augusta, ME 04330
Telephone: 207-626-3860

MARYLAND
Maryland Institute for EMS Services
653 West Pratt Street
Baltimore, MD 21201-1536
Telephone: 410-706-3666

MASSACHUSETTS
Department of Public Health, Office of EMS
2 Boylston Street, 3rd Floor
Boston, MA 02116
Telephone: 617-753-7300

MICHIGAN
Michigan Department of Community Health
Division of EMS and Trauma Services
201 Townsend Street, 6th Floor
Lansing, MI 48913
Telephone: 517-241-0179

MINNESOTA
MN EMS Regulatory Board
2829 University Avenue, Southeast Suite 310
Minneapolis, MN 55414-3222
Telephone: 651-201-2800

MISSISSIPPI
Mississippi Department of Health
PO Box 1700, 570 East Woodrow Wilson, Annex 309
Jackson, MS 39215-1700
Telephone: 601-576-7380

MISSOURI
Department of Health & Senior Services,
 Bureau of EMS
1617 Southridge
Jefferson City, MO 65102
Telephone: 573-751-6356

MONTANA
EMS & Trauma Systems Program,
 MT Department of Public Health &
 Human Services
PO Box 202951
Helena, MT 59620-2951
Telephone: 406-444-3895

NEBRASKA
State Department of Health, Division of EMS
301 Centennial Mall South, 3rd Floor
Lincoln, NE 68508-2529
Telephone: 402-471-2159

NEVADA
Nevada EMS
4150 Technology Way, Suite 200
Carson City, NV 89706
Telephone: 775-687-7590

NEW HAMPSHIRE
Department of Safety, Bureau of EMS
33 Hazen Drive
Concord, NH 03305
Telephone: 603-271-4568

NEW JERSEY
Department of Health & Senior Services, Office of EMS
PO Box 360, 50 East State Street
Trenton, NJ 08625
Telephone: 609-633-7777

NEW MEXICO
EMS Bureau, Department of Health
2500 Cerrillos Road
Sante Fe, NM 87505
Telephone: 505-476-7701

NEW YORK
State Department of Health, EMS Bureau
433 River Street, Suite 303
Troy, NY 12180-2299
Telephone: 518-402-0996

NORTH CAROLINA
Office of EMS, Department of Health &
 Human Services
701 Barbour Drive, PO Box 29530
Raleigh, NC 27603
Telephone: 919-855-3935

NORTH DAKOTA
Division of Emergency Medical Services,
 ND Department of Health
600 East Boulevard Avenue, Department 301
Bismarck, ND 58505-0200
Telephone: 701-328-2388

OHIO
Ohio Department of Public Safety
PO Box 182073
Columbus, OH 43218-2073
Telephone: 614-466-9447

OKLAHOMA
EMS Division, State Department of Health
1000 Northeast 10th Street
Oklahoma City, OK 73117-1299
Telephone: 405-271-4027

OREGON
Emergency Medical Services & Trauma Systems,
 Health Department
800 Northeast Oregon Street, Suite 465
Portland, OR 97232-2162
Telephone: 971-673-0520

PENNSYLVANIA
Bureau of EMS
7th and Forster Streets
Room 1032, Health & Welfare Building
Harrisburg, PA 17120
Telephone: 717-787-8740

RHODE ISLAND
Division of EMS, Rhode Island Department of Health
3 Capitol Hill, Suite 306
Providence, RI 02908-5097
Telephone: 401-222-2401

SOUTH CAROLINA
Emergency Medical Services Section,
    Department of Health and Environmental Control
2600 Bull Street
Columbia, SC 29201
Telephone: 803-545-4204

SOUTH DAKOTA
South Dakota Department of Health
Emergency Medical Services
118 West Capitol Avenue
Pierre, SD 57501-2000
Telephone: 605-773-4031

TENNESSEE
Division of EMS, Tennessee Department of Health
425 Fifth Avenue North, 1st Floor
Nashville, TN 37247
Telephone: 615-741-2584

TEXAS
EMS & Trauma Systems Coordination Office
Department of State Health Services
1100 West 49th Street
Austin, TX 78756-3199
Telephone: 512-834-6700

UTAH
Bureau of EMS, Department of Health
PO Box 142004
Salt Lake City, UT 84114-2004
Telephone: 801-538-6435

VERMONT
EMS Division, Department of Health
PO Box 70, 108 Cherry Street, Room 201
Burlington, VT 05402
Telephone: 802-863-7310

VIRGINIA
Division of EMS, Department of Health
109 Governor Street, James Madison Building,
    Suite UB-55
Richmond, VA 23219
Telephone: 804-864-7600

WASHINGTON
Department of Health, Office of EMS and Trauma,
    Lisensing and Certification
PO Box 47853
Olympia, WA 98504-7853
Telephone: 360-236-2847

WEST VIRGINIA
State Trauma and Emergency Care System, Office
    of EMS
350 Capitol Street, Room 426
Charleston, WV 25301
Telephone: 304-558-3956

WISCONSIN
Department of Health and Family Services, Division
    of Public Health
1 West Wilson Street, Room 133
Madison, WI 53701
Telephone: 608-266-1568

WYOMING
EMS Program, State of Wyoming
Hathaway Building, 4th Floor
Cheyenne, WY 82002
Telephone: 307-777-7955

PUERTO RICO
Puerto Rico Emergency Medical Services
State Emergency Medical System
PO Box 2161
San Juan, PR 00922-2161
Telephone: 787-754-2550

U.S. VIRGIN ISLANDS
Division of Emergency Medical Services
48 Sugar Estate
Charlotte Amalie, USVI 00802
Telephone: 340-776-8311

NOTES

NOTES

NOTES

Special FREE Offer from LearningExpress

LearningExpress guarantees that you will be better prepared for, and score higher on, the EMT-Basic exam

Go to the LearningExpress Practice Center at www.LearningExpressFreeOffer.com, an interactive online resource exclusively for LearningExpress customers.

Now that you've purchased LearningExpress's *EMT-Basic Exam for Firefighters*, you have **FREE** access to:

- A **full-length EMT-Basic practice test**
- **Immediate scoring** and **detailed answer explanations**
- A **customized diagnostic report** to benchmark your skills and focus your study

Follow the simple instructions on the scratch card in your copy of *EMT-Basic Exam for Firefighters*. Use your individualized access code found on the scratch card and go to www.Learning ExpressFreeOffer.com to sign in. Start practicing online for the EMT-Basic exam right away!

Once you've logged on, use the spaces below to write in your access code and newly created password for easy reference:

Access Code: _____   Password: _____